Socioeconomic Impact Management

Also of Interest

The Socioeconomic Impact of Resource Development: Methods for Assessment, F. Larry Leistritz and Steven H. Murdock

Nuclear Waste: Socioeconomic Dimensions, Steven H. Murdock, F. Larry Leistritz, and Rita Hamm

Guide to Social Assessment: A Framework for Assessing Social Change, Kristi Branch, Douglas A. Hooper, James Thompson, and James Creighton

Social Impact Assessment and Monitoring: A Cross-Disciplinary Guide to the Literature, Michael J. Carley and Eduardo Bustelo

Public Involvement and Social Impact Assessment, Gregory A. Daneke, Margot W. Garcia, and Jerome Delli Priscoli

Integrated Impact Assessment, edited by Frederick A. Rossini and Alan L. Porter

Applied Social Science for Environmental Planning, edited by William Millsap

Social Impact Analysis and Development Planning in the Third World, edited by William Derman and Scott Whiteford

Nuclear Power: Assessing and Managing Hazardous Technology, edited by Martin J. Pasqualetti and K. David Pijawka

**Science, Technology, and the Issues of the Eighties: Policy Outlook,* edited by Albert H. Teich and Ray Thornton

*Available in hardcover and paperback.

A Westview Special Study

Socioeconomic Impact Management: Design and Implementation
John M. Halstead, Robert A. Chase, Steve H. Murdock, and F. Larry Leistritz

The authors of this book present a comprehensive analysis of impact management for such large-scale resource and industrial development projects as power plants, mines, and nuclear waste disposal facilities. An overall framework for designing an impact management program is presented and specific recommendations for implementing management measures are provided. This book is unique in that it provides a conceptual framework for choosing among alternative approaches in designing a management system, as well as offering practical guidance for implementing such systems.

John M. Halstead is a research assistant in the Department of Agricultural Economics at North Dakota State University, where Robert A. Chase is a research associate. Steve H. Murdock is head of the Department of Rural Sociology at Texas A&M University. F. Larry Leistritz is professor of agricultural economics at North Dakota State University and is author with Steve Murdock of *The Socioeconomic Impact of Resource Development* (Westview 1981).

Socioeconomic Impact Management

Design and Implementation

John M. Halstead, Robert A. Chase,
Steve H. Murdock, and F. Larry Leistritz

Routledge
Taylor & Francis Group
NEW YORK AND LONDON

First published in paperback 2024

First published 1984 by Westview Press, Inc.

Published 2019 by Routledge
605 Third Avenue, New York, NY 10158

and by Routledge
4 Park Square, Milton Park, Abingdon, Oxon OX14 4RN

Routledge is an imprint of the Taylor & Francis Group, an informa business

Library of Congress Catalog Card Number: 84-051866

Publisher's Note
The publisher has gone to great lengths to ensure the quality of this reprint but points out that some imperfections in the original copies may be apparent.

ISBN 13: 978-0-367-28784-9 (hbk)
ISBN 13: 978-0-367-30330-3 (pbk)
ISBN 13: 978-0-429-30659-4 (ebk)

DOI: 10.4324/9780429306594

Contents

Tables and Figures

TABLES

FIGURES

Preface

Large-scale industrial and resource development projects are affecting many areas in the United States and other nations. Some of the types of projects having substantial effects on nearby communities include energy resource development in many of the western states and Canadian provinces, water projects in the northwestern and southwestern United States, offshore petroleum development in the North Sea and Arctic regions of Canada and Alaska, metal mining and smelting in Australia, and power plant construction in New Zealand. These developments present both opportunities and problems for the areas where they are located. While resource and industrial development projects often offer the benefits of new jobs and provide a stimulus to the local economy, they also may lead to rapid population growth--frequently creating problems that many rural communities are not prepared to effectively manage.

The economic, demographic, public service, fiscal, and social effects (*socioeconomic impacts*) of large-scale development projects have been extensively examined by both researchers and decision-makers in recent years. A growing number of these analyses and case studies provide insights concerning the effects of such activities on communities located near project sites. A common theme that emerges from such analyses is that, in the absence of detailed local planning and access to financial and technical assistance from external sources (e.g., the developer or federal, state, or similar levels of government), large projects will frequently create substantial problems for their host communities. Among the most pervasive of these community problems are a lack of adequate housing to meet the needs of the incoming project workers and their dependents, and inadequate public sector revenues to support the provision of needed services.

Such impacts can lead to several problems for the larger society as well. First, the basic principles underlying society's conceptions of social and economic justice and equity may be severely challenged because socioeconomic impacts may be inequitably distributed such that some segments of society (e.g., the elderly, residents of rural areas) are forced to bear an inordinate share of the costs of large-scale projects. Second, inadequate housing, public services, and similar infrastructure problems may lead to increased rates of labor absenteeism and turnover, decreased worker productivity, and thus to increased development costs. Finally, because of the actual or perceived inequity in the distribution of project-related costs and benefits, residents in areas near the project site may actively oppose the project. If such opposition becomes an accepted strategy for citizens in reacting to proposed projects, it may become nearly impossible to establish projects that have some objectionable characteristics but are essential to the continued operation of developed industrial societies, or it may lead to the location of such sites in politically expedient but technically undesirable (e.g., less safe or more expensive) locations. Thus, the need is readily apparent to examine those measures which can be employed to alter the effects of project development on nearby communities, reducing those effects which are generally viewed as undesirable and enhancing those changes which are deemed beneficial.

Despite a growing consensus that socioeconomic impacts are important and must be addressed, however, the processes for effectively coping with such project effects have received only limited attention in the literature. Even though the characteristics of the socioeconomic changes resulting from large-scale projects and methods for projecting such effects have been the subject of numerous analyses, the mechanisms which can be employed to influence the socioeconomic impacts of large-scale projects have received only cursory treatment. Those reviews of "impact mitigation" which have appeared typically discuss only a few selected types of impact management measures or review only a few selected cases where developers or communities have taken an active role in influencing project outcomes. Thus, such studies have seldom attempted to draw, and have even failed to provide reviews that are in an appropriate form to allow the formulation of, the generalizations essential to establishing a scientific approach to impact management. In addition, such analyses have tended to be theoretically uninformed, providing no systematic framework to delineate and evaluate alternative mitigation approaches and the interrelationships between alternative approaches.

For both policymakers and social science analysts, then, there is a critical need for a single source that provides an integrated analysis of impact management principles and practices for large-scale projects. This work is an attempt to address this need. Specifically, it attempts to (1) outline several conceptual frameworks for designing impact management programs, (2) identify situations which create a need for impact management, and (3) examine the key components of impact management systems, with attention to both conceptual bases for choosing among alternative approaches and practical considerations in implementing them. The work thus represents an attempt to provide a conceptual framework for the development of a scientific approach to impact management, a basis for identifying impact management problems, and information and references useful in designing management programs.

The work is intended to address the needs of private and public sector officials engaged in project development, public officials concerned with project permitting and growth management planning, and social scientists involved in the analysis of impact issues and problems. That such an effort can be only partially successful is evident, given the complexity and rapidly changing nature of this field. In an area of study as rapidly developing as this, information presented in many areas may soon become dated. However, it is our hope that such an effort, by summarizing the state-of-the-art in the management of socioeconomic impacts of resource developments, will serve to improve that art as well.

J.M.H., R.A.C., S.H.M., and F.L.L.

Acknowledgments

In completing this work, the support and encouragement of several entities have been invaluable. The Department of Agricultural Economics and the North Dakota Agricultural Experiment Station at North Dakota State University and the Department of Rural Sociology, the Texas Agricultural Experiment Station, and the Center for Energy and Mineral Resources at Texas A&M University have all provided support for this effort and receive our sincere appreciation.

We wish to thank the many persons who assisted in the preparation of the manuscript. Thus, the clerical assistance of Patricia Bramwell, Cindy Danielson, Becky Dethlefsen, Jan Johnson, Pedra Meeks, Ona Richards, and Jackie Snortum is gratefully acknowledged. We also wish to thank Debbie Tanner, Carol VavRosky, and Steve Stark for the graphics. We extend special thanks to Lori Cullen, who tirelessly typed the entire manuscript and coped cheerfully with numerous revisions. We extend very special appreciation to Brenda Ekstrom, our technical editor, whose suggestions greatly improved the readability of the manuscript and whose countless hours of editing, indexing, proofreading, and general production assistance made its completion possible.

We also extend our appreciation to numerous colleagues and associates who reviewed and suggested revisions that have clearly improved the manuscript. In particular, we wish to thank Don Albrecht, Audrey Armour, Molly Brady, Jim Finley, Rita Hamm, Natalia Krawetz, Reg Lang, Arlen Leholm, and Jay Leitch.

J.M.H., R.A.C., S.H.M., and F.L.L.

1 Introduction to Socioeconomic Impact Management

Any attempt to evaluate the management of the socioeconomic impacts of resource and industrial development will necessarily involve examination of a broad range of conceptual and pragmatic considerations. It is therefore necessary to begin the discussion by specifying (1) the rationale behind the focus of the work, (2) the specific focus and limitations placed on the effort, (3) an overview of impact management approaches, and (4) the basic organization of the text.

RATIONALE FOR AN EVALUATION OF SOCIOECONOMIC IMPACT MANAGEMENT METHODS

A number of concurrent trends have led to increased development of resource extraction and conversion facilities and industrial plants in rural areas with small populations and limited infrastructure. Changes in energy markets which have occurred over the last decade have resulted in increased emphasis on the development of domestic resources in the United States and several other industrialized nations. Because the most economically attractive deposits of these energy resources, including coal, oil sands and oil shale, conventional oil and gas, and uranium, are often located in areas remote from major population centers, substantial numbers of energy extraction projects are being developed, or proposed for development, in such areas (Moore 1982; Brealey and Newton 1981; Gartrell et al. 1980; Dixon 1978; Murdock and Leistritz 1979). Many energy conversion facilities, such as electric power and synthetic fuel plants, also are being sited in remote areas. These trends can be attributed both to economic factors, which in some cases favor the siting of such plants close to their fuel source, and also to environmental considerations which discourage the siting of these facilities near populous areas (Santini, South, and Stenehjem 1979; Warrack and Dale 1981; Metz 1982a). Growing world demand for other minerals likewise has led to development of numerous new mines. Because the mineral deposits located near major industrial centers generally were the first to be developed, the most attractive remaining resources are often now found in remote areas (Metz 1982a; DePape 1982). Finally, recent trends toward industrial decentralization, which are evident in a number of industrialized nations, have led an increasing number of firms to locate new manufacturing facilities in rural areas (Summers et al. 1976; Summers and Selvik 1979; Lonsdale and Seyler 1979).

As important as the rural location of many of these facilities is in determining their relative impacts on siting areas, their size in comparison to the economic and demographic bases of such areas is equally significant. Many new projects can be expected to require construction work forces numbering in the thousands and a permanent operation-and-maintenance force of several hundred to several thousand (Gilmore et al. 1982; Warrack and Dale 1981; Brealey and Newton 1981; Murdock et al. 1983). When such large-scale projects are developed in sparsely populated areas far from large urban centers, they present both benefits and problems to the communities nearby. Such projects often lead to long-desired increases in local employment and to general economic growth in the area. However, the total magnitude of economic growth associated with such projects, the rapidity of the fluctuations of such patterns during the lifetime of the project, the public service demands created by growth, and the uncertainty of the timing and specific location of many of the impacts create severe planning problems for local areas.

For example, the construction of energy facilities in sparsely populated rural areas has sometimes led to a doubling or trebling of population in nearby communities in only a few years with rapid growth beginning as early as the first year of construction (Gilmore et al. 1982). This growth often fluctuates widely during the development period with the most substantial increases occurring during the construction phase, followed by relative stability during the facility's operation, and by rapid population decline during the postoperation phase (Murdock and Leistritz 1979). Similar patterns of growth are often associated with the construction of large military installations and industrial facilities.

Because public service needs fluctuate with population, local areas are often faced with the difficult decision of whether to build facilities to meet the anticipated requirements during a project's construction phase and then face the possibility of substantial excess capacity during the operational phase or simply to attempt to get by during the construction phase and build to meet the long-term needs resulting from the project. Added to such difficulties is the fact that local officials often must plan with the realization that the demands for new services resulting from a new project are likely to precede the revenues from it (Gilmore et al. 1976), along with the realization that changes in the project's construction schedule or in the settlement patterns of new workers can often change the expected impacts (Murdock et al. 1978). Uncertainty regarding the impacts that may actually be experienced may have a major influence on the response of the local public sector to project-related needs (Krawetz 1981). Public officials often are understandably reluctant to increase public debt if it is not clear that future increases in the tax base will be sufficient to repay the debt without substantial tax increases. Similarly, underwriters and rating services are reluctant to participate in bond issues when significant uncertainty is involved. Many public finance decisions in impact areas are thus limited by the uncertain nature of such developments and their resultant impacts (Murdock and Leistritz 1979).

The uncertainty often associated with such large-scale projects also may inhibit the private sector from responding adequately to the new needs. Project-related inmigration may create the need for an expansion of an area's housing stock which is far beyond the capacity of local builders (Newton 1982). Yet, uncertainty regarding whether the project will actually take place, when it will begin, and whether it is possible that it will be developed only to be later abandoned as infeasible--together with uncertainty regarding potential impacts at the community level--may cause developers from outside the area to be reluctant to initiate major housing projects. Similarly, uncertainty concerning the magnitude and permanence of growth may discourage the local trade and service sector from expanding to meet growing demands.

As a result, communities affected by large-scale projects frequently experience periods during which housing, public services, and private sector retail and service capabilities are less than adequate to meet the needs of the expanded local population. Such situations have sometimes led to dissatisfaction on the part of both long-term residents and newcomers and to a general feeling that the local quality of life has been degraded (Myrha 1980; Dixon 1978; Gilmore and Duff 1975a). These feelings, in turn, have contributed to increased rates of labor turnover and absenteeism, decreased worker productivity, and increased development costs (Metz 1983; Gilmore 1976). Thus, project proponents, as well as the affected communities, have reason to be vitally interested in ensuring that the demands imposed by new development can be accommodated without undue strain.

Within the last few years, another form of socioeconomic impacts associated with large-scale projects also has become apparent--the impacts of facility closure. In several localities, unanticipated decreases in the demand for a facility's product have abruptly changed an anticipated future of robust economic growth into one of mass unemployment, plummeting housing values, and fiscal shortfalls (McGinnis and Schua 1983; Halstead, Chase, and Leistritz 1983). The causes of facility closures, shutdowns, and cancellations have included depletion of mineral deposits, reductions in regional demand (e.g., for electricity), declining prices and an unfavorable outlook in the world market (e.g., for oil, uranium, and such metals as copper, molybdenum, and iron), high interest rates and financing difficulties, unfavorable governmental regulation and taxation policies, plant obsolescence, and basic structural economic changes (Metz 1983; Halstead, Chase, and Leistritz 1983). Structural economic change describes a combination of forces, including rising labor costs, increasing transportation costs, and shifts in the locus of major markets, which have the overall effect of reducing an area's comparative advantage in the production of a specific product. These structural changes, which give rise to opportunities to increase profits by shifting operations to an alternative location, appear to be a major cause of extensive manufacturing plant closings in the north central and northeastern United States (Bluestone and Harrison 1982).

Whatever the cause of a facility shutdown, impacts on the community can be substantial, particularly if the plant is the area's major employer. The most obvious and immediate impact is the loss of jobs provided by the facility. Other local businesses may experience the negative multiplier effects of the closing, because of both curtailment in purchases by the facility from local businesses and reduction in the demand for consumer goods and services caused by loss of the plant's payroll. In some cases local trade and service firms will find it necessary to lay off workers or even to go out of business. Depressed area housing markets may create problems for workers who desire to leave the area in search of better employment opportunities (Halstead, Leistritz, and Chase 1983). Local governments typically experience losses in property, sales, and income tax revenues. These reductions in public sector revenues may be particularly problematic because they often occur at the same time that demands for public assistance and selected other forms of public services may be increasing as a result of the substantial number of unemployed workers in the community.

Responses to facility closures have sometimes included grants by the firm to local governments, severance pay or early retirement provisions for workers, a variety of financial and technical assistance from senior levels of government, and local efforts to attract new industry (Halstead, Chase, and Leistritz 1983). In addition, the community impacts associated with shutdowns have stimulated proposals for state or federal legislation to require firms to provide advanced notice and various forms of assistance to workers and communities (Bluestone and Harrison 1982; McKenzie 1982). Finally, closure problems have led some analysts to examine alternatives to the single-industry community (DePape 1983; Brealey and Newton 1981). Although the most appropriate public policy responses to closures are still a subject of considerable disagreement, it is certain that policymakers will be more sensitive to these problems when new projects are proposed in the future and will demand very careful management of these projects by their developers.

Historical Precedents for Impact Management

Although the need for impact management has been discussed more frequently in recent years, antecedents for activities of this type go back several decades. Notable among the early examples of activities which are now often termed impact mitigation were the efforts of various mining and other resource development companies in establishing housing and support services (i.e., "company towns") for their workers and the initiatives of the U.S. Department of Defense in providing impact assistance to communities affected by major military facilities (Metz 1982a; Leistritz, Halstead, Chase, and Murdock 1982).

Construction of self-contained communities, or company towns, was commonplace in the United States in the 1800s, and followed the precedents set in the United Kingdom (Metz 1982a; Knight 1975). Between 1850 and 1940, thousands of company towns were built to accommodate miners, loggers, and construction workers. Even though company towns and company-owned housing in general have decreased in popularity, new town development and direct company provision of permanent housing are still practiced occasionally in remote areas (Metz 1982a; Holmes and Narver 1981). Similar development of worker housing and support services by resource companies also has been practiced frequently in remote areas of Canada and Australia (DePape 1983; Brealey and Newton 1981; Robinson 1982).

Early instances of providing temporary living accommodations for construction workers were most frequently associated with railroad construction (Knight 1975). For example, during construction of Canada's transcontinental railways between 1903 and 1914, more than 3,000 temporary work camps housing about 200,000 men were utilized (Parkinson et al. 1980). Similar temporary housing arrangements have been utilized during construction of dams, military installations, and other large facilities and during oil field development in remote locations in both the United States and Canada (Olien and Olien 1982).

The impact assistance activities of the Department of Defense (and its predecessor agencies) began with the Lanham Acts of 1940 and 1941. These acts authorized the Federal Works Administrator to provide housing and a broad range of community facilities in order to avoid shortages which would impede national defense activities (President's Economic Adjustment Committee 1981). The Lanham Acts' rationale for community assistance, to avoid "the imposition of an increased excessive tax burden or an unusual increase in the debt limit of the taxing or borrowing authority," is remarkably similar to the standards adopted for recent military projects (President's Economic Adjustment Committee 1981) and for some power plant construction projects (Watson 1977). During the period from 1941 to 1945, impact assistance expenditures totaled $456 million ($2.6 billion in 1980 prices), or about 3 percent of total military base investments.

Early efforts to provide housing and support services when projects were being developed in remote areas generally were initiated by the project proponent. Except in those cases where a federal agency was the project developer, federal and state governments typically played little, if any, role in such efforts. Governmental involvement increased somewhat over time in such areas as regulating work camps to ensure conformance with public health, safety, and food processing standards. Likewise, unions became active in demanding more adequate living conditions for their members (Parkinson et al. 1980). Substantial involvement by government in mandating and reviewing industrial activities, however, was only to occur with the passage of environmental policy laws by several of the industrialized nations.

Another development which would subsequently influence impact management efforts was an evolution in workers' attitudes. Resource project workers came to expect higher quality housing and public services and more extensive recreational opportunities than had often been present in the early company towns. Moreover, these workers demonstrated an increased willingness to relocate if their expectations were not met. This change in workers' attitudes suggested that, during periods when skilled labor was in high demand, housing and associated services and amenities would become an important incentive for attracting and maintaining a productive work force (Metz 1982a; Parkinson et al. 1980; Brealey and Newton 1981).

During the 1970s, the socioeconomic impacts of large-scale projects became the subject of increasingly stringent regulatory requirements. In the United States, the National Environmental Policy Act of 1969 (NEPA) and state environmental and facility siting legislation mandated the preparation of environmental impact statements (EISs) for major projects (Council on Environmental Quality 1973, 1978). Further, after a period of virtual neglect in the early 1970s, the social and economic impacts of development are now receiving substantial attention not only in EISs but also in the overall siting and permitting process (Watson 1977; Luke 1980). Similar requirements have emerged, as either a formal mandate or an informal process, in a number of other countries (Lee and Wood 1978; OECD 1979; Wandesforde-Smith 1979; Kennedy 1980; Carpenter 1981). Thus, there is a trend toward institutionalizing socioeconomic impact considerations into the overall project planning and approval process (Watson 1977; Fookes 1981b; DePape 1982). Project proponents are increasingly being required to institute measures to reduce the costs and dislocations which facility development may impose on nearby communities, to compensate local jurisdictions and/or individuals, and/or to increase the local benefits associated with the project. These requirements frequently are formalized as conditions attached to project siting permits, lease agreements, or other necessary governmental approvals (DePape 1982; Ellis 1982; Watson 1977).

The environmental regulatory processes which emerged during the 1970s marked a major turning point in socioeconomic impact management efforts. By requiring that socioeconomic impacts be evaluated (impact assessment) and plans for avoiding or alleviating undesirable effects be prepared (impact mitigation), environmental laws assured that the socioeconomic effects of large-scale projects would receive more systematic attention. In fact, the environmental regulatory process has been largely responsible for formalizing socioeconomic impact analysis as a legitimate field of inquiry.

Beneficiaries of Impact Management

The rationale for devoting scarce resources to impact management activities has not only resulted from legislative mandates, however. Such efforts are also often justified because of their effects on (1) the communities affected by a project, (2) the firm or agency responsible for project development, and (3) society as a whole. While each of these entities has somewhat different stakes in the outcome of the development process, it can be shown that each stands to benefit from an effective impact management effort.

From the viewpoint of the affected communities, impact management efforts are essential in order to avoid the potentially disruptive effects of development. Results of rapid growth, such as overstrained public facilities, revenue shortfalls, poorly planned or uncontrolled housing development (e.g., poorly maintained mobile home parks), and a general feeling that the local quality of life has been degraded, have been widely publicized (Gilmore 1976; Cortese and Jones 1977; Dixon 1978). Community leaders are frequently aware of such potential problems and place a high priority on avoiding them (Halstead, Leistritz, and Chase 1983). In addition, an impact management program can be viewed in a more positive light as an opportunity to utilize development-induced change as a mechanism to further community goals (e.g., improved facilities and services). Finally, local planners and decision-makers often recognize that an effective impact management and planning process is essential not only to meet immediate needs and to solve short-term problems but also to ensure the community's long-run viability. Thus, sound physical and financial planning may be necessary during a period of rapid growth in order to avoid a legacy of future service problems and fiscal difficulties (Murray and Weber 1982).

The firm or agency responsible for project development can also anticipate both short- and long-term benefits from an effective impact management program. First, such efforts may serve to build local support for the project, thus enhancing prospects for approval by regulatory bodies and reducing the potential for litigation and associated delays (Luke 1980; O'Hare et al. 1983). Second, a well-designed impact management plan that helps to ensure adequate housing and services for the project work force can be expected to enhance recruitment and retention and to improve worker morale and productivity (Metz 1980; Myhra 1980; Holmes and Narver 1981). Although the benefits accruing to a developer from a more productive work force are difficult to quantify, initial estimates suggest that the benefits are likely to be impressive and may more than offset the costs of mitigation efforts in some cases. For example, in evaluating alternative impact management options for a large energy facility sited in a remote location in the western United States, Harvey (1982) concluded that provision of housing and associated infrastructure (a new town) near the site would result in benefits of about $7,800 per year for each project construction worker living in the new town. The benefits from providing such accommodations, which would allow workers to avoid a long commute, were comprised of reductions in premium pay and per diem allowances (56 percent), reduced worker turnover (15 percent), reduced absenteeism (13 percent), and increased overall productivity (16 percent). Similar benefits (per worker) were estimated for the project's operating period. A final factor which may encourage developers to implement impact management programs is their desire to avoid adverse community impacts (and associated publicity) which might affect their future projects. Thus, publicity of the type associated with rapid-growth impacts in the Rock Springs, Wyoming, area may have negative effects on the developer's prospects for obtaining siting approval for a subsequent project (Myhra 1980).

From the viewpoint of society as a whole, it might appear that communities which are chosen as sites for major resource development facilities are fortunate and likely to receive "windfall benefits." Indeed, the fact is well documented that such facilities often do provide substantial benefits in terms of increased tax base (Halstead and Leistritz 1983a; Shields et al. 1979; Purdy et al. 1977), attractive jobs for local workers (Wieland et al. 1979), stabilization or augmentation of local population, and enhancement of local services and facilities (Murdock et al. 1982; Rathge et al. 1982). However, the expanding socioeconomic impact literature also reveals that large-scale resource projects may also impose hardships (i.e., costs in excess of benefits) on some nearby communities (e.g., those not sharing in the project-related tax revenues), on selected groups within the community (e.g., fixed income groups), and/or during selected time periods (e.g., the project construction period) (Weber and Howell 1982; Gilmore et al. 1982; Murdock and Leistritz 1979). Further, it must be recognized that (1) some facilities are <u>generally</u> viewed as undesirable locally, although beneficial on a regional basis (e.g., hazardous waste facilities), and others (e.g., strip mines, nuclear power plants) may be considered unfavorable by a substantial segment of the local population; and (2) local residents have gained increased leverage for opposing such facilities (e.g., through NEPA) and are increasingly willing to do so (O'Hare et al. 1983).

From the societal viewpoint, then, there are at least three justifications for support of efforts to require developers to mitigate, or compensate for, the adverse impacts of their projects. First, and probably most important, is the fact that in the absence of mitigation or compensation measures, "desirable" projects (from a societal viewpoint) may be stymied because of local opposition. If local groups feel that a proposed project is detrimental to their interests, they are likely to organize in opposition to its development; such opposition is frequently effective (O'Hare et al. 1983). Two socially inefficient outcomes may result from such "adversary" siting procedures: (1) it may prove to be impossible to locate a project essential to society anywhere, or (2) the project may eventually be developed but at a less than optimal (e.g., more costly, less safe) location. An impact management program, including compensation and/or incentives for local interests, has the potential to aid in resolving such siting dilemmas (O'Hare et al. 1983; O'Hare 1977).

A second reason why impact alleviation measures may be encouraged is that by requiring developers to internalize the external costs associated with their facilities (through specific measures to prevent or compensate for adverse impacts), such costs are made more visible and society is more assured that the project meets the "net benefits" criterion (i.e., that total benefits to society exceed total costs).

The third major consideration which may lead to public (i.e., societal) support for impact management measures is that of equity. It has been noted that the equity argument for compensation is weaker than the efficiency argument (O'Hare et al. 1983). This is because of conflicting interpretations of what is meant by equity or fairness. While the concept of *procedural justice* would always appear to support impact mitigation/ compensation actions, *allocative justice* may or may not favor such an approach depending on the distributional outcomes of such actions (i.e., are the "poor" being asked to compensate the "rich"?). From a practical political standpoint, however, there appears to be a general reluctance to impose large losses on small and identifiable segments of society (Morell and Magorian 1982). In fact, Thurow (1980) argues that political reluctance to impose clear economic losses on specific groups is a major cause of inertia in the policymaking process.

Equity considerations are further complicated when the siting of a facility exposes those living in the vicinity to the slight probability of very significant adverse effects (as in the case of a toxic chemical spill). In such cases, it is ultimately necessary for decision-makers to determine what level of risk is "acceptable" (Petak 1980). It is clear that public judgements concerning the levels of risk which are acceptable depend in large measure on whether the risk is assumed voluntarily or involuntarily; the decision to accept risks voluntarily appears to imply that there are corresponding benefits which are considered "worth the risk" (Morell and Magorian 1982). To the extent that an impact management program alters local perceptions of the benefits associated with facility siting, then, it may also affect local opinions concerning the acceptability of project-related risks. Overall, equity as well as efficiency considerations tend to encourage public support for impact management efforts.

In sum, the importance of a greater emphasis on impact management is reflected by the growing recognition among policymakers and social science analysts, the large number of historical and legal precedents, and the benefits for siting areas, developers, and society as a whole. Until very recently, however, the approaches that can be taken to influence the socioeconomic effects of large-scale projects have received little attention in the literature. In addition, the articles and reports that have been prepared often are difficult to locate and are typically site- or topic-specific. That is, they tend to be concerned with impact management for one type of development at a given location or to deal with only one type of impact management measure. As a result, it is extremely difficult to discern general strengths and weaknesses of various management approaches or the situations in which each might most appropriately be applied. Given the diversity of recent experiences with various aspects of impact management and the probable need to carefully manage future developments, a comparative review and evaluation of the efficacy of various approaches in different settings is essential. Such a comparative analysis, drawing on experience from several countries, should prove valuable in suggesting not only the relative effectiveness of alternative approaches but also, and perhaps more importantly, the specific circumstances under which various methods are likely to be most useful in the future.

Because past descriptions of socioeconomic impact management techniques have generally failed to take account of the cumulative and interactive effects of multiple impact management measures, they provide little insight concerning which approaches can be expected to complement each other and which will tend to negate each other. Perhaps the most serious shortcoming of past efforts, however, is their failure to suggest comprehensive frameworks for the evaluation of management alternatives--frameworks which are critical both as guides to the disparate literature in the area and as bases for systematically designing or evaluating impact management programs. Thus, while several authors have attempted to provide comprehensive guides for impact assessment (Bisset 1980; Chalmers and Anderson 1977; Finsterbusch and Wolf 1981; Tester and Mykes 1981; Leistritz and Murdock 1981), no similar guide is available as an aid in designing or evaluating impact management efforts.

For both the policymaker and the social science analyst, then, the need for a consolidated single source reference on the impact management process is evident, particularly if such a source provides the following:

1. A discussion of the circumstances which create a need for impact management, including an evaluation of the salient factors that are likely to affect the nature and magnitude of each type of impact and thus to influence the needs for impact management
2. An overview of conceptual frameworks for designing impact management programs and for identifying key components of such management systems and the interrelationships among these components
3. An examination of each of the key components of an impact management system, the specific management measures applicable to each component, the factors to be considered in choosing among alternative approaches, and pragmatic considerations in implementing them

This book is an attempt to provide such an information source that addresses the needs of decision-makers and research analysts. The general as well as the specific elements of its focus are discussed below.

SPECIFIC FOCUS AND SCOPE

The focus of this book is on the management of the socioeconomic impacts of resource development in rural areas. In addition, it attempts to describe some of the conceptual, methodological, and implementation considerations associated with impact management methods. The way each of these elements is delimited in the effort is discussed below.

Impact Management

As with most new fields of study, the analysis and management of socioeconomic impacts has spawned its own set of specialized terminology. Among the terms which have become central to most discussions of socioeconomic impacts are *impact assessment*, *impact mitigation*, and *impact management*. *Impact assessment* describes the process of first projecting the nature and magnitude of the economic and social changes likely to result from project development and then evaluating the significance of these effects (Wolf 1981; Leistritz and Murdock 1981).

The term *impact mitigation* came into widespread usage following its inclusion in NEPA. The NEPA interpretation of *mitigation* has become relatively broad, encompassing "(a) avoiding the impact . . ., (b) minimizing impacts . . ., (c) rectifying the impact by repairing, rehabilitating, or restoring the impacted environment, (d) reducing or eliminating the impact over time . . ., or (e) compensating for the impact by replacing or providing substitute resources or environments" (Council on Environmental Quality 1978). There has been a common tendency, however, to view impact mitigation in the more narrow context of merely "reducing or eliminating negative impacts" (O'Hare et al. 1983; Urban Systems, Inc. 1980).

In the context of formulating appropriate responses to the potential socioeconomic effects of large-scale resource or industrial development projects sited in rural areas, the concept of *impact mitigation* described above appears too narrow. Rather, broader and more comprehensive approaches are needed to encompass measures that enhance the project's local benefits, provide for various forms of compensation (e.g., monetary, in-kind) to local interests, and reduce or eliminate negative effects. Hence, we, as well as others (Gilmore et al. 1982; Berkey et al. 1977), believe that the term *impact management* is a more appropriate description. *Socioeconomic impact management* may thus be defined as the development of procedures and programs to ensure both the equitable and timely distribution of benefits and the avoidance and/or amelioration of negative socioeconomic effects of industrial activities or projects (Gilmore 1983).

Socioeconomic Impacts of Large-Scale Projects

Impact is often an ambiguously used term, frequently evoking negative connotations, which denotes change of some kind. For the purposes of this work, we define *impact* as the phenomena of rapid change in established economic, demographic, and social structures, usually geographically localized, caused by large-scale, precipitous growth or decline in an area's economic base--in other words, impacts on the man-made rather than the natural environment. Although the impacts of all large-scale development projects have some common characteristics, the nature of these effects also can be expected to differ substantially depending on the characteristics of the project, the site area, and the inmigrants associated with the project. Thus, the impact of a given project will differ depending on whether the site area is rural or urban, sparsely or densely populated, whether its economic base is agricultural or industrial, and whether the new inmigrants to the area are similar to or different from the indigenous residents of the area. The impacts of a project also are likely to differ for individual locales within the general area of project influence. These factors increase the complexity of impact management.

Resource Development in Rural Areas

The term *resource development* is used very broadly in the analysis and discussion to include the development of any previously undeveloped resource in an area. Emphasis is given to natural resources, such as energy, minerals, and water, and to industrial developments involving new uses of human resources, such as the labor supplies of rural areas. Resources thus refer to both physical and human resources.

Emphasis also is placed on development occurring in *rural* areas. In part, this reflects the fact that an increasing number of resource development projects are being located in rural areas. It also reflects the authors' primary experience and training. Although impact management principles are similar for urban and rural areas, some differences in emphasis are essential because of the differences in means and economies of scale that affect the provision of services and other factors in rural areas. References will be made to differences in impact problems encountered and appropriate management responses for various types of areas, but emphasis will be placed on impact management techniques for rural areas.

The geographical focus of the work is restricted primarily to impact management in the United States and Canada. Socioeconomic impacts experienced in other countries (particularly the lesser-developed countries and those with centrally planned economies) would differ in many respects, and the institutional framework for dealing with such impacts also would be quite variable. To expand the book to a worldwide focus thus was deemed infeasible. In addition, the authors' experience in resource development is principally with the United States and Canada. Examples from other nations, such as Australia, New Zealand, and the United Kingdom, are introduced to illustrate contrasting or alternative approaches to impact management that might be applicable to some North American situations.

Management of Socioeconomic Impacts

Even though a large number of types of impacts are likely to result from resource development, the focus of this work is on those related to *socioeconomic* dimensions, including the economic, demographic, public service, fiscal, and social effects of development. The discussion deals specifically with impact management, which is seen to involve efforts to both anticipate and alleviate those project effects that are generally perceived as undesirable and to enhance effects which are deemed beneficial.

Conceptual Considerations

Although impact management is largely applied and action oriented, one of the major emphases of the present work is to suggest that conceptual frameworks can be developed and usefully applied to the impact management process. In this effort, a conceptual framework means a systematically organized set of concepts and propositions that improve the ability to explain, understand, and predict socioeconomic outcomes (Blalock 1969). The use of such a framework improves both the ability to anticipate likely areas requiring careful management and the actual management of community impacts. The development and application of such frameworks thus form a major goal of the effort.

Methodological and Implementation Considerations

Methodological and implementation considerations can include a broad range of factors. The *methodological* considerations of interest here are limited to a general discussion of the key features of various impact management approaches, the issues or problems most adequately addressed by each, the factors likely to influence the success of each approach, and the resource commitments and costs associated with each. *Implementation* considerations emphasized in the work relate to factors which must be considered in attempting to initiate specific impact management measures in various settings. Constraints to implementation which may be posed by federal, state, or local legislation, by union and general management practices, and by other institutional factors are discussed.

The work thus attempts to provide a relatively comprehensive overview of the pragmatic, conceptual, and methodological dimensions of the impact management process as they apply to large-scale resource developments in rural areas. Although its areal focus is somewhat limited, it should prove useful to a wide range of community, industrial, and research analysts.

OVERVIEW OF IMPACT MANAGEMENT APPROACHES

Because much of the focus in the remainder of the work will be on the description of alternative impact management procedures, it appears useful to provide a brief overview of the impact management efforts which have been initiated to date. These efforts reflect a variety of approaches with respect to who participates in the process and their roles and responsibilities, the forms of assistance provided, and the intended purposes of such assistance. Thus, the discussion below briefly examines the levels of government (i.e., the type of authority), the use of financial and technical assistance, and the compensation, enhancement, and monitoring dimensions of impact management. This discussion will serve as a useful guide to the reader in examining the remainder of the work.

One important basis for comparing and contrasting impact management efforts is the source of *authority* to implement or require impact management measures (Cole et al. 1983; Gilmore 1983). It is the exercise of various forms of legal authority by the different levels of government, more than any other factor, that has been responsible for the "new era" in impact management. Federal, state (or provincial), and local governments all have utilized their respective authority to require impact management efforts. In the United States, the federal government's authority to play a role in impact management comes primarily from NEPA. To date, the federal role has been quite limited because most of the agencies preparing EISs do not require mitigation of any impacts off the site of the activity they are considering (Gilmore 1983). Federal regulatory agencies such as the Nuclear Regulatory Commission and the Federal Power Commission have sometimes required mitigation efforts as a condition of project licensing (Watson 1977), and agencies like the Department of Defense sometimes provide community assistance payments when the agency is the project proponent. Recent examples of such projects are the deployment of the Trident and proposed deployment of the MX weapons systems (President's Economic Adjustment Committee 1981). Considering the federal role overall, however, it appears that, at least in the United States, the federal government has often been unresponsive to socioeconomic impact management needs.

In some other countries, the federal government has assumed a larger role in impact management. In Canada, for instance, federal authority stems primarily from the Environmental

Assessment and Review Process (EARP), established by a Cabinet decision in 1973. Almost all projects involving federal agencies or federal resources are subject to the EARP, and a number of major reviews have included substantial emphasis on socioeconomic impact assessment and impact management planning (Marshall and Scott 1982). Federal assumption of a major role in development planning has not always proved an unmixed blessing, however. In Scotland, for example, some observers believe that the national government, in an effort to encourage rapid development of North Sea oil resources and thus increase energy self-sufficiency and foreign exchange earnings, has often overridden local interests (Moore 1982).

States and provinces have played a major role in forcing impact management needs to be addressed. In the United States, large-scale energy resource development has led several western states to pass energy facility siting legislation. In such states as Wyoming and North Dakota, the siting process has served as a basis for negotiation and joint planning between industry, and state and local officials. Requirements that specific management activities, such as worker housing and grants and loans to local governments, be undertaken have been attached as conditions for granting siting permits (Ellis 1982; Halstead, Leistritz, and Chase 1983).

Likewise, several Canadian provinces have taken an active role in impact management. For example, the province of Saskatchewan has incorporated specific requirements concerning local employment and business participation in the lease agreement for a new uranium mine (Amok/Cluff Mining Ltd. 1981). The provinces of Alberta and British Columbia also have assumed central roles in planning for new or rapidly expanding communities in oil sands and coal development regions (Paget and Rabnett 1981; Young 1981).

Some local governments have used their planning and zoning authority as a means of requiring resource development firms to provide impact assistance. In Rio Blanco County, Colorado, local zoning provided the authority enabling the county to negotiate a comprehensive impact management agreement with a firm which proposed to develop a coal mine (Halstead, Leistritz, and Chase 1983). Similar use of local planning and zoning authority has occurred in such widely separated locations as Skagit County in Washington, the town of Yakutat in Alaska, and the Shetland Islands in Scotland (Cole et al. 1983; Martin 1983).

Another key component of almost every impact management program is obtaining *financing* for needed facilities and services. During periods of rapid growth, local jurisdictions typically face significant cash flow problems as major increases in expenditures are needed during, or even prior to, the project construction period, whereas substantial growth in tax revenues may not be realized until several years later (Murdock and Leistritz 1979). Local governments often have difficulty in borrowing the funds necessary for infrastructure expansion because of institutional constraints such as debt limits and also because of the uncertainty often associated with large development projects. As noted previously, this uncertainty also may restrict the ability of housing developers and local businesses to obtain needed capital.

The principal sources of financing for most impact management efforts have usually been senior levels of government and/or the firm(s) proposing the resource development project. In the United States, the federal government has provided a significant amount of financial resources for improving public service infrastructure in impacted communities. Most of these funds, however, have been made available through categorical grant programs which are not specifically targeted to the needs of rapid-growth areas. A considerable level of local expertise, as well as persistence, has been required for communities to benefit from these programs, and hence these programs generally are not regarded as a dependable source of financial assistance (Auger et al. 1978).

Some state governments have provided substantial levels of financial aid. For example, several western states, including Colorado, Montana, North Dakota, and Wyoming, have earmarked a portion of their mineral severance taxes to aid affected communities (Murdock and Leistritz 1979). In some states (e.g., North Dakota), state grants and loans have been the primary source of financing for community facilities, while in others (e.g., Colorado, Wyoming), industry also is expected to provide direct assistance to communities. Financing from industry has taken a variety of forms, including prepayment of taxes, loans, loan guarantees, and outright grants to local jurisdictions (Metz 1983).

Another serious need of many communities preparing for development of a major project is *technical assistance*. Small rural communities often lack the technical capability to assess and plan for impacts of a major project, the legal expertise to negotiate with industry, and the administrative capability to expand services. Senior levels of government, particularly the state or provincial level, often have attempted to provide such assistance. Likewise, industry has assisted through donations of personnel and by funding planning and facility design studies.

An issue that frequently arises in developing impact management agreements is the mechanisms to be employed to *compensate* individuals and groups that suffer project-induced costs or losses. Some compensation requests are conceptually simple to resolve because established legal precedents apply (e.g., the case of landowners whose property is taken in the course of development). Other compensation cases are more difficult, such as when recompense is sought for the disruption of traditional lifestyles or for the loss of amenities that are difficult to value quantitatively. There are some recent examples, however, of attempts to develop creative solutions to such problems. For example, Petro-Canada Exploration (PEX) recently developed a plan for compensating trappers whose activities would be affected by the company's proposed coal mine in British Columbia. The PEX plan includes provisions for trapline relocation, habitat protection, or trapline enhancement as well as cash payments (Petro-Canada, Inc. 1982).

Another dimension of impact management which is receiving increased attention is measures to *enhance* the *local benefits* associated with project development. These efforts have been focused primarily on increasing the number of area residents who obtain project jobs, enhancing the opportunities of local businesses to obtain project construction and supply contracts, and encouraging development of local businesses with backward or forward linkages to the resource development project. This aspect of impact management appears to have received greatest attention in connection with mining projects in northern Canada (DePape 1982).

Impact management efforts have increasingly included a system for *monitoring* changes in areal economic and social conditions as project development progresses. The need for these monitoring systems is widely recognized because such uncertainties as the project's timetable, labor force requirements, worker demographic characteristics, and settlement patterns often cause anticipatory impact assessments to be a rather imperfect guide for impact management (Gilmore et al. 1982). Although the importance of the information that can be gained through monitoring is widely recognized, the systems that have been implemented to date differ greatly in the indicators evaluated, the mechanisms for and frequency of data collection, and the nature of analysis performed, as well as in other respects (Leistritz and Chase 1982). The developer is expected to play a key role in the implementation of most monitoring systems, because of unique access to vital information, such as the number and characteristics of project workers.

Other important components of many impact management programs include industry's provision of transportation, temporary housing, and sometimes permanent housing. As noted earlier, some activities of this type predate the current interest in more comprehensive impact management. Efforts undertaken recently in these areas sometimes have been the result of impact management agreements covering a broader range of mitigation activities, but in other cases these measures were implemented at the initiative of industry to enhance work force recruitment and retention.

These are some of the major approaches that have been reflected in recent impact management efforts. Whether explicitly or implicitly, these considerations must be addressed in designing and implementing such efforts in the future.

ORGANIZATION OF THE TEXT

The text consists of nine chapters in addition to this introductory chapter. Each of these chapters is devoted to a particular topic (except for the concluding chapter). The chapters are organized in the order that the issues they address are likely to be considered in an impact management process. Within each chapter, the key issues related to the impact management aspect being considered are briefly examined. Specific approaches applicable in addressing these issues are then examined, and the factors to be considered in choosing among alternative approaches are discussed.

Chapter 2 examines several conceptual schemes for approaching and guiding the impact management process. Based on general systems theory, conflict theory, and exchange theory, these frameworks delineate conceptual structures that point to the need to view impact management as a total process involving the assessment, management, and monitoring of multiple impact types and phases at key points in the community development process. The chapter points out the major components that form the basis of the discussion in subsequent chapters.

Subsequent chapters discuss the roles of assessment, mitigation, and monitoring phases of impact management, and the forms and types of management measures (e.g., incentives, compensation measures) that can be used in addressing each of the five basic impact types (economic, demographic, public service, fiscal, and social) during each major project phase (project planning, project construction, project operation, and project closure). Thus, each of Chapters 3 through 9 addresses an important category of management measures.

In Chapter 3, the impact assessment process is examined. Special emphasis is placed on the importance of beginning the impact evaluation process early in the project planning cycle, preferably during the site selection phase. An overall approach to the analysis of community acceptance problems is outlined, and general guidelines for impact projection and evaluation are presented.

The critical issue of interaction and negotiation between the developer's organization and the potential host community during the facility siting process is examined in Chapter 4. Alternative approaches, including both new concepts and traditional approaches to such interactions, are discussed and illustrated with examples of successful and less than successful experiences in connection with development of large-scale or controversial projects. This chapter gives special emphasis to the role of community development and public participation processes in creating an atmosphere conducive to project siting and the successful implementation of an impact management program. The importance of existing community perceptions, institutions, and organizations in determining the most appropriate approach to implementing a program of community interaction is examined in depth.

In Chapter 5 specific institutional mechanisms which may be utilized in implementing and formalizing the developer-community interaction process are examined. Alternative means of implementing such agreements (e.g., as conditions attached to project permits or leases, or as formal agreements between various levels of government) are examined, and typical features of agreements which have been implemented are reviewed. The effects of these agreements in providing compensation to local interests and/or creating incentives for cooperation in project development are analyzed. Finally, the key role of monitoring mechanisms in assuring compliance with key agreement features and/or in guiding the implementation of impact management measures is discussed.

The sixth chapter deals with the project management options which can be employed to reduce the community-level impacts associated with relocating (inmigrating) workers and their dependents and/or to enhance the local benefits associated with project development (for example, through increased levels of local employment). Specific management options examined include altering the facility's design or construction schedule, implementing training and/or preference programs to increase the percentage of local workers hired, and encouraging long-distance commuting as an alternative to relocation (an approach which may be particularly applicable during project construction). In addition, the special difficulties resulting from the sudden fluctuations in population size that often occur during the construction and closedown phases of projects are examined.

Chapter 7 is the first of two dealing with the need to enhance the capability of local communities to cope with project-related growth and change. Specifically, this chapter reviews options for managing project-related effects on public sector services as well as on private trade and service firms. Special attention is given to the role of advanced planning to avoid problematic impacts (such as housing shortages and inadequate community infrastructure), to enhance the use of existing public facilities, and to increase the ability of local firms to capture project benefits for the community. Specific examples of measures which have been or could be used to facilitate expansion of housing and community infrastructure are reviewed. This chapter is one likely to be of widespread interest to community and regional planners and community leaders.

The closely related topic of financing community development is addressed in Chapter 8. This chapter identifies the problems that may be encountered in both public and private sectors because of the timing and jurisdictional distribution of public sector revenues and costs, the limited access of both public and private sector entities to outside capital markets, and the substantial levels of uncertainty often associated with the development of the project and its local growth implications. The strengths and limitations of numerous options for overcoming these problems are evaluated (including grants, prepayment of taxes, bonding and other forms of borrowing, and user charges for the public sector along with the various conventional capital sources and public-private partnerships for the private sector).

The ninth chapter deals with the special problems inherent in, and the need for innovative responses to, project shutdown, slowdown, closure, or cancellation. Experiences of a number of communities, each confronted with closure of a major industry or cancellation of a large-scale project, are examined. Alternatives available in planning for and subsequently coping with such situations are presented. In addition, the broader policy issues associated with industry closure are examined, including those currently being debated in connection with the "shutdown legislation" being discussed in several states.

The conclusion of the work summarizes the key points presented in earlier chapters and speculates about the future of socioeconomic impact management. A concerted effort is made to ascertain future critical socioeconomic management issues in large-scale facility siting and to suggest future directions that research on impact management dimensions must take to address these issues.

The topics addressed in the text are broad in scope and inclusive of only some of the many aspects of socioeconomic impact management. They represent, however, very important aspects of the impact management process.

2
Theoretical Perspectives for Impact Management

The discussion in this volume clearly establishes impact management as an applied process that requires sensitivity to the characteristics of the project, the siting area, the parties at interest, and other dimensions unique to a given project in a given area. It is, in fact, a process in which the interaction of the unique characteristics of a project and siting area are likely to require different management patterns for each project-site combination. Given such conditions, it may appear unusual to include this chapter because theoretical perspectives are attempts to discern commonalities of patterns across events and places. That theoretical discussions are unusual in the impact management literature is evident from any assessment of the existing literature in impact management (Gilmore 1983; Metz 1980). The practice of impact management has been largely atheoretical, and there have been virtually no attempts by researchers or academicians to use existing frameworks to examine impact management processes. Thus, neither the historical development of the field of impact management nor the phenomena to which impact management processes apply points to the inclusion of a theoretical discussion in a volume such as this.

The purpose of this chapter, however, is to suggest that the use of theoretical perspectives can enhance the ability to understand the dynamics which occur during impact events and impact management processes. In addition, the use of theoretical perspectives may lead to the development of more effective and sensitive impact management plans. Specifically, the chapter first presents a discussion of some of the major impact management issues for which the use of theoretical perspectives may provide insight and clarification. The next section presents several theoretical perspectives with relevance for impact management. The final section demonstrates the utility of such frameworks for addressing the key aspects of impact events and processes that are examined in the remainder of the volume. The chapter makes no attempt either to develop or to comprehensively apply a given theoretical perspective to the impact management process. The discussions of theoretical perspectives are very general and intended for use by impact management practitioners, not social theorists. They describe only some of the many ways in which theoretical perspectives can be applied to the management process. However, given the paucity of attempts to develop and utilize theoretical perspectives in impact management, they can be seen as a first step toward demonstrating the utility and need for theoretical development in the field. The chapter is therefore an attempt to expand, rather than to comprehensively delineate, the theoretical dimensions of the field of impact management.

THE ROLE OF THEORY IN IMPACT MANAGEMENT

The traditional roles of theory in increasing one's understanding and ability to explain and predict a phenomena (Stinchcombe 1968; Popper 1959; Zetterburg 1965) are as important in the area of impact management as in other areas of analysis. As applied to impact management, these roles suggest that theoretical perspectives can assist in addressing the following key impact management dimensions:

1. What areas should be included in the impact area and in the impact management process?
2. Who should be included in the interaction involved in impact management?
3. What is the nature of the processes likely to occur in the interaction between the parties involved in the process?
4. How will impact-area residents react to project-related changes?
5. What entities or mechanisms can respond to and address the changes likely to occur as a result of a project and be used to mitigate or compensate the area for irreversible changes in its social and economic structure?

Each of these dimensions involves a number of issues for which existing theoretical perspectives provide alternative explanations. The issues related to these dimensions will be briefly discussed prior to the description of theoretical perspectives applicable to impact management.

The issues surrounding the identification of the area likely to be impacted by a project are numerous (Murdock and Leistritz 1979; Leistritz and Murdock 1981). Impact areas can be defined in terms of the residences of persons who may be directly and indirectly employed at the site, in terms of the parties directly or indirectly affected by a project, or in numerous other ways. As a result, delineations using commuting zones, functional economic areas, legal jurisdictions, and cultural areas have been utilized (Finsterbusch et al. 1983). How far the boundaries of such areas should extend from the project site and how the areas influenced by a project can be delineated are interlaced with questions of who should make such delineations and of how direct the influences must be for an area or a people to be considered as impacted by a project. When key resources such as water, air, or special cultural areas are involved, the resolution of such issues becomes particularly difficult. As demonstrated below, different theoretical frameworks provide different perspectives that may be extremely useful in suggesting the criteria that should be used in delineating the impact area.

The issues surrounding who should be involved in the management process are equally difficult to resolve. Questions arise about whether only those directly affected and resident in the area, or all those with an interest in the area and its human and natural resources, should be involved. In the latter case, questions concerning which entities (e.g., which interveners) from outside the area should be involved become extremely difficult to resolve. Equally important are issues related to the proper roles of industry and local, state, and federal governments in the impact management process. Closely related to these concerns are questions of how various parties can be and should be involved. How does one ensure that the public is adequately involved in the process, and when is that involvement most effective and appropriate? If properly used, theoretical perspectives can play a useful role in identifying the potential parties of interest in impact events and those parties likely to be most effective in bringing about the resolution of problems within the management process.

Impact management is inherently processual, but the nature of the processes that should and will occur is far from evident. To what extent is conflict between the parties of interest inevitable? How can cooperation be brought about between parties with differing points of view? To what extent can compromises be reached and to what extent is it simply necessary to recognize that some parties are likely to lose resources as a result of a major project development? These are only some of the types of process issues that may affect impact management. Again, theoretical perspectives can provide a means of discerning the nature of the processes likely to occur and of the means of increasing the likelihood of the occurrence of different types of processes.

The process of identifying the probable project-related changes may also benefit from theoretical guidance. Whether such changes should be seen as brief alterations in an area's overall organization that will soon be rectified or as representing changes that will permanently alter the structures of an area's socioeconomic and sociocultural bases is unclear. In the same way, issues related to the normalcy of such changes and to whether or not such changes will lead to changes in the relative positions of social and economic groups or to uniform changes for all groups in the social structure often go unresolved. The exposition of such patterns of change remains the major goal of many social science theories, and their use in the management process can assist the practitioner in identifying and preparing for the alternative courses of change that may appear in the development process.

The final issue areas are of key concern to impact management. It is critical to resolve issues such as whether or not mitigation and compensation should be effected through key interest groups, such as industry or local communities, or whether such processes are best done through the use of existing institutional bases in the impact area or through the creation of new and separate authorities and mechanisms. The use of theoretical perspectives can help to identify key area characteristics that suggest which mechanisms may be most effective in a given impact area.

The resolution of these issues is critical to any impact management process. This volume will demonstrate that the lessons learned from other areas are often useful guides for a new application of a management process. Incorporating theoretical perspectives in impact management may also help analysts anticipate the course of such events and resolve issues during project development. Some of the theoretical perspectives that can be applied and how such applications may be useful in the management process are described below.

THEORETICAL PERSPECTIVES APPLICABLE TO IMPACT MANAGEMENT

The range of sociological and economic theories that can be applied to impact management is extensive. In this discussion, we present only a few of these theories.

1. Functional, Ecological, and Systems Theories
2. Conflict Theories
3. Social and Economic Exchange Theories

The attempt is, thus, exemplary, and no claim for inclusiveness or exhaustiveness is made. In the discussion which follows, the general tenets of each perspective are described; their application to the impact management process is discussed in the next section.

Functional, Ecological, and Systems Theories

The functional, ecological, and systems theoretical perspectives, though clearly differentiated in the formal social sciences literature (Parsons 1968; Hawley 1950; Buckley 1967), are similar and can be considered as a common perspective for purposes of this effort. Each of these perspectives views localities as being composed of a set of interacting and closely interrelated factors. Such factors include not only the physical features but also the economic, social, and cultural systems, as well as the individual acting members (residents) of the area (Parsons 1968). Central to these perspectives is the idea that the units of "the system of interrelationships" are functionally related to each other with the parts interacting to perform key functions, such as economic support (or sustenance-maintenance) (Gibbs and Martin 1959), socialization of members to the area's socioeconomic and cultural bases, and governance (i.e., to ensure control of group members) (Turner 1974).

Each of these perspectives maintains that a key to understanding how any setting functions is to identify the functional parts of the system, establish how such parts interact, and delineate how the system changes. For these theorists, the key system parts are those that address key functions; the interrelationships between these parts are largely a result of the pursuit of functions needed by the members of the system, and the changes are largely a result of outside or exogenous forces. Change is seen as a disturbance to an otherwise harmonious system and as being accommodated by subtle shifts in system parts. Residents of the area are seen as aligning or adapting their actions in relation to such functions and as taking their status from, and as having their resources determined by, their relation to the key functions of the system.

These theorists maintain that one can discern the system of an area and distinguish it from other systems by identifying the key functional parts of the system and the means by which these key parts interact cooperatively. By knowing these factors, one can discern how residents in an area will react to changes in the system to make the system function. Although the proponents of these related perspectives differ substantially both in the roles they see for individual actors in the system (Parsons 1968; Hawley 1950; Duncan 1964) and in the key functions identified in the system (Merton 1968), they share a belief in the feasibility of system identification and in the existence of system functionality.

Conflict Theories

Conflict theorists (Dahrendorf 1959; Simmel 1956; Coser 1956) maintain a perspective that is quite different than the functional, ecological, and systems perspectives. To conflict theorists, the major social process is one of conflict over resources. Groups are formed to more effectively compete for such resources, and groups and individuals receive their status and their ability to influence others in relation to their control of resources. Although popularly associated with the works of Karl Marx (Mills 1948), the perspective is much broader than his works demonstrate. Central to the theory is the view that social and economic systems undergo a continuous process of change as groups (and individuals within groups) compete for the limited resources in an area.

For conflict theorists, the key to understanding the social and economic nature of an area is to understand the area's resource base and the social and economic stratification system that has evolved around that resource base. It is equally important to understand the effects of a given social change, to know how resources will be altered, and to know how people's awareness (or consciousness) concerning such resources will be altered by such a change. By examining how key interest groups react to that change and by determining how the relative power of such groups changes, it is possible to discern the effects of a social change on the affected area.

Exchange Theories

Exchange theories, although primarily associated with the sociologist George Homans (1950), can be seen in a broader sense as a set of theories derived from behavioral psychology, sociology, and basic economics. Such theories stress that human behavior in a setting reflects persons' attempts to maximize the rewards (or maximize the utility) they receive from being involved in a set of actions or events. Whether discussed in terms of rewards or returns and profits, the basic premise of this perspective is that persons will seek involvement in a social and economic event only if they perceive that they will benefit (or be rewarded) from the involvement. They will continue to be involved only if they continue to be rewarded.

For exchange theorists, understanding events in an area and how a given social change will be received requires a careful analysis of the rewards that a setting is offering its residents and of how such rewards will be affected by a given change. Such rewards include not only monetary factors but also numerous social factors, such as prestige, power, and appreciation. To understand an area and how it will be affected by a given event, it is essential to examine the patterns of exchange existing in an area and to discern how such patterns will likely be changed by the event. Both the frequency and the quality (and equality) of such exchanges form central areas of analysis for those using the exchange perspective.

In summary, each of these three broad sets of theories can be applied to nearly any social or economic setting, and each can be used to arrive at an explanation of what is likely to occur as a result of a given action. The explanations they provide and the elements on which they focus may vary widely, however.

Thus, functional, ecological, and systems theorists tend to focus attention on the identification of how key parts of (or functions in) a system change as a result of an action. They see the system as responding as a unit to accommodate the alterations required among system parts. These theorists focus on the effects of an action on system inputs, the interrelationships among system parts, and the effects on outputs of the system.

Conflict theorists concentrate on interest groups and power groups in the area. How an action changes the relative power and the relative resources of these groups is a central focus. At the same time, the use of conflict theory may lead to a confrontational perspective on the nature of the interaction likely to exist between groups responsible for an action and those responding to an action.

Theorists using the exchange perspective tend to seek ways to identify how a given action will affect existing patterns of exchange. Unlike the conflict theorists who see interaction as basically conflictual, exchange theorists see interaction as an exchange of rewards. Thus, an event will be consequential to the extent that it affects the patterns of exchange and the material and nonmaterial rewards received as a function of such exchanges. The major focus is not on the system (as in functionalism) nor on the parties in the system (as in conflict theory) but on the interaction among groups and parties in an area.

The differing emphases of each perspective provide a wide range of ways of perceiving the appropriate design for impact management. Although they do not suggest the superiority of any one design, they can indicate some of the elements that should be taken into account in the design and implementation of an impact management program.

THE APPLICATION OF THEORETICAL PERSPECTIVES TO IMPACT MANAGEMENT

The perspectives summarized above can be applied to key impact dimensions to assist in interpreting impact management events and processes. They can also be used to suggest the key components of those factors that are discussed in the rest of this volume.

Functional, Ecological, and Systems Perspectives and Impact Management

The functional, ecological, and systems perspectives have been applied to the examination of impact events. In fact, much of the early impact assessment work on social indicators reflects systems and functional theories (Fitzsimmons et al. 1977; Finsterbusch and Wolf 1981), and it has been proposed that the ecological framework may be usefully applied to guide the socioeconomic impact assessment process (Murdock 1979). Yet, these theories have not been systematically applied to impact management, despite the fact that they have numerous ramifications for the management process.

The application of these perspectives indicates that impact management must take the characteristics of the system into account. As such, the relevant impact area for impact management is that area that contains functionally linked parts. The use of functional economic areas or commuting zones as approximations of impact areas reflects such perspectives.

In addition, however, these frameworks suggest that all systems are interrelated with yet other systems which are parts of still larger systems. According to the proponents of these perspectives, an attempt should therefore be made to locate the linkages that exist between the impact area's system and other systems and to bring elements that represent these linkages into the impact management process. The use of such perspectives suggests, for example, that if the community maintains numerous industries and other sources of employment (such as federal government employment) that are headquartered outside the community, then an attempt to bring representatives of the parent systems into the management process may be appropriate.

The functional, ecological, and systems perspectives also indicate that the effects of a management action must be traced throughout the system's linkages. For example, the effects of a given mitigative action taken for one group of residents must be examined in relation to other elements within the system. The effects of mineral or other resource developments should be assessed for landowners, as well as for those who rent farm lands. The implications of the establishment of a separate authority for impact management should be examined in light of existing governmental and nongovernmental institutions. In sum, the use of these perspectives points to the need to carefully examine the implications of actions for the system's interrelated parts.

These frameworks further suggest that the key actors in the management process should be those closely tied to an area's key functions and institutions. Thus, financial, religious, business, educational, and other leaders should be involved in impact management as should those involved in the key industries of the area (e.g., farm operators in an area dominated by farming, plant managers or owners in an area dominated by manufacturing). In addition, these perspectives imply that linkages exist between even seemingly diverse functions and that an analysis of the project's effects and the effects of impact management on these linkages should be made. For example, it may be essential to examine what will happen to the traditionally close relationships (linkages) between agriculture and financial institutions in an area, if financing demands from a newly developed minerals industry are extensive.

The functional, ecological, and systems perspectives also indicate that an area's general system will seek to accommodate changes to the system by using existing mechanisms. From these perspectives it can be argued that impact management processes will be more successful if they draw on existing parts of the system rather than create new entities that must find a new functional niche in the system. New entities are likely to require greater adjustments than the enhancement of existing system parts. These perspectives, thus, suggest that attempts to seek cooperation among existing governmental and other units will provide the most effective means of implementing a management process.

These frameworks further suggest that the greater the compatibility between the changes a project induces in a system and the existing elements and processes of the system, the greater the likelihood that the project will not disrupt the system. For example, an area with a history of resource development and with an existing economy based on resource exploitation probably will react less negatively to a new resource-intensive development than an area without such characteristics. The compatibility of the project with the existing components of the impact area's system can, thus, be examined as a means of identifying the area's (system's) likely reaction to a project.

The functional, ecological, and systems perspectives also suggest the use of multidimensional mechanisms in the impact mitigation process. This process should include measures to lessen the magnitude of both the changes likely to impact the system and the differences between project-related factors and the existing characteristics of the system. This process should attempt to strengthen and enhance existing mechanisms to better manage project-related changes and should include attempts to compensate individuals or groups whose place in the system has been negatively impacted by the project. In the terminology often used in these perspectives, the mechanisms used in the impact management process should be ones that seek either to maintain the equilibrium of the system or to re-establish the system's equilibrium if it has been disrupted. Efforts to lessen project-related impacts by reducing the size of the inmigrating work force, to strengthen existing institutional mechanisms, and to compensate persons negatively impacted by a project are clearly supported by the use of these frameworks. Finally, given the importance of system integrity for its proper functioning, the use of such perspectives strongly suggests the need to establish a mechanism to monitor changes so that forces likely to disrupt the system's equilibrium can be addressed.

The functional, ecological, and systems perspectives strongly point out the need for a holistic viewpoint on impact managment. Their use provides recognition of the fact that impacts are not simply events that affect a few persons in an impacted area and that impact management cannot involve only the provision of housing or of financing, but must be seen as a complex process that is sensitive to the social, economic, and cultural relationships that exist in impacted areas. The use of these theories provides a broad encompassing perspective which is necessary for the adequate design and implementation of an impact management system (Gilmore 1983).

Conflict Theory and Impact Management

The conflict perspective suggests that the areas and parties to be included in the management process should not be limited by geographic boundaries, but rather selected in terms of their power within the area. If an area is largely autonomous, then few, if any, parties outside the local area would be appropriate for inclusion in the management process. On the other hand, national or even international bodies may appropriately be involved if the area's social and economic patterns are determined by such entities. The critical area and parties of interest are those that presently control resources or compete for them. Equally important, the use of this perspective suggests that to identify who should be involved in the process, analysts should determine how and which resources will change. Any such change will involve competitors, so, if beneficiaries of project development exist, "relative losers" are also present. This interest group approach to identifying the appropriate players in the impact management process can serve to sensitize one to the fact that nearly any action leads to benefits for some persons or groups and costs for others in an area.

Using the conflict perspective also implies that the introduction of a project into an area can nearly always be expected to result in some conflict because it introduces new resources and new competing groups into an area. It points to the need to see the impact management process as an arbitration process. Unlike the functional, ecological, and systems perspectives that emphasize the role of cooperation between existing elements, using conflict theory suggests the need to ensure that as many existing elements as possible are compensated to minimize the competition that will ensue over new resources. Finally, because the use of a conflict perspective tends to entail a viewpoint of existing social and economic systems as involving marked inequity and a less than equitable distribution of resources, its use will usually involve the analysis of how the existing systems of have and have nots will be affected by a project's development. Such an analysis may lead to the suggestion that although it is disruptive to the existing order, the project will increase equity in the system--a conclusion unlikely to be reached from a systems perspective. Although an analysis of the distributional dimensions of a development may also lead to the conclusion that a project will increase inequity in the system, the emphasis placed on such an analysis is largely missing from a functional perspective, but clearly essential in impact management.

The use of a conflict perspective also suggests that project-related changes will receive a diversity of reactions from area residents, depending on the relative benefits they expect to receive from the project. Support can be anticipated from those who expect to receive increased resources, and opposition from those who lose resources. Equally important, however, is the fact that conflict theories suggest that it is not the absolute gain or loss of resources, but gains and loses relative to other groups that may affect the nature of reactions to a project. Thus, the fact that a resource is added to the range of resources of one group is often sufficient to foster conflict. For example, a new development may do little to the resources of farm groups or local residents in a developing area, yet the fact that it reduces the relative advantages of such groups may lead them to oppose it. Employing conflict theory can assist analysts in recognizing the importance of relative costs and benefits and status gains and losses in an area.

The use of a conflict perspective also points to the importance of compensation in the mitigation process. Because resource changes result in relative losses and gains, compensation measures may be necessary. In addition, because dominance patterns tend to be perpetuated by those in power, it may be necessary to develop mechanisms to assist the most disadvantaged in an area through means that require little involvement of the local power structure. The conflict perspective, thus, clearly implies a stronger role for outside entities than the functional, systems, and ecological perspectives.

Using the conflict perspective suggests the need for those involved in impact management to enter the process with sensitivity to the possible existence of conflict among interest groups. Although some of its dimensions are clearly contradictory to those in the functional perspective, its emphasis on identifying interest groups and the costs, as well as the benefits, of development and its emphasis on the need to analyze the impacts of a project on the distributional system of relative costs and benefits provide additional, rather than conflicting, considerations for use in analyzing the impact management process.

Exchange Theory and Impact Management

The use of an exchange perspective indicates that the impact management process should be seen primarily as an interactive process among groups desiring differential forms of rewards. It requires an examination of the impact process in terms of the groups that will interact and in terms of the rewards each will receive in the development process. This perspective has been usefully applied by Howell et al. (1983) to the examination of the public participation process, but has not been generally applied to impact management.

From the exchange perspective, the relevant impact area is that involving the groups that will interact in the management process. As with the conflict perspective, the area of interest is not necessarily geographically bounded, but rather selected to include those involved in key interactive processes. In terms of the parties to be involved in the management process, this perspective emphasizes not only the need to identify such key interactive groups as the developer, the directly and indirectly impacted parties, the governing (both formally and informally) bodies, and "the public," but also the need to see that the initial and continued involvement of such groups will be determined by the material and nonmaterial reward structure for such involvement. Thus, as Howell et al. (1983) note, the crucial role of public involvement in the management process will be determined in large part by the perception by such groups that they can, in fact, affect the course of events.

The critical point provided by this perspective in regard to the interaction process is that involvement of important interest groups cannot be assured nor maintained without a reward system. Using exchange theory in the impact management process suggests that interactions between interest groups should not be initiated by impact managers unless there is recognition of the fact that a two-way flow of influence and power must accompany such interactions.

The use of exchange theory also points to the management process as a continuous, fluid process of interaction which is unlikely to involve a fixed set of actors (as is sometimes indicated by functional and systems theorists) or of protagonists (as suggested by conflict theorists). Rather, the process is an ebb and flow of information and reactions to that information. For the impact manager, the exchange perspective points out the need for a strong emphasis on information dissemination and responsiveness (a form of reward) to solicitations for information exchange.

The use of the exchange perspective also suggests that local reactions to a project will be a function of the rewards received by the residents of the impact area. In addition, it implies that effects that are aggregatively beneficial will not necessarily lead to project acceptance. Rather the basic tenets of exchange theory point to an area as involving individual actors, each seeking to maximize the rewards he receives. As a result, the use of this perspective would suggest the need to look for means to distribute the rewards of project development among a wide range of area residents.

Using exchange theory indicates that the most effective impact mitigation mechanisms are likely to be those that provide a broad base of both material and nonmaterial rewards. According to exchange theorists, existing agencies cannot be expected to simply assume the responsibilities for such actions, particularly if they are asked to administer systems that they had little part in designing. Agencies, like individuals, need to perceive themselves as being involved in mechanisms through exchanges with other entities (i.e., the need to be rewarded). Thus, the fact that mitigation programs are sometimes poorly administered by agencies that were simply "assigned" responsibilities for them is not surprising from an exchange perspective.

In summary, the use of the exchange perspective indicates the importance of meaningful, mutually rewarding exchange between entities involved in the impact management process. It emphasizes the importance of a wide range of material and nonmaterial rewards and of information dissemination within such exchanges. Finally, it suggests that the tenet that actions must be rewarding to those who perform them must be recognized not only in the discernment of the beneficiaries of impact mitigation, but in all phases of the administration of impact management systems.

Although the perspectives discussed in this chapter represent only some of the many social science theories that can be applied to the impact management process, their use demonstrates the general value of theoretical guidance in impact management design and implementation. Thus, the functional, ecological, and systems theories point to the need for a holistic perspective on impact management and for one that emphasizes the need to trace the effects of a given action on the interrelationships that exist in a system. In like manner, they point to the utility of seeing impact events as being actions imposed on an area--actions that require adjustments by the major components of an area--and of viewing impact mitigation as a means of maintaining, repairing, and monitoring a total system. The use of the conflict perspective points to the need to identify the parties likely to be impacted by a development, to recognize the importance of relative, as well as absolute, benefits and losses, and to analyze the distribution of costs and benefits among groups within the area. Finally, the exchange perspective suggests the need to seek meaningful rewards for those involved in the impact management system, to see the importance of information flows in the system, and to recognize the importance of the equality of exchange in any interaction process. Together, then, using theoretical perspectives provides an understanding of, and sensitivity to, dimensions of the impact process that cannot be obtained from merely a descriptive perspective.

Finally, the use of these perspectives provides an orientation from which to view the topics covered in the remainder of this volume. No matter what theoretical perspective one wishes to apply, a key starting point is the discernment of the magnitude of the changes that the project will bring. Chapter 3, thus, provides an essential starting point for any impact analysis. In like manner, reductions in the numbers of project-related inmigrants reduces the magnitude of impacts that will affect the impacted area; the contents of Chapter 6 are, thus, consequential from any of the perspectives described above.

From the functional, ecological, and systems perspectives each of the remaining chapters addresses a key concern. Chapter 4 utilizes the role of key functions as a means of identifying those who should be involved in the public participation process. Chapters 5, 7, and 8 focus on the means for strengthening the system's parts to adapt to, and manage, the impacts of a development. Finally, Chapter 9 deals with the critical issue of a system's context after the development is ended. Taken as a whole then, the volume can be seen as examining the inputs to, the parts of, and the final state of a socioeconomic system as it is impacted by a major exogenous force of change.

The discussion in the volume also attempts to remain sensitive to the conflict perspective. Each of the chapters illustrates the areas where conflicts have arisen and the nature of conflicts between interest groups. The chapters of the volume can be seen as identifying the means by which competing interest groups have managed the changing patterns of resources created by project-related activities--key parts of any application of the conflict perspective.

Finally, from the exchange perspective the volume provides a useful chronicling of the means by which rewards for involvement in the impact management process and for those positively and negatively impacted by a project can be equitably distributed. Thus, the chapter on public participation deals specifically with the need for equality in exchanges; the chapters on institutional mechanisms, on enhancing existing infrastructures, and on financing point to the successes, as well as the failures, involved in using such systems when the rewards of the system are marginal or unevenly distributed. Finally, the chapter on shutdowns can be seen as addressing the ultimate question of what are the endpoint rewards for an area for hosting a project.

The topics of the remainder of the volume are enhanced by an understanding of the theoretical perspectives described above. Although the discussion in the rest of the volume is largely descriptive, the theoretical perspectives delinated in this chapter should be seen as integrally related to the concerns delineated in the remainder of the volume.

CONCLUSIONS

The discussion in this chapter attempts to demonstrate that the use of a theoretical perspective, though seldom forming a part of the discussion in works on impact management, is important for understanding the management process and for effectively designing and implementing impact management plans. It attempts to demonstrate such utility with three theoretical perspectives as they apply to key impact dimensions and notes that the content of this volume provides insights into the components of such theories as they apply to impact management. Although it represents a simplistic beginning for the process of theory development in the field of impact management, this chapter provides contexts to use in examining the impact management process and one basis for additional theoretical developments and applications.

3 Initiating Impact Management: Where to Begin?

Implementing an impact management program for a large or controversial facility inevitably involves an intense process of interaction between the developer(s) of the facility and representatives of the siting area or areas (e.g., local and state citizens and public and private officials). The successful initiation of this process is important for both developers and residents of the siting area. Unless the process is initiated in a careful and deliberate manner, developers are likely to fail to anticipate events that may make a technically feasible project pragmatically infeasible and/or lead to costly delays in construction. Furthermore, community residents may not become aware of the positive and negative aspects of project development before critical decisions about the siting process have already been made. The process by which developers become familiar with the siting area's characteristics and siting area residents become familiar with the characteristics of the project is often referred to as the *scoping* process (Wolf 1983). This process also includes a preliminary assessment of the likely impacts of the project at the proposed site and tentative (and sometimes contradictory) decisions by developers and residents about whether the project should proceed at the proposed site.

In general, then, this scoping process can be seen as involving three phases:

1. A familiarization phase
2. An assessment phase
3. An evaluation phase

During each of these phases developers and resident groups must use a variety of information and procedures to obtain the data necessary for their decision-making processes. The purpose of this chapter is to discuss some of the elements that should be examined and to delineate the methods that can be usefully applied in each of these three phases of the scoping process.

THE FAMILIARIZATION PHASE

The familiarization phase involves a preliminary issue identification and impact evaluation. Such an analysis provides a mechanism for identifying potential risks and costs, as well as benefits, to local interests associated with project development and for bringing these factors to the attention of project developers and residents while the project is still in the feasibility study stage (Gilmore et al. 1982). It also serves as an initial step toward identifying the impact assessment and management activities that will need to be undertaken should the project proceed. Because developers and residents come to this phase with different informational needs, the elements addressed in this phase are different for developers and for residents of potential siting areas.

For developers, socioeconomic analyses conducted during this phase will typically include a comparison of alternative sites, using analytical approaches which emphasize simple calculations, secondary data, and professional judgement, rather than elaborate mathematical models and extensive local contact. The emphasis on simple calculations and generalized estimates is accentuated by the fact that the information about key project characteristics (e.g., employment levels) available early in the project planning process may be only a very rough approximation of the final values.

One element the developer will wish to assess is community acceptance. An essential first step in the analysis of community acceptance problems is to identify key interest groups, sometimes termed parties-at-interest to the development (Gilmore et al. 1982), and to determine their concerns. Although it is important to identify the major potential sources of effective opposition (Luke 1980), groups that could provide local support also should be recognized (Gilmore et al. 1982). Environmental and neighborhood groups also must be considered because such entities can provide effective support for or opposition to a development effort. The concerns of the area's key economic groups, such as farmers, fishermen, and local retailers, also should be evaluated. In areas that are popular locations for vacation or retirement homes, it may be critical to understand the characteristics and feelings of these seasonal residents (Luke 1980). Useful insights concerning key interest groups often can be obtained by examining past facility siting efforts in the area. Hearing records and newspaper accounts typically indicate the groups providing testimony and the issues emphasized.

Another key step in evaluating acceptance problems is analyzing the state and local regulatory process through which project approval must be obtained. The forums where decisions approving or rejecting a facility will be made should be identified. Then the history of past project reviews should be examined to determine not only the procedural standards of each forum but also any precedents and guidelines that have been established in the permitting of past projects. Impact issues that have been important in the review of past projects should be given special attention.

In addition to analyzing recent expressions of community attitudes and the current status of the regulatory process, it is important to evaluate shifts in attitudes and changes in the political and regulatory climate. The effect of recent events on decision-makers' attitudes should be considered. For example, in some areas the effects of national economic recession and local plant closings have resulted in decreased concern regarding the impacts of economic and population growth. At the same time, greater attention is being given to the potential vulnerability of communities dependent on a single industry and to the potential for encouraging spin-off industries associated with an initial development project, in order to enhance local economic benefits.

Once the key issues and concerns of local interests have been identified, a preliminary evaluation of potential socioeconomic effects at each site can be undertaken. In many cases, evaluations of other environmental impacts may be conducted concurrently. In order to ensure that socioeconomic impact assessment and management receive appropriate attention on a continuing basis, it is desirable that a designated individual or group within the developer's organization be assigned specific responsibility for these tasks (Luke 1980).

For the residents of potential siting areas the familiarization phase is equally important. Although developers may wish to conceal their initial site evaluations from communities for a variety of reasons (e.g., to allow for acquisition of land at lower prices), residents of potential siting areas should be prepared to actively solicit information about the project from its developers as soon as the community(ies) becomes aware that it is being considered as a potential site. Early recognition is important whether the area wishes to take steps to attract or steps to resist the siting of the project.

The information essential to the decision-making process of siting area residents includes such obvious elements as the name of the developer and the type of project being sited as well as more subtle types of information that may require a substantial amount of research. Included among the latter types of information are the following: the nature of the developer's relationships with other communities in which it has sited facilities; the developer's past record concerning impact mitigation and compensation; the likely long-term economic feasibility of the project; the relative stability of demand for the facility's product; the size and timing (phasing) of the facility's work force; the developer's record in regard to providing employee training for residents in siting areas; the alternative locations (in addition to the residents' own community) being considered for project development; and the relative feasibility of each of the alternative sites in terms of objective and widely used criteria for site selection (Lonsdale and Seyler 1979). Given this and similar information, the residents of siting areas can begin to evaluate the likely costs and benefits of the project for their area.

During the familiarization phase it is essential that an organizational entity be empowered by the community to represent the community's interests in soliciting information from and about the developer. Industrial development boards and commissions can often play this role as can other community groups and officials. Often the most difficult organizational aspect for the community and for potential developers is deciding who represents the community in such interactions. Although this issue is not easily resolved, communities are well advised to prepare for such contingencies by identifying a group or entity to represent them (Weber and Howell 1982).

PRELIMINARY ASSESSMENT OF SOCIOECONOMIC IMPACTS

The principles for, and methods of, assessing impacts are similar for the developer and for siting area residents. The following discussion can thus be seen as describing methods and procedures useful to either group.

The preliminary evaluation of socioeconomic impacts, like subsequent and more detailed efforts, consists of two principal tasks--impact projection (prediction) and impact evaluation. *Impact projection* involves utilizing appropriate techniques of economic, demographic, and social impact analysis to predict or forecast the likely effects of project development on key economic and social indicators (Wolf 1981). These projections are *conditional forecasts* based on specified assumptions concerning both key features of the project (e.g., employment levels) and future trends in the area's *baseline* (i.e., without project) economic, demographic, and social conditions. The *impacts* associated with project development are estimated by comparing the values of each variable of interest in the projection which assumes that the project is established (*with project* or *development* scenario) with the corresponding values from the forecast that assumes that the project is not developed (*baseline* scenario). *Impact evaluation* consists of comparing estimated project-related *requirements* (e.g., for housing and public services) with the site area's *capacity* for meeting these needs (Gilmore et al. 1982).

Key Factors in Impact Estimation

Impact projection relies heavily on three sets of factors. These are the characteristics of (1) the project, (2) the site area, and (3) the inmigrating project workers. Several works describing impact projection methods and procedures have been published (Leistritz and Murdock 1981; Tester and Mykes 1981; Chalmers and Anderson 1977; Murphy and Williams 1978; Denver Research Institute 1979; Finsterbusch et al. 1983), and a number of comprehensive and integrated impact projection models have been developed (for a review of such models, see Leistritz and Murdock 1981 and ECOS Management Criteria 1982). The time and cost requirements for utilizing such sophisticated projection models are likely to be extensive however. In the early scoping stages of impact management planning, therefore, there is a need for a simplified framework for identifying key variables and developing initial approximations of potential impacts as a guide to project planning. Such initial estimates can be valuable as a general indication of the relative importance of socioeconomic issues, in comparison to other environmental concerns, and thus as a basis for determining the level of resources to be budgeted for subsequent socioeconomic impact assessment and management activities.

Project Characteristics. The characteristics of the development project are clearly central to impact projection. Among the key characteristics of such projects are their physical locational features, particularly the extent to which their effects emanate from a central location, and the relative size of their construction and operational work forces. Thus, one means of categorizing projects is with regard to these dimensions. Projects can be seen as being one of the following:

1. Point:operating--these developments are concentrated in one area and have both significant construction and operation work forces. Examples include power plants, mines, and manufacturing facilities.
2. Point:limited-operating--projects with significant construction, but very little operating, employment. Hydro-generating facilities (dams) are a typical example of this type of project.
3. Linear--a project with significant construction employment dispersed over a long corridor, generally creating only transitory impacts in any one area. Examples of this type of project include oil or gas pipelines, transmission lines, and highways. Such projects also typically have few, if any, operating employees.
4. Multiple-point--typical examples of this type of development include mineral exploration and oil and natural gas development. Although the cumulative impacts of exploration may be considerable, the high mobility of the exploration crews may serve to disperse socioeconomic impacts over a wide area.

The prototypical rapid-growth situations often discussed in the impact literature, such as Rock Springs, Wyoming, are generally associated with point developments. In some ways, the point:limited-operating projects are the most challenging from an impact management standpoint, because project-related growth will be both substantial and temporary during the construction phase but have limited long-term operational effects that allow for a return on construction period investments.

Whatever the basic type of project, other features that will be important in determining the socioeconomic effects of development include its employment, investment, procurement patterns, and resource requirements. Project employment requirements (including total work force needs, the timing of those requirements, and skill levels) are a key to determining the number of workers and dependents likely to migrate into the site area. The level of investment in project facilities is typically a major factor in determining the local tax revenues generated by a development. Procurement patterns (i.e., the amount and types of goods and services purchased from local firms) are the major determinant of the project's indirect economic effects. Finally, the project's resource requirements, such as use of land and water, may in large measure determine the potential for competition with other local economic interests.

Characteristics of Site Area. Just as important as the characteristics of the project is the nature of the site area. Of primary importance is the magnitude of the local labor pool, relative to project employment requirements. While potential site areas require specialized analysis to determine their exact characteristics in this regard, three general classes of sites can be usefully distinguished:

1. Rural and remote--located in a sparsely populated area outside commuting range of major population centers.
2. Rural with commuting potential--located in a sparsely populated area but within commuting range of major population centers.
3. Urban--located within or on the outskirts of a major population center.

What constitutes a major population center is, of course, relative to the size of the project. A community of 10,000 population may provide a substantial local labor force for a project with a total work force of only a few hundred whereas a major synthetic fuel facility or large defense project employing 5,000 to 10,000 workers would require an area with a much larger population base to accommodate its labor requirements.

The key issue clearly is the extent of local labor availability (and local capacity to accommodate inmigrants) relative to the demands imposed by project development. In general, as Warrack and Dale (1981) point out, there is a proportionality of impacts such that the larger the project and the smaller the population of the area relative to the project, the larger the project's impacts on the community's(ies') infrastructure and management capabilities (see Figure 3.1).

Even though the total population residing within commuting distance of the project site provides a useful proxy for local labor availability, other factors also should be considered. Skill levels of existing residents will be critical in determining their suitability for project employment. For example, the extent of inmigration associated with recent power plant construction projects in North Dakota and northern Minnesota was substantially

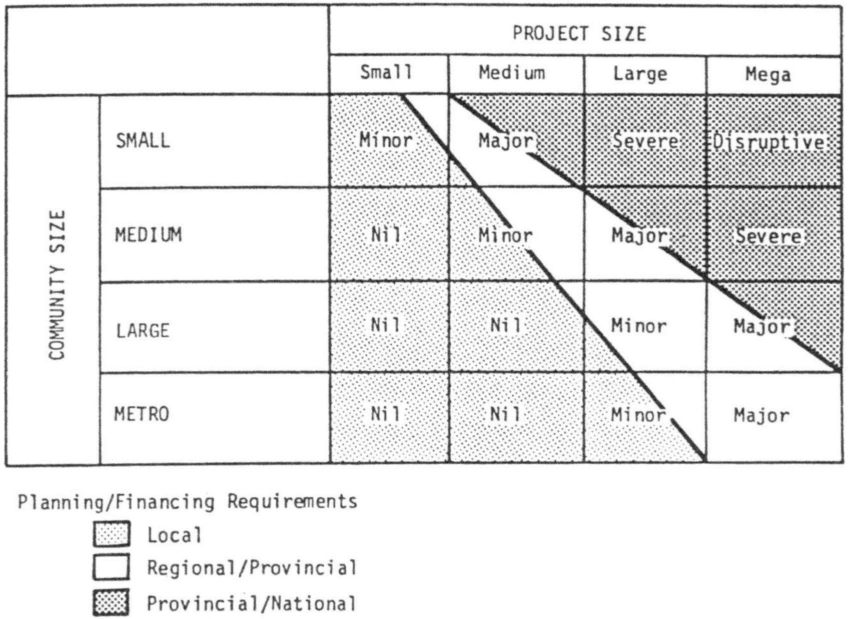

Figure 3.1. Project/community proportionality matrix

SOURCE: Adapted from Warrack and Dale (1981).

less than might have been anticipated for these relatively remote locations because each region had a substantial pool of experienced construction craftsmen (Gilmore et al. 1982). Likewise, the local labor market situation, reflected in levels of unemployment and underemployment, will affect the extent to which project employment requirements can be met through local recruitment.

The area's economic structure will be a major determinant of a project's secondary economic effects. In areas with well-developed trade and service sectors, the propensity of project workers to purchase goods and services locally will be higher, and the extent of project procurement of supplies and materials from area sources also may be greater. Thus, secondary employment and income multipliers will generally be larger in areas with more diversified and self-sufficient economies (Leistritz, Murdock, and Leholm 1982).

The adequacy of the area's existing public and private sector services and infrastructure also will influence the impacts experienced. Communities that have modern facilities with significant excess capacity may be able to accommodate substantial inmigration with little strain. In other areas, however, present services may be barely adequate to meet the needs of existing residents. Adequacy of public and private sector services also may influence inmigrants' residential location choices between towns in an area. State and local tax structures can greatly affect the magnitude and timing of revenues derived from a new project, which in turn will largely determine the fiscal resources available to local jurisdictions for public service and facility expansion.

Characteristics of Inmigrants. Finally, the impacts of the project will vary with the characteristics of the inmigrants who come to the area as a result of the project. If these inmigrants are similar in their characteristics (e.g., age structure, race/ethnicity, income, education), social perspectives, attitudes, and values to indigenous residents, the area is likely to experience less dramatic impacts than if inmigrating and indigenous residents are different in these regards. Thus an examination of the likely characteristics of inmigrating workers and their families and a comparison of these characteristics to those for indigenous residents can provide useful information about the likely impacts of a project on a siting area.

Essential Steps in Impact Projection

Although impact projection clearly is a complex task and a complete impact assessment typically will require substantial quantities of locally derived data and take many months to complete, a number of estimation steps are common to almost all such assessments. Given the scoping intent of this initial phase, the impact analyst may choose to focus on these key steps and to rely largely on secondary data and on experience gained through impact evaluations for similar projects developed in analogous areas. The purpose of this section is to identify some of these key steps and to suggest cost-effective approaches to approximating potential impacts.

This brief discussion is, of course, intended to be only a very general guide to a very complex analytical process. Persons attempting to develop impact estimates, even at this preliminary stage, should become familiar with the extensive literature in the field (for example, see Tester and Mykes 1981; Leistritz and Murdock 1981; Finsterbusch and Wolf 1981; Denver Research Institute 1979; ECOS Management Criteria 1982; and Chalmers and Anderson 1977). Impact analysts also should be aware of the extensive number of case studies dealing with various types of large-scale development projects (for example, see Pijawka and Chalmers 1983; Gilmore et al. 1982; Dunning 1981; Fookes 1981a; Malhotra and Manninen 1980; Chase and Leistritz 1983; and Halstead and Leistritz 1983b).

Nearly all of the methodologies employed in impact assessment, however, include several key steps. All begin with information on the project's direct employment and other indicators of its direct stimulus to the local economy and then, from these, forecast numerous other impact dimensions including:

1. Secondary employment effects
2. The number of project-related workers migrating to the area
3. The number and characteristics of the inmigrating population
4. The settlement patterns of the inmigrants
5. The increases in housing and service requirements at the community level
6. The level of fiscal resources required to expand the community's infrastructure

Approaches to estimating these effects are discussed in the paragraphs which follow.

Secondary employment (also sometimes termed indirect and induced employment) effects of development refer to additional employment created in various trade and service sectors of the local economy as a result of purchases of goods and services by the developer and project workers. The magnitude of secondary employment effects is frequently estimated by an employment multiplier, which relates the change in secondary employment to the level of direct project employment. The key factor determining the magnitude of the employment multiplier is the propensity of project workers and the developer to purchase goods and services from local firms. The extent of local purchases often depends on the ability of local firms to supply a variety of goods and services. Areas with more diversified economies thus tend to have larger multipliers. (For further discussion of factors influencing multiplier values, see Leistritz, Murdock, and Leholm 1982; and Leistritz and Murdock 1981.)

Recent research indicates that, when large projects are sited in rural areas, their local secondary employment effects may be quite small, particularly during the project construction phase. For example, construction phase multipliers in the range of 1.1 to 1.5 (indicating from 0.1 to 0.5 secondary jobs per project construction job) have been reported for power plant construction in the United States and New Zealand (Gilmore et al. 1982; Pijawka and Chalmers 1983; Fookes 1981a). Corresponding operation phase multipliers are reported to be in the range of 1.3 to 2.5 (Gilmore et al. 1982; Leistritz, Murdock, and Leholm 1982).

Once total project-related employment requirements have been estimated, the next step is to determine the percentage of these jobs that may be filled by persons already residing in the area, and conversely the proportion likely to be filled by workers migrating into the area. Rates of local recruitment can be expected to differ significantly depending on the magnitude of project-related employment relative to available local labor and also on whether local workers possess the skills needed for project jobs.

Levels of local recruitment experienced by similar projects developed in analogous areas may provide a useful benchmark for estimating local employment at a new facility. For example, surveys of project construction work forces indicate that local workers may comprise as little as 20 percent or as much as 80 percent of the total (Mountain West Research 1975; Malhotra and Manninen 1980; Dunning 1981), with the higher rates of local recruitment generally being associated with smaller projects and those located in more populous areas. Similar surveys of coal mine and power plant operations (permanent) work forces indicate that local workers typically make up 40 to 80 percent of the total work forces (Wieland et al. 1979; Hooper and Branch 1983; Browne, Bortz, and Coddington 1982). Such surveys also indicate, however, that under some circumstances very specialized workers, such as many construction craftsmen, are willing to commute substantial distances (e.g., 60 to 90 minutes one way) on a daily basis. In addition, such research indicates that company-sponsored training programs may substantially increase local recruitment of permanent employees. (For a more detailed discussion on these topics, see Chapter 6.)

After the number of project-related jobs that will be filled by inmigrating workers has been estimated, the demographic characteristics of these workers and their dependents must be determined in order to estimate the inmigrating population. As with local hiring, studies of previous developments can provide insights regarding worker characteristics. For example, such studies of energy and water development projects in the western United States suggest that the median age for relocating construction and operations workers typically is between 30 and 35 and that most of these workers (60 to 80 percent) are married (Wieland et al. 1979; Browne, Bortz, and Coddington 1982; Chase and Leistritz 1983). Some of the married construction workers, however, may not bring their families with them to the site area. The percentage of married construction workers not accompanied by dependents has ranged from 25 to 50 percent (Dunning 1981; Chalmers 1977; Malhotra and Manninen 1980). Such information from past projects can provide a basis for estimating the likely magnitude and composition (i.e., age and gender) of the project-related inmigrating population (Murdock et al. 1982).

Having estimated the extent of population influx associated with project development, the next critical step is to evaluate the likely settlement patterns of the inmigrants. Research to date suggests that, while gravity models utilizing community population and distance from the project site as explanatory variables are useful for evaluating the relative attractiveness of various communities to project workers (Murdock et al. 1978; Wieland et al. 1979), such factors as the availability of housing and the adequacy of public and private sector services also must be considered (Murdock et al. 1982). In fact, some small communities with limited infrastructure, although located in close proximity to project sites, have been largely bypassed by inmigrants who preferred to reside in somewhat larger communities located farther away. There also is a tendency for inmigrating construction workers to reside in larger towns farther from the project site, in comparison to permanent operations-and-maintenance workers.

When the number and characteristics of inmigrants likely to reside in each of the area's communities have been estimated, attention can be turned to analyzing the housing and public service needs that will result from project-related population growth. Generally, the greatest effort in this step is focused on those communities that are anticipated to experience the highest growth rates. Special attention is given to comparing housing and service needs with the community's capacity to accommodate them. Although the evaluation of service requirements is a complex task (Jones and Murdock 1978), published per capita standards often can be utilized in making an initial analysis (for example, see Leistritz and Murdock 1981). Case studies of other areas affected by project development also can be useful in identifying the types of services likely to experience the greatest increases in demand (for example, see Gilmore et al. 1982; Murdock et al. 1981; Leistritz and Maki 1981).

If the service and facility requirements imposed by project-related growth appear likely to substantially exceed a community's existing capacity, an initial attempt should be made to estimate the fiscal implications of service and facility expansion. Although only general estimates of such costs will be possible during this initial screening phase, case studies can provide insights concerning costs incurred in similar development situations (for example, see Gilmore et al. 1976; Murdock and Leistritz 1979; Halstead and Leistritz 1983a).

IMPACT EVALUATION

Perhaps even more important than estimating the nature and extent of socioeconomic changes that project development may stimulate is evaluating the capacity of a potential site area to cope with these effects. Unfortunately, the methods of impact evaluation are much less well-defined than those for impact projection. Most experienced impact analysts appear to agree that the essence of such evaluation is the comparison of project-related *demands* (e.g., for housing, services, and social assimilation of newcomers) with the *capacity* or *capability* of the area's economic, governmental, and social systems for meeting these needs (Gilmore et al. 1982). Determining an area's capacity for meeting the demands imposed by growth, however, is a very challenging task, and few formulas or guidelines appear to be generally applicable. At best, then, it is only possible, here, to suggest some key factors that should be considered.

Because many community adjustment problems associated with facility development are related, directly or indirectly, to the magnitude and rapidity of associated local population growth, a useful starting point in the evaluation process is to compare projected growth patterns with those which the affected communities have experienced in the past. The outlook for areal demographic change in the absence of project development also should be considered as such baseline changes could either offset or accentuate project-related problems. Finally, projected growth patterns can be evaluated in the light of other communities' success in coping with similar growth rates.

In comparing projected and historical growth patterns, it appears that communities which have some recent experience in dealing with growth-related needs may be better equipped to recognize and respond to such needs in the future (Murdock et al. 1982). On the other hand, areas with long histories of stable or declining population may be less able to respond effectively, particularly if lead time is limited. At the same time, however, the analyst must consider the effects of past population change on a community's current service capacity and fiscal resources. Thus, a community that has recently experienced a significant population decline may have considerable vacant housing and substantial excess capacity in its more capital-intensive service facilities (e.g., schools, water, and sewer), whereas in a town with a recent history of substantial growth, services and public budgets already may be strained.

The area's baseline population outlook also should be examined. Project-related growth may pose greater problems for an area that is experiencing substantial growth from other sources than for an area experiencing stable or declining population. The considerable time periods often required for planning large projects accentuate the importance of examining baseline projections for potential site areas; such information often is readily available from local planning groups or state agencies. Further, while trends in total population are important, projected changes in population composition also should be examined. For instance, in some areas characterized by overall population stability, the school-aged population is projected to decline rapidly (because of previous decreases in birth rates), suggesting that excess capacity in the local schools may exist.

Although most observers agree that higher rates of growth lead to greater community adjustment problems, there are few precise guidelines regarding the rates beyond which local response capacities may be strained. A recent study of federal defense facilities concluded that growth impact problems are likely to be most serious for communities with less than 5,000 population and with an annual growth rate of 7 percent or more (President's Economic Adjustment Committee 1981). A similar study of energy development areas in the western United States concluded that growth rates of more than 10 percent annually are hard to accommodate while rates of 15 to 20 percent have led to near chaos in unmanaged rural growth situations (Gilmore et al. 1975). Even though such observations provide some basis for identifying potential problem situations, it is important to remember that communities may differ significantly in their capacity to accommodate growth, because of the factors noted earlier. Further, the timely availability of appropriate external assistance may allow for effective response to rather high growth rates. For instance, in the town of Washburn, North Dakota, population more than doubled between 1975 and 1980 because of the construction of a power plant nearby. The consensus of local officials and community residents, however, was that this growth had been manageable, largely because substantial fiscal resources (i.e., grants and loans) had been available from the state's Coal Impact Office and a careful planning process had been undertaken (Leistritz and Maki 1981).

The evaluation of projected population growth may suggest a need to examine the effects of development on the area's housing market and on the ability of local governments to provide public services. If projected housing needs substantially exceed present housing supply, the potential for rapidly expanding the housing stock should be evaluated. Key factors to be considered include the availability of suitable land, the production capacity of local builders, and the adequacy of existing financing arrangements. (For further discussion of these issues, see Chapter 7.)

Evaluation of public services should include special attention to those services and facilities for which expansion is characterized by substantial lead time and/or large investments such as schools and hospitals. Investment requirements should then be compared to the fiscal resources of the affected jurisdictions, including project-related tax revenues, bonding capacity, and existing programs for assistance from senior levels of government. (For a detailed discussion, see Chapter 8.)

Although concerns regarding the adequacy of housing and local services are prevalent in development situations, it also is important to evaluate impact projections in light of specific local issues. The analysis of residents' attitudes, discussed previously, can prove valuable in discerning specific concerns that may arise if a project is proposed for development there. For instance, local economic interests may be fearful that the project will compete for key resources. As an example, the capability of coal companies to reclaim strip-mined land became a key issue in agricultural North Dakota during its recent history of coal development (Hertsgaard and Leistritz 1983). Similarly, in some areas of Scotland, companies engaged in North Sea oil development agreed to *minimize* their hiring of local residents in order to limit competition with local businesses for available labor (Sewel 1983).

CONCLUSIONS AND IMPLICATIONS

The essence of impact evaluation is to identify gaps between the demands imposed by project-related growth and the capability of the host area to respond to those demands. If such gaps are identified, impact management measures designed to restore the balance between capacity and requirements may be needed. The final step in the initial analysis of potential project effects thus should be identification of impact management measures that may be appropriate and preliminary estimation of the cost of such efforts. It also is important at this point to develop estimates of the time and cost likely to be associated with public participation, negotiation, and the implementation of impact management measures and to reaffirm responsibility for community acceptance activities. The estimated time and cost for these community activities then can be incorporated into the project's critical path charts and capital budgets.

Finally, the initial scoping of socioeconomic impacts and management responses should provide valuable background for subsequent public participation, impact assessment, and negotiation activities.

4
Public Participation and Negotiation in Facility Siting

Once a decision has been made to site a project, the process of interaction between developers and siting area residents, described in the preceding chapter, is likely to intensify. In fact, this process has become increasingly formalized in legally mandated public participation programs involving developers and various publics. Such programs are required under the provisions of the National Environmental Policy Act (NEPA), by numerous state and local agency statutes, and under the operating guidelines of many siting and other authorities. In addition, public sentiment often sees such programs as a part of the publics' right to know and participate in the events shaping their communities. Public participation and public participation programs have thus become a central part of the impact management process as seen by governments and the public.

From the standpoint of the developer it is equally apparent that

> today, industry cannot indulge in the luxury of siting its facilities or developing natural resources in areas where there is no risk of community rejection. Such areas probably are nonexistent. In every situation, there is some threshold of impacts or perceived impacts at which the siting of a facility will be seriously questioned or opposed (Luke 1980).

It is no longer possible for a developer to simply make the decision of where a project will be sited and annouce it as a *fait accompli* to the siting area. This "decide-announce-defend" model (Ducsik 1982) has become increasingly difficult to implement. Rather as Serie et al. (1983) note, the siting process has frequently become not only one that involves the determination of technical suitability and licensability but also one that requires regional and community political support. Despite the growing necessity to engage in public participation, however, many developers face the process with considerable trepidation. Although the lack of such programs can clearly lead to delays in project construction or even to project cancellation (O'Hare et al. 1983; Morell and Magorian 1982), it is not clear whether in a majority of instances the advantages of early and substantial public participation outweigh the disadvantages. Participation, in fact, may bring added costs in time and money and lead to increased conflict. Fookes (1981d) has described the path to local participation as a "mine field," Ducsik (1981) describes the two-sided nature of the process of citizen participation as being both an "Aladdin's Lamp" and a "Pandora's Box," while Hadden et al. (1981) have succintly pointed to both the advantages and disadvantages of the participation process for developers (see Table 4.1). For developers, then, the public participation process is clearly essential, but its benefits are less obvious than for the siting area publics.

TABLE 4.1.
Costs and benefits of public participation

Benefits	Costs
Fulfills rights of citizens	Requires time
Provides a check on government	Requires money
Allows priorities to be set	Reduces decision-making efficiency
Encourages leadership development	Reduces rationality of the decision-making process
Puts emphasis on issues rather than party loyalty	Requires organization or representation of the unorganized
Brings citizens in closer contact with industry/government--reduces alienation	Increases conflict by bringing in new viewpoints
Encourages citizens to accept industry/government decisions	

SOURCE: Hadden et al. (1981).

Whether viewed from the perspective of the developer or that of the publics in siting areas, it is clear that neither the dimensions that should be included in, nor the parameters that should guide, the public participation process have been adequately established. The process of public participation is, in fact, an area that is as much an art as it is a science and one in which the ideals of democracy have played as significant a role as empirical observation in establishing its principles and practices (Christenson and Robinson 1980). As a result, the answers to such questions as who should be involved in a public participation program, when such involvement should occur, and what the appropriate forms and types of that involvement should be have been addressed in a variety of ways (Howell et al. 1983). The literature surrounding the process has thus been characterized by case studies and delineations of alternative but largely untested approaches to, and perspectives on, the participation process. There is no one widely accepted approach to public participation and only limited literature to draw on in evaluating alternative approaches (Ducsik 1984).

Although it is not possible to delineate a single best approach to public participation, it is a vital part of the impact management process and its consideration is essential for any work describing impact management. Thus, in this chapter we examine public participation. Because the state of knowledge concerning public participation is so limited, no attempt is made to provide a comprehensive overview of the subject. Rather the intent is to provide a discussion that both points to the importance of the public participation process and notes an emerging body of literature that is attempting to delineate principles for designing and implementing such programs. In light of this, we examine specific case studies of both unsuccessful and successful public participation programs to discern characteristics that appear to be associated with success, examine several alternative perspectives on public participation, and finally attempt to formulate general principles that may be useful in designing and implementing public participation programs. Given the state of knowledge in this area, the reader must recognize, however, that the discussion is intended to be largely exemplary rather than definitive.

EXAMPLES OF FAILURE AND SUCCESS IN PUBLIC PARTICIPATION

The Nuclear Waste Disposal Controversy

The problem of how to deal with the high-level radioactive waste from commercial and defense activities has been under study since the military began generating wastes in the 1940s (Murdock et al. 1983). A consensus has been reached by most of the scientific community that deep-mined geologic repositories in salt, basalt, granite, or volcanic tuff are the best method for permanent disposal (U.S. Department of Energy 1980). Potentially suitable areas for exploration have been identified in Washington, Utah, Mississippi, Louisiana, Nevada, Texas, Michigan, and Wisconsin. However, the long-lived nature of these wastes and perceived dangers of transportation and handling accidents or groundwater contamination have made the prospect of hosting these facilities highly undesirable in the eyes of residents of potential host states (Murdock et al. 1983).

The need for effective public participation has been stressed by both private and public officials working in the federal government's waste isolation program (Abrams and Primack 1980; Hadden et al. 1981). However, several of the states involved in the siting process maintain that the U.S. Department of Energy has bypassed state government and the general public in selecting potential sites. This has helped lead to an adversarial relationship between the states and the federal government (George 1983).

The Utah Experience. The bedded salt formations of the Paradox Basin of eastern Utah have been characterized as an area which could potentially host a high-level nuclear waste repository. Some activities of the Department of Energy (DOE) and its contractors, however, have aroused political opposition to siting a repository in the state. For example, the state has been forced to resort to the Freedom of Information Act to obtain copies of studies done by DOE in the Paradox Basin. These difficulties in obtaining information have also hampered the state's attempts to provide review comments on such studies. Other problems noted included:

> publication of a draft national siting plan half-way through the completion of the work outlined in that plan; the publication of siting criteria after specific sites have been identified; failure to complete phases in a step-wise process before moving on; failure to follow through on commitments to environmental impact statements and failure to adhere to original time schedules because of stated need to fast track the program (Christofferson 1983).

The state has concluded that DOE's efforts at site evaluation were "insincere" and done only to "legitimize decisions already made" (Christofferson 1983). The end result may well be legal confrontation and extensive political disputes.

The Wisconsin Experience. Although Wisconsin is not currently considered a candidate for the first repository, its granitic formations make it a possibility for future study. As in Utah, however, the preliminary activities of DOE and its contractors in the state have been perceived as being performed without adequate notice to local or state jurisdictions.

The state has charged that DOE has undertaken activities in Wisconsin without informing appropriate units of state government. In addition, it has been charged that DOE has made references to a particular support document in state-federal meetings which was later found to only be in draft form and to contain several serious flaws and omissions. The department has also been charged with being reluctant to release documents for review by state officials (Walsh 1982).

One of these incidents caused a member of the State Planning Council[2] to declare that "this action jeopardizes DOE's credibility concerning the concept of consultation and concurrence"[3] (Symon 1980). This person further stated that it was essential for the State Planning Council and Executive Heads of State Government to be informed of all intentions and procedures involving proposed radioactive waste disposal.

A summation of the state's position is provided by the first section of State Assembly Bill 555, which creates a radioactive waste review board, a radioactive waste policy council, and a radioactive waste technical council.

> The legislature finds that the state is not assured that the federal Department of Energy will consider the unique features of the state and the needs of the people of the state when assessing the state as a potentially suitable location for the long-term disposal of . . . radioactive waste. . . . Neither is the state assured that the federal Department of Energy will ensure adequate opportunity for public participation in the assessment process.

Given this loss of credibility, interaction between the parties has taken on a somewhat adversarial role. Without more communication and cooperation between DOE and the state, impact management may become difficult.

The case of high-level nuclear waste repository siting provides an example of a very difficult siting process. The perceived dangers of such a project and the very long-term potential problems associated with it make its acceptance by a siting area difficult under the most positive of circumstances. For such a project public acceptance may not occur even when public participation programs have been successfully designed and implemented. It is evident, however, that the public participation programs utilized in the siting process to date have been limited in a number of ways that illustrate important principles that appear to be necessary in public participation programs. Thus, in both the case of Utah and Wisconsin the potential developers have failed to allow for

1. open sharing of information between themselves and local siting area publics,
2. independent technical reviews of their technical documents, and
3. consistency in policy statements and practices.

Although these circumstances often arise because the developer wishes to ensure that all information has been fully verified prior to its release to the public, hesitancy to release information for review is often perceived as an attempt to conceal information. When such events are coupled with changes in schedules and time commitments, the developers are likely to lose credibility and may be perceived by the public as lacking integrity. The case of high-level nuclear waste repository siting thus suggests that the above three principles must be evident in a successful public participation program (Walsh 1982; Symon 1982; Halstead 1982).

Siting Hazardous Waste Facilities

An example of a more successful public participation program can be illustrated with the case of hazardous wastes in Colorado and Idaho. Although such wastes are clearly perceived as less dangerous than high-level nuclear wastes, the cases described below do provide examples of success in the siting of facilities that are generally perceived as negative.

The Case of Naturita, Colorado. The town of Naturita in southwestern Colorado was recently selected by Chem-Nuclear, Inc. as a prime candidate for a low-level radioactive waste disposal site. Although the site was subsequently dismissed for other technical reasons, Chem-Nuclear's approach to siting proved very successful in eliciting community support.

Officials from Chem-Nuclear initiated a public information program well before the final siting decision had been made. In addition, public contacts were frequent, taking the form of one-to-one briefings, small group presentations, and public hearings. Company representatives also met with news media personnel and dispersed informational material. Equally important, company decision-makers displayed a commitment to incorporating the public's views into the siting process (Serie et al. 1983).

A key facet of Chem-Nuclear's process was developing an air of credibility and trust. Because the planning process was initiated early in the project's development, local residents were kept up-to-date on company activities. As a result, local residents and officials perceived that they had been adequately informed about the project and had had an influence on key decisions. At the time the project was rejected, the public of the area were quite positive about the need for the project and the credibility of Chem-Nuclear.

The Experience of Wes-Con. One of the most difficult siting problems in the wake of such events as Love Canal (New York) and the "Valley of the Drums" (Kentucky) is finding a location for a hazardous chemical waste disposal facility. Numerous towns throughout the country have reacted to the problem by passing ordinances prohibiting hazardous waste facilities within their borders (Morell and Magorian 1982; O'Hare et al. 1983). The prospects of possible environmental and health damages, noxious odors, and unsightly landscapes seem to far outweigh any anticipated economic benefits. How then, in 1973 and 1979, did Wes-Con, Inc. site two hazardous waste disposal facilities with very little opposition?

Wes-Con's disposal philosophy involved waste storage in abandoned missile silos in rural Idaho. The first site, 10 miles from Grand View, Idaho, (1980 population, 260), is two miles from the nearest rancher and surrounded by Bureau of Land Management grazing lands.

During the time Wes-Con was completing its environmental assessment and applying for a site conditional use permit, the company took the initiative to solicit support from the county commissioners (although they had no legal leverage over the site) and the local Cattlemen's Association. Once construction began, Wes-Con hired local residents for the management staff, donated salvage materials to community groups and citizens, and invited visits to the facility. In addition, the company provided free disposal of local hazardous wastes (mostly pesticides), provided area ranchers free use of their heavy equipment, and agreed not to accept any controversial wastes (for example, nuclear wastes and nerve gas). Wes-Con's major site management decisions were deferred to state agencies to maintain political support and public credibility. Finally, the company purchased a fire truck and made it available for use by local ranchers and farmers.

Wes-Con's second experience near the town of Bruneau (20 miles away, 1980 population, 100) was located within the same county (Owyhee) as the Grand View site. Again, Wes-Con approached local officials and organizations for support and offered services and benefits to the community. Local politicians and civic leaders saw the Bruneau facility as an extension of the Grand View site and gave their approval. After a public hearing for a conditional use permit and subsequent incorporation of improved operating features into the site, the facility began operating in 1979 with no local opposition (O'Hare et al. 1983).

These examples of the siting of low-level nuclear waste sites in Colorado and hazardous wastes in Idaho are illustrations of success in public participation programs. Although the auspices (i.e., private versus public developers), the nature of the materials being handled, and the characteristics of the siting areas are different than those noted in the cases of high-level waste repository siting, these cases are also clearly different in the public participation approaches that have been used in the siting process. Differences in the hazardous waste cases include the following:

1. Early initiation of public participation activities
2. Provision of extensive information to members of the public
3. Open access to developers by members of the public and media
4. Allowance for public input prior to the completion of key decision-making processes
5. Provision of additional community incentives and benefits for accepting siting

In sum, then, these cases suggest that open communication between developers and the public may be instrumental to the development of effective public participation programs.

THEORETICAL APPROACHES TO PARTICIPATION AND NEGOTIATION

The preceding case studies illustrate that failure to involve the public in siting decisions can lead to serious problems in the siting process. Conversely, early and effective public involvement can circumvent many of these problems. These and similar principles underlie many of the prevailing approaches to the design of public participation programs. As a further means of delineating essential elements of such programs in this section, we present several attempts to formulate general principles of public participation.

Designing A Citizen Participation Program

Arnstein (1969) has developed a hierarchy of citizen participation levels. This "ladder" (Figure 4.1) characterizes grades of involvement from nonparticipation to citizen control. Only the top three rungs--citizen control, delegated power, and partnership--involve substantial input into the decision-making process. In general, Arnstein maintains that unless the public is involved at a level that allows them to influence decisions, they are unlikely to accept and remain involved in a public participation program.

Black (1983) has found that citizen participation programs have been given low priorities in federal legislation and, in general, have occupied the lower (nonparticipatory) rungs of the ladder. Black has also identified four steps in the decision process where citizen input is especially valuable to the developer: (1) problem identification--local residents may have more intimate knowledge of a given situation; (2) evaluation of alternatives--citizens can identify unacceptable options in the project's cost-benefit analysis, thereby reducing conflict and litigation later; (3) review of draft recommendations--in this way, official recognition of the final report becomes a function of public support; (4) public support--citizens who have worked intimately with the program have more of an interest in seeing it completed.

In order to gain higher levels of participation and for citizens to affect project decisions, Howell et al. (1983) have identified three key attributes which a program must have to stimulate and sustain public participation: (1) a situation in which the costs of involvement are minimized; (2) maximization of the rewards associated with involvement; and (3) the establishment of a climate of trust among the citizens that perceived rewards will be delivered. These attributes are similar to the questions which Serie et al. (1983) have proposed that the public will raise regarding a project, namely:

1. How will I benefit from the project?
2. Will it hurt me, or future generations?
3. Why should I trust you?

Again, the importance of the developer's (or government's) *credibility* is evident.

To insure that public participation programs provide for open communication and community input, Howell et al. have identified 16 principles of effective citizen participation (see Table 4.2). Principles 1-3 suggest that a public participation program is best

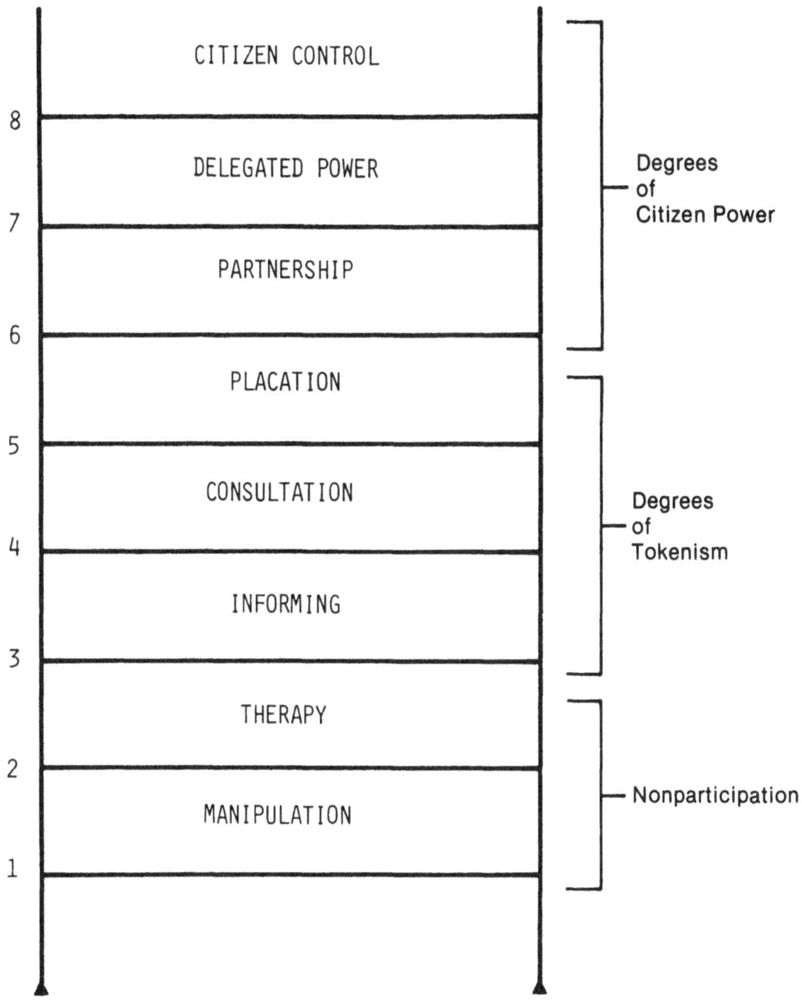

Figure 4.1. Eight rungs on a ladder of citizen participation

SOURCE: Arnstein (1969).

TABLE 4.2.
Sixteen principles for an effective public participation program

1. Employ an objective community development specialist

2. Include strong support by key leaders in the affected area

3. Draft a written agreement to define responsibilities of all parties early in the program

4. Analyze and consider local social and political conditions prior to implementing the program

5. Foster cooperation with local organizations

6. Carry out an extensive information and education program

7. Have the program organized and carried out by a representative citizen committee, including informal social group representatives

8. Trust will quickly dissolve if the public perceives it is being asked to ratify a decision already made

9. Early and continuous involvement of citizens in the site characterization process is a necessity

10. Two-way dialogue must be maintained

11. Public trust can be maintained only if citizens perceive that project officials are responsive to area needs

12. The program should be implemented so that citizens can use their time efficiently and constructively

13. Communication should be clear, concise, and noncondescending

14. Citizens must be treated as highly valued consultants

15. Public recognition can be used as a reward for participants

16. The product of the program should be a written document which clearly communicates local sentiment to decision-makers

SOURCE: Howell et al. 1983.

seen as a formal rather than an *ad hoc* effort. Principle 4 speaks to the need to recognize local social conditions. For example, public participation processes for the Susitna dam project in Alaska had to be structured to accommodate fishing and tourist seasons, as well as to facilitate transportation access for residents of the far-flung project impact area (Blunck 1983). Principles 5 and 6 point to the need for active dissemination of information. Principles 7 (inclusion of local groups in the process) and 14 are essential for reaching the upper rungs of Arnstein's participation ladder. Principles 8-11 are essential in fostering the trust and credibility factors needed for a successful program. Principles 12 and 13 are "cost-minimizing" steps, and involve structuring processes so that citizens can effectively utilize the time spent in the program. Finally, Principles 14-16 help maximize the rewards of participation to citizens.

Delli Priscoli (1979) has identified four points which an agency should consider in devising a public involvement strategy. First, realize that initial dissonance may arise. Second, make decisions about how much sharing of decision-making can or should be done. Third, link the participation programs to the actual decision-making. Finally, take steps to insure that citizen involvement techniques are appropriate, in time and money, to the type and level of decisions being made.

Fookes (1981d) has drawn some general conclusions and guidelines from observations of experiences gained during the siting of the Huntly and Waikato Power Stations in western New Zealand. These have been summarized into two basic "needs" and six assumptions that Fookes suggests must be considered when designing a participation program.

In general, people affected by a project have two basic needs. The first is *information*--keeping the public up to date on the status of the project. The other need is to maintain a *dialogue*--a two-way line of communication. Local people need to be directly involved in the decision-making process.

The first two assumptions are that (1) the public needs to be represented by a range of interest groups, of which local body representatives are only one, and (2) the public is *not* a homogeneous body, but a conglomeration of diverse interests and individuals. These two assumptions attempt to answer the question of who should be involved in a participation program.

The next three assumptions address the question of how to involve the public. Fookes suggests that (3) committees provide a recognized machinery for public involvement, but there are other ways which should complement formal committees, (4) local representatives do not automatically function as information channels, nor do they necessarily reflect local attitudes and values adequately, so supplemental channels are needed, and (5) the news media play an important role in local participation arrangements.

The final assumption addresses the question of how much to involve the public. Fookes notes that (6) people involved in the participation opportunities must be clearly aware of where the responsibility for final decisions rests.

As a general observation, Fookes emphasizes that involved people must believe that decisions are still being made, and that they are not being presented with a *fait accompli.* He answers the question of when to involve the public quite succinctly: "while there is still room for proposers to change their minds in light of new information" (Fookes 1981d).

Goals of a Citizen Participation Program

The preceding formulas and case studies have presented both reasons to engage in citizen participation and frameworks for building such a program. Given this *raison d'etre* for public participation programs and the theoretical means for implementation, the final question is, what exactly should such a program do? In other words, what are the *goals* of citizen participation?

Two such goals, each benefiting both parties (though not always equally!), are generally seen as objectives of the process.[4] These are (1) an improvement in the planning process and (2) the building of "informed consent" for the project in question. Each idea is described in turn.

Improved Planning. Morell and Magorian (1982) emphasize that programs need not be implemented "merely to gain approval and support for a particular policy." Rather, they should also contribute to error detection in the decision-making process. Susskind (1980) has concluded that policy designers may misinterpret or overlook critically important facts. Therefore, a participation program could provide two means of error detection: (1) as a check of technical accuracy of planning and a chance to provide additional information and (2) as a means of infusing the planning process with representative values and political goals (Morell and Magorian 1982). If a participation program addresses these issues, the chances of reaching socially optimal siting decisions are enhanced.

Building Informed Consent. While improved planning processes for facility siting and development will benefit society as a whole, project developers generally have a more immediate concern: getting their plant (mine, smelter . . .) built. Participation programs will certainly not guarantee that a project's opponents will be converted to a pro-project stance. What Bleiker (1983) has called informed consent is not really consent at all, since a project's opponents are still against the proposal. Rather, through an effective participation program, the project's opponents are persuaded to go along with the proposal (however reluctantly); that is, opponents are convinced not to use their (*de facto* or *de jure*) veto power over the project (Freudenburg and Olsen 1983). A key feature of this concept is to eliminate uninformed or misinformed opposition and consent. (Further elaboration on the informed consent philosophy is provided in IPMP [1983].)

CONCLUSIONS AND IMPLICATIONS

The case studies and alternative approaches presented in this chapter cover a variety of circumstances and issues. In spite of the differences of locale or author, several points recur with sufficient frequency to suggest several principles that appear to be essential in implementing a public participation program. For convenience, these can be divided into design issues and general program objectives.

Design issues address the means that the participation program uses to answer the questions of who, how, when, and how much. The case studies reviewed indicate that units of state and local governments, local citizens' groups, various local individuals, and sometimes even regional or national groups should take part in the program. Howell et al. (1983) and Fookes (1981d) both emphasize this point. These groups and individuals must have both well-defined participatory roles and a continuous and comprehensive flow of information. The crucial timing factor is emphasized by the state of Utah's contention that it is being asked to legitimize decisions already made in the nuclear waste repository siting process. Participation should occur when there is sufficient lead time so that project plans can still be altered. Howell et al. (1983), for example, note that trust will quickly dissolve if the public perceives it is being presented with a *fait accompli*. The final design issue addresses what influence the public should have in the final decision. Although there are different views on this dimension with some suggesting the ultimate decision rests with the developers (see Fookes 1981d and Serie et al. 1983) while others (e.g., Howell et al. 1983) suggest that the public must also have the right to reject a project, all agree that the public's role must be clearly recognized at the initiation of the program. Finally, all appear to agree that the participation programs must be closely and visibly linked to the decision-making process, and that participants should be treated as valued consultants.

The general program objectives include three ends: minimization of costs of participation, maximization of benefits of participation, and establishment of credibility. The first two aims are designed with the intent of maximizing both participation in and the productivity of the program. The final objective, credibility, is perhaps the most important of all. In the Utah and Wisconsin case studies, damaged credibility of the project developer has led to legal and political problems. Conversely, the cultivation of local trust in Idaho and Colorado greatly facilitated the siting process. Both Serie et al. (1983) and Howell et al. (1983) emphasize the importance of the credibility factor and note that it is interwoven in virtually all developer-community interactions. Effective, comprehensive public participation programs can both improve the planning process and build a base of informed consent for the project. This atmosphere of cooperation, in turn, may expedite the siting process and insure that siting area residents' concerns are met. It is thus essential to socioeconomic impact identification and management planning.

In conclusion, citizen input can help to identify socioeconomic impacts and concerns. However, public participation, while related to socioeconomic impact assessment, is not a substitute for it. Participation programs essentially ask whether people like a proposed project, while impact assessment evaluates what a project will do to them (Freudenburg and Olsen 1983). The participation process sets the stage for implementation of the strategies described in the following chapters.

NOTES

1. Throughout this chapter, the terms "public participation," "citizen participation," and "local participation" will be used interchangeably.

2. The State Planning Council on Radioactive Waste Management was established under Executive Order No. 12192 to provide advice and recommendations on ways of resolving specific institutional issues related to the management of radioactive wastes (Riley and Hess 1981).

3. "Consultation and Concurrence" as defined by the Interagency Review Group on Radioactive Waste Management was to provide states with "a continuing ability to participate in activities at all points throughout the course of the activity (i.e., siting, constructing, operating, and decommissioning a high-level nuclear waste repository) and, if it deems appropriate, to prevent the continuance of federal activities" (ONWI-87 p. 1 1980). This term has since been changed to "Consultation and Cooperation."

4. The two parties are the developer (government or private industry) and the local community and other informed groups.

5 Institutional Mechanisms in Impact Management

The impact management process involves a number of formal and informal procedures for managing impacts. Those which provide formal legal mandates or mechanisms for managing impacts can be broadly referred to as institutional mechanisms. Numerous legal and institutional mechanisms affect the siting, construction, and operation of a major facility, as well as the impacts of a project on a facility's host community. National legislation such as the U.S. National Environmental Policy Act (NEPA) of 1969 has affected resource development through imposition of environmental standards which projects must meet. In addition, subnational governments often impose requirements on project developers before granting construction permits. Increasingly, then, compliance with these institutionally imposed requirements has become a major part of the development process, and knowledge of the characteristics of such requirements is a necessary prerequisite for an effective impact management program. A discussion of institutional issues, as well as the mechanics of actual arbitration, monitoring, and compensation agreements, is therefore an essential part of any description of socioeconomic impact management planning.

As with many aspects of impact management, however, no comprehensive discussion of institutional mechanisms in impact management exists, and as a result, no commonly accepted criteria for classifying such mechanisms has been developed. In general, institutional mechanisms can be seen as the means by which the public(s) attempts to control either the project's location or its impacts. These attempts have generally taken the form of siting and taxation legislation intended to regulate all projects of given types or specific forms of agreements aimed at addressing the unique issues of a particular project. In order to understand institutional mechanisms as they affect the impact management process it is essential to understand each of these three general forms of institutional mechanisms.

This chapter is therefore divided into three descriptive sections plus a conclusions and implications section. The first section deals with state and local siting laws and ordinances which affect a project's socioeconomic impacts on a community. The second discusses the states' role in revenue provision to impacted communities through severance taxes and trust funds. The third section discusses community-developer agreements and procedures, and is comprised of three subsections on compensation, monitoring, and arbitration. The conclusions section evaluates strengths and weaknesses of these institutional mechanisms and proposes some guidelines for future efforts. Because of substantial regional variation in the applications of these mechanisms, emphasis is placed on the description of programs in selected areas. The intent is thus to identify central features of such mechanisms by describing the diversity of means that have been used to implement them.

STATE AND LOCAL SITING LEGISLATION

Various permitting processes and siting laws have been developed in response to the need to control growth and the location of certain necessary (though sometimes noxious) facilities. As of 1979, 27 states had enacted siting laws, and 12 others were considering implementation. Only six of these laws specifically address socioeconomic impacts although many require consideration of related factors such as impacts on aesthetic and historical resources (Auger and Zeller 1979). In the energy-rich regions of the West and Southwest, these vary from a statewide approach employed by Wyoming to the Colorado process that leaves permitting requirements to county-level government. In the East, where major problems have been encountered in attempting to site hazardous waste and similar facilities, several states have passed legislation to facilitate siting. A national study of siting laws and regulations found that the failure to provide for socioeconomic impact assessment was the most significant gap in many state regulatory systems, a gap which could successfully be filled by comprehensive siting acts (Auger and Zeller 1979). In Canada, such siting agreements are usually less formal.

Although the specific requirements of most siting acts vary, they all address certain key features common to each: (1) the level of government which has jurisdiction over issuance of the siting permit, (2) the size and/or type of facility covered under the act, (3) the limits of power for granting or refusing permits and imposing permitting conditions, and (4) the type and form of public hearings, review, and negotiation mandated. Since knowledge of these four dimensions is essential to understanding the nature of facility siting acts, these dimensions are used below as the basis for comparing legislative siting provisions in various areas.

Level of Jurisdiction

Levels of jurisdictional control on large-scale projects differ widely. In the western United States (Auger et al. 1978), North Dakota and Wyoming, for example, have state siting commissions. In Colorado, siting permits are issued at the county level. The most efficient level of control will probably depend on expertise and political power available to state and local governments--powers which vary widely. For example, the Wyoming Industrial Development Information and Siting Act was a major force in securing socioeconomic impact mitigation commitments from the developer of the Laramie River Power Station, commitments which the local community would not have been able to obtain by itself (Susskind and O'Hare 1977). The state of Alaska is able to exert control over development by virtue of state ownership of resource lands and tidelands. Since the state exercises this level of control and benefits directly from resource development, the state assumes responsibility for most socioeconomic impact management (Auger et al. 1978). Conversely, Rio Blanco County, Colorado, was able to impose substantial mitigation requirements on the developer of its Deserado mine as conditions for granting a siting permit (Western Fuels, Inc. 1981). Finally, in some states, communities can procure financial assistance from companies through the use of contract zoning, by which zoning changes are granted in return for specific actions by the developer. Although the preparation of such contracts may require a level of professional expertise not available at the local level in many rural areas (Barrows and Charlier 1982), such contracts provide a useful way of controlling land use around sites.

Resource developments in Canada generally fall under provincial and local control. The exceptions to this are developments which impact (1) bodies of water overlapping more than one province, (2) Indian lands, and (3) federal lands. In such exceptions, the federal government is involved through the Federal Environmental Assessment and Review Process, which ensures that environmental and social consequences of these projects are addressed (Didur 1983; CCREM 1982).

When state and federal issues are involved, jurisdictional authority is less clear. While the National Environmental Policy Act provides for assessment of socioeconomic impacts, actual mitigation requirements have generally been placed on developers by local or state governments. However, in the case of certain facilities, such as nuclear power plants, coastal facilities, or nuclear waste repositories, state and federal roles in the siting process may overlap. State-specific lines of responsibility in the siting process are sometimes not well defined, although the recent trend has been toward more state involvement in the process (Auger and Zeller 1979). Auger et al. (1978), in a study of 11 energy-producing states, found that the extent to which federal assistance for impact management is expected relates to the nature of the project. If the project is on state land or occurs with state encouragement, local and state governments tend to take responsibility for impact management, whereas if the project is federally backed with little direct benefit to the state, management is viewed as a federal responsibility. However, the federal government may not be responsive to local needs or comprehensive of the local situation (Gilmore 1983).

This lack of responsiveness and clear delineation of responsibility--in short, noncooperation between state and federal governments--has led to delay and duplication in the siting process, particularly in the EIS and hearing process. In some instances of unattractive, federally sponsored facilities (such as a high-level nuclear waste repository), state-federal interaction has taken on an adversarial form (Halstead et al. 1982).

Size of Facility

Types of facilities covered under these agreements are usually divided into size classes based on (1) production (e.g., electricity generated, gas produced, barrels of oil refined), (2) employment, or (3) cost of the facility. In addition, the type of facility covered (e.g., thermal power plant, transmission line, etc.) is specified by some of these acts (Auger and Zeller 1979). For example, the North Dakota Siting Act applies to electric-generating plants of 50 Mw or larger, plants refining 100 mcfd or more of gas, and plants refining 50,000 barrels or more of oil per day. In Wyoming, any plant with construction costs of $50 million or more falls under the provisions of the siting act. Local permitting standards also vary widely; for example, Garfield County's (Colorado) permitting ordinances cover facilities employing 200 or more workers (Garfield County 1983).

Wyoming's cutoff level has received some criticism because it applies only to large facilities and does not take into account smaller facilities whose cumulative impacts may be severe (Susskind and O'Hare 1977; Hyman 1982). The state has no desire to change these standards, however (Ellis 1983). County standards may be more efficient at controlling smaller, diverse projects, assuming sufficient expertise for administering these standards is available and that the project does not impact a multicounty area.

Limits of Power

Typically, a siting commission has the authority to grant conditionally or to refuse to grant permits. Conditions imposed may include environmental, social, and economic provisions, which often mandate specific socioeconomic mitigation actions. Wyoming's Industrial Development Information and Siting Act requires that a developer prove that the facility will not pose threat of injury to "the environment nor to the social and economic conditions of inhabitants or expected inhabitants in the expected area" (State of Wyoming 1981). Similar requirements for mitigation are imposed by the North Dakota Facility Siting Act, while impact ordinances in Rio Blanco County, Colorado, are designed to protect the "health, safety, morals, convenience, order, prosperity, and general welfare of present and future inhabitants" (Rio Blanco County 1979). This ordinance translates into requirements for developers to mitigate impacts on such matters as schools, law enforcement, waste disposal, housing, traffic, and area property values. The Massachusetts Hazardous

Waste Facility Siting Act (1980) differs from these other acts in that the state essentially serves as monitor and arbitrator between the site developer and the local community. This Act has not entirely avoided the issue of state vs. local control, which poses a potential problem wherever the state has final authority in the siting decision.

Provincial government involvement in Canadian resource development varies from province to province. In Alberta, for example, the Minister of the Environment has the authority to require both an EA (Environmental Assessment--the equivalent of the U.S. EIS) and a social impact assessment (SIA) for a proposed development--a power known as "double discretion." In British Columbia, the Environment and Land Use Act (RSBC 1979) requires that developers assess the social and economic aspects of their project, which may lead to fulfilling requirements for mitigation and compensation. The Act is administered by the Environment and Land Use Committee, which is chaired by the Minister of the Environment (CCREM 1982). Some local governments involved in energy development also utilize the option of contract zoning (Siefried 1983).

Public Participation

The final facet of most siting acts is their provision for public participation and negotiation in the siting process. In North Dakota, the Public Service Commission conducts extensive reviews and holds public hearings to determine that construction and operation of the facility in question will produce minimal environmental and socioeconomic effects (State of North Dakota 1981). Recent efforts to streamline the bill's provisions for transmission line construction, so that only one set of hearings was required for corridor selection and line routing (rather than the present provision for two), were met with strong popular and political opposition by groups who felt their opportunity for input would be reduced (Thompson 1983). Thus, opportunity for public participation is viewed as an important facet of this bill.

The Massachusetts Hazardous Waste Facility Siting Act (1980) provides for a final community-developer agreement which specifies terms, conditions, and provisions under which the facility shall be constructed, maintained, and operated. Compensation levels for adverse impacts are to be negotiated between the developer and the impacted communities. If it is determined that an impasse has been reached, the council may settle the matter through binding arbitration. One problem with the Act is that it provides for a very rough preliminary screening of siting proposals to eliminate any obviously unfavorable sites suggested and to spare the administrative expense of review. While projects which pass this so-called "feasible and deserving" criterion are subject to extensive environmental review and public scrutiny later in the process, some groups and individuals charge that the siting commission is ignoring public concerns by granting this initial approval. As of mid-1983, no facilities had reached final siting approval, so the Act's constitutionality has yet to be challenged in court (Clark 1983).

As the above examples illustrate, facility siting laws take a variety of forms, and show substantial variation in the jurisdictional levels, size of facilities, range of factors, and the degree of public participation they mandate. This degree of variety is, in fact, an item of information of utility to both developers and the public. For developers, this variability clearly demonstrates the need to carefully analyze the legislative as well as technical aspects of alternative sites and the political as well as the economic feasibility of project development. For the public this variety suggests that legislative control of projects is possible and can be tailored to the unique needs of a wide variety of settings. For both developers and the public it is evident that siting legislation presents a challenge for compliance and enforcement and is likely to play an increasingly important role in impact management in the future.

STATE FINANCING OF ENERGY IMPACT MANAGEMENT

Methods of financing the upgrading and expansion of services to accommodate energy development take a variety of forms. In the western United States, several states (discussed below) impose taxes on minerals extracted and power produced, then redistribute part of the revenues at a local level.

North Dakota imposes a production tax on large coal gasification and coal liquefaction plants. This is in lieu of all property taxes except for those on the site on which the plant is located. The state also imposes an excise tax on electricity produced, and a severance tax on coal of about $1.00 per ton (Coon et al. 1983). These revenues then are divided among the state general fund, a state trust fund, the state Energy Impact Office, and the county where the coal was produced. Most revenues to local governments for impact management come from the Energy Impact Office (Voelker 1981).

Colorado, Montana, Wyoming, and Utah all impose some type of property tax on generating facilities. Colorado imposes a severance tax on coal based on tonnage mined, similar to North Dakota. Montana and Wyoming severance taxes are based on the mine-mouth[2] value of the coal (Voelker 1981).

Colorado's formula for distribution of severance tax proceeds is similar to North Dakota's. Funds are divided among the state's general fund, the local government severance tax fund, and the state severance tax trust fund. Montana's severance tax funds are principally divided among the state constitutional trust fund, state general fund, local impact fund, and educational trust fund.

Generally, impacted communities face severe financing problems in relation to education, road systems, and sewer and water systems. These account for about 60 to 70 percent of state and local government expenditures (Voelker 1981). Although these percentages may not be this high for all communities, the three largest expenditure items are usually for these areas (Leistritz and Maki 1981; Halstead and Leistritz 1983a). Revenue distribution systems, such as those described, are designed to insure that enough funding returns to local governments to offset the costs of rapid growth and expansion. In North Dakota, this system seems to have worked well (Halstead and Leistritz 1983a). Although studies have shown that the total revenue available for impact management generally is sufficient in western states, cities and school districts may not be as well off financially as state and county governments due to distributional problems (Stinson and Voelker 1978). (These and other revenue-providing systems and methods are discussed in Chapter 8.)

Severance taxes have thus formed a major source of funding to support impact assistance. These taxes differ substantially in their means of assessment, and the extent to which they are distributed directly to siting areas also varies widely. They have been instrumental, however, in providing necessary support for such public services as education, road systems, and sewer and water systems. Such taxes appear to provide a flexible and effective mechanism for addressing impact financing needs, although there is considerable debate on the subject. Further discussion of severance taxes is provided in Chapter 8.

COMMUNITY-DEVELOPER AGREEMENTS

In some cases, general siting and revenue legislation are not sufficient to address the specific needs of an impact area. In such situations, special legal agreements may be necessary. The state, local, provincial, and federal ordinances discussed previously in this chapter provide the foundation for community-developer negotiation. From the general provisions of these statutes, ground rules are laid from which specific siting conditions can be constructed. These agreements often involve at least three aspects. The initial compact may spell out provisions such as payments to be made to school districts or other units of local government as *compensation* for the facility's negative socioeconomic impacts. A second aspect involves a *monitoring* program to determine whether actual project impacts are more or less extensive than anticipated by the initial projections and if so whether the impact management plan needs to be reformulated. The final element the agreement may contain is a provision for *arbitration* should disputes over interpretation of the agreement's terms arise. Each of these three aspects is briefly discussed below.

Compensation

Development of any large-scale resource development facility will invariably lead to costs that exceed benefits for some local groups and communities. Compensation mechanisms may therefore be in order to redress individuals and groups who experience such effects. Compensation can be defined as including monetary payments or other forms of benefits to local interests as a form of recompense for project-induced costs or losses. Compensation, which seeks to make affected parties as well off as they were prior to development, can be contrasted with *incentives*, which provide benefits above and beyond the costs incurred (Halstead et al. 1982; Carnes et al. 1982; U.S. Environmental Protection Agency 1980).

Compensation measures have generally taken one of four basic forms: (1) monetary, (2) conditional, (3) in-kind, and (4) offsetting (Leistritz et al. 1982). Direct monetary payments are the form of compensation most frequently employed. For example, this mechanism is often used to compensate landowners whose property is taken in the course of development. Likewise, direct payments have often been made by developers to local governments to compensate for construction-phase fiscal deficits.

Conditional compensation mechanisms are implemented only if a particular circumstance occurs. For example, a developer might post a surety bond or acquire liability insurance as a guarantee that facility closure and clean-up costs will be covered or that compensation will be provided in case of a facility-related accident.

In-kind compensation typically involves replacement of lost amenities. For example, a developer might dedicate lands to the community for park and recreation purposes, or contribute funds for wildlife habitat preservation as compensation for recreational opportunities foreclosed or habitats disturbed by development (O'Hare et al. 1983). This type of compensation was recently employed in Montana, where the Montana Power Company paid $1.65 million to the state to purchase conservation easements as a condition for siting a 400-mile power line in western Montana (*Dakota Country* 1983).

A final form of compensation can be termed "offsetting compensation." This compensation concept recognizes that some adverse effects of development are virtually impossible to prevent (e.g., loss of small town atmosphere) but that creation or enhancement of benefits in other areas (e.g., attractive job opportunities, enhanced local business participation in development activities, and improved community facilities) may in some sense offset the negative effects. This concept is being increasingly employed as an impact management strategy with some Canadian resource communities, and it appears worthy of consideration for more widespread application (DePape 1982).

An effective compensation plan can be seen as being composed of several steps. First, potential benefits and costs must be determined during the assessment phase. Second, the impacted groups entitled to receive compensation must be identified. This step involves identifying each individual or group that desires compensation, evaluating the basis and validity of the claim, and determining the level of compensation to be paid. Third, methods of payment must be chosen (grants, guaranteed loans, etc.). Finally, the terms of payment must be specified.

The literature suggests that at least five types of local groups may claim to be entitled to some form of compensation (Halstead et al. 1982):

1. Local landowners whose property is taken for facility development
2. Nearby landowners whose property may be diminished in value
3. Local governments which experience significant fiscal deficits
4. Low income and fixed income groups affected by local inflationary effects of development
5. Environmental groups

The precedents for compensation differ substantially among these types of claimants; compensation appears to be most prevalent for the first and third categories. In most cases, negotiation between the developer and the affected parties will be vital in reaching a mutually agreeable settlement.

The level of compensation necessary to address tangible impacts, such as stresses on schools, public services, and housing, is usually quantifiable through impact modeling techniques, though actual financial settlements are often subject to intense negotiation. For example, Western Fuels, Inc. made substantial payments to local governments in Rio Blanco County, Colorado, to offset impacts of its Deserado Mine and Moon Lake Power Plant. These payments, which totaled over $6.5 million, were distributed among town and county governments, school districts, park and recreation districts, and the library and hospital. In addition, the company agreed to upgrade roads and bridges in the area. Finally, a system was installed to monitor project impacts; if impacts were more severe than originally predicted, a formula was developed to provide for additional compensation payments.

Less tangible impacts may also occur to an area's cultural and social systems. In British Columbia, Petro-Canada Inc. (PEX) attempted to alleviate the impacts of its Monkman Coal Project on traditional lifestyles such as trapping and fishing. The process set up a trappers' compensation committee (TCC) composed of the trapper, a PEX representative, and a mutually agreed upon third party. Once a damage claim is submitted, the TCC may award compensation for exploration impacts, trapline relocation, operation impacts, and a once-only trapline grant. By this plan, PEX intends to maintain the cultural traditions of the area natives, and to insure the individual trappers' livelihood (Petro-Canada, Inc. 1982).

The impacts involved in these compensation agreements in Rio Blanco County and in British Columbia are all specific to the project areas. However, other groups may legally intervene in the siting process for broader reasons, such as disagreement with the type of facility constructed (e.g., nuclear power plants or certain controversial defense facilities), the need for the facility's product (for example, a power plant or dam supplying excess energy), or the environmental damage the facility will inflict. Some of these groups may be especially hard to compensate for damages. For example, an anti-nuclear group may be opposed to a proposed nuclear power plant for ideological reasons and reject any plan offering financial compensation in return for withdrawing opposition. Such attempts at compensation may even be treated as bribes (O'Hare et al. 1983). In these cases, in-kind, conditional, and offsetting compensation measures may be more appropriate.

A recent informative example of offsetting compensation is provided by the 800 Mw Sherco 3 Power Plant in Minnesota. The need for the facility was challenged by both the state Department of Energy, Planning, and Development (DEPD) and the Minnesota Public Interest Research Group (MPIRG). Faced with the prospect of costly delays and uncertainty as to whether the litigation would be resolved favorably, the utilities decided to negotiate and settle with the intervening parties. The objective of DEPD and MPIRG was to ensure that the utilities committed themselves to a least cost energy strategy combining electric generation, conservation, load management, and alternative energy sources. The utilities were to prove that construction of Sherco 3 would not lessen their commitment to these goals (Miller 1983).

The agreement of June 1982, reached after 5 months of hearings, involved certain concessions by DEPD and MPIRG. Both agreed to file no additional testimony in the hearings, accepted a January 1, 1988 in-service date for Sherco 3, and if a Certificate of Need were granted, agreed not to seek rehearing or appeal of that decision.

In return for these concessions, the utilities agreed to numerous conservation and management policies. These included reduction of SO_2 (sulfur dioxide) emissions from its other plants, investment and research in alternative energy production methods, and additional conservation research and financial incentives (such as rate breaks) (Northern States Power et al. 1982).

Monitoring

While preproject impact assessments play an essential part in the impact management process, preliminary projections of such project impacts as local population growth and work force settlement patterns are sometimes inaccurate, occasionally by large margins (Gilmore et al. 1982; Braid 1980). These inaccuracies do not necessarily stem from problems with impact projection techniques, however, since unexpected changes in a project's construction schedule can substantially affect the timing and magnitude of work force inmigration, altering the assumptions under which the original projections were made. Such possible deviations from the original forecasts thus point to the need for a system to monitor a project's development. Such a system can provide accurate, timely information to decision-makers to insure that the impact management plan is achieving its desired results or, if unexpected developments are occurring (e.g., project work force is substantially greater than or less than expected), to provide the information necessary to revise the original management plan.

In general, there are two reasons for designing and implementing a monitoring plan. First, some states and localities mandate that a monitoring plan be implemented before a construction permit is granted. For example, utilities constructing energy projects in Mercer County, North Dakota, were required by the state facility siting act to monitor socioeconomic impacts of the developments (Halstead and Leistritz 1983a). Likewise, utilities involved in the construction of the Laramie River Power Station near Wheatland, Wyoming, implemented a monitoring program for local project impacts as a stipulation of the permit granted by the Wyoming Industrial Siting Council (Western Research Corporation 1983).

The second reason for implementation is perhaps the more important from a management standpoint; that is, the use of the monitoring system as a management and research tool. As noted, this system can determine whether a project's impacts are more or less severe than originally predicted, and pinpoint areas of impact (such as housing or educational facilities) that need further attention. Baril (1981) has noted three types of monitoring systems used by Ontario Hydro of Canada. The first, called the information sponge, is primarily passive in nature and merely notes changes in indicators from one period to the next. The second, target tracking, requires setting a target (based on a plan, policy, or objective) and collecting data to identify discrepancies between actual conditions and the target. The third type, rolling target, is a variation of target tracking. This method allows for changing targets as new information becomes available, and is the most active of the three systems.

Variations of the target tracking theme have been applied in the United States at several development sites. For example, utilities involved in the Missouri Basin Power Project were able to demonstrate, through the project monitoring system, that construction impacts at the Laramie River Station were not as severe as originally anticipated, and thus the local Project Area Coordinating Committee granted the utilities permission to expand the size of their construction work force. The work force had previously been limited to a maximum ceiling based on projected impacts (Western Research Corporation 1983). In Rio Blanco County, Colorado, payments by Western Fuels, Inc. to the county to mitigate the impacts of the company's energy developments in the area were directly tied to the level of the socioeconomic indicators monitored by the system (Halstead, Leistritz, and Chase 1983).

In addition to its management functions, the monitoring plan can be designed so as to provide background data on sociological characteristics of workers for future research. Such a system was employed at the Huntley Power Project in New Zealand (Fookes 1981b).

When designing a monitoring plan, four elements must be considered: indicators (variables) to be monitored, data collection mechanisms, frequency of data collection and reporting, and communities to be monitored. A brief discussion of each follows.

Indicators Monitored. Data collected by the monitoring system can be divided into two categories: project characteristics and community characteristics. Project characteristics include information on size, location, and characteristics of the project work force, and the stage of project completion. Community characteristics include changes in population, school enrollments, housing stock and occupancy, and local revenues. The actual variables monitored will vary according to the goals of the plan (Leistritz and Chase 1982).

Data Collection Procedures. Collection of work force data will require some form of survey instrument. Most monitoring systems rely on entry surveys taken at time of hiring or periodic surveys once the project is underway. Entry level surveys usually have a high rate of compliance; however, the information collected may become outdated as the worker adjusts to life in the community. The periodic survey provides more accurate data and also provides information on worker use of and satisfaction with area services. However, these advantages must be weighed against difficulty in implementation and possibly lower response rates than an entry survey. Whichever form of survey is chosen, care should also be taken to insure that the questionnaire is as short as possible, with carefully defined questions, since it is usually self-administered. The cooperation of the company is also an important element in a successful monitoring system.

Frequency of Data Collection and Reporting. These features will vary according to the nature of the project and possibly the permitting stipulations. A project which is subject to wide and rapid swings in employment levels will probably require more frequent collection efforts. Collection and reporting periods vary from annual and semi-annual to quarterly and monthly.

Selection of Communities to Monitor. The decision of which area communities to monitor involves a tradeoff, since each additional area monitored will generate additional information at possibly substantial extra cost. Initial selection of communities should be based on preliminary predictions of impact incidence. The monitoring system should be designed with the flexibility to add or delete communities from the plan (Leistritz and Chase 1982).

In general, the information gathered by the monitoring plan should be in a form reflecting changes at the level of individual jurisdictions. It is also useful if this information is in a form to facilitate comparison of present and projected service demands with existing and projected facility capacity.

In conclusion, an effective monitoring system should emphasize analysis and interpretation of information rather than mere collection of volumes of data. The system should link the data collected to priority issues and expected impacts.

Arbitration

Although preliminary assessments attempt to provide a comprehensive plan for dealing with project impacts, it is often impossible to foresee certain events in a project's development. Facilities such as hazardous or nuclear waste disposal sites may generate unanticipated environmental, psychological, or health problems while changes in a project's work schedule may alter the timing and magnitude of population increases. Some agreements, such as the Deserado agreement discussed earlier in this chapter, tie fluctuations in project impacts directly to the monitoring/compensation system. Some project impacts, however, may be more difficult to quantify or predict. In these cases, a flexible system of management may be necessary. When one party believes that levels or types of compensation are inappropriate at some stage of a project, negotiations between the developer and the affected groups may break down. In this case, it is necessary to have a mutually agreed upon system of arbitration to provide the final, binding decision. The following example outlines one approach to arbitration which has proven successful since its implementation in 1977. Examples of other systems are provided by the James Bay (1976) and Ontario Hydro agreements (Proctor and Redfern 1979).

The Northern Flood Agreements: A Case Study in Arbitration. These agreements between the Government of Manitoba, the Manitoba Hydroelectric Board (Hydro), the Northern Flood Committee, Inc., and the Government of Canada as represented by the Minister of Indian Affairs and Northern Development, were consummated in December 1977, to provide a forum for communicating and resolving impact issues resulting from Hydro's Lake Winnipeg Regulation and Churchill River Diversion Project. One of the key aspects of this agreement is its statement of need, which addresses the uncertainty of many project impacts.

> Uncertainty as to the . . . [Project's] effects . . . is such that it is not possible to foresee all the adverse impacts . . . nor to determine all those persons who may be affected by it, and therefore it is desirable to establish through the offices of a single arbitrator a continuing arbitration instrument, to which any person adversely affected may submit a claim, and as well as to fully empower such arbitrator to fashion a just and appropriate remedy. (Northern Flood Agreement 1977)

Compensation provisions of the agreement provide for several types of payment. Each acre of Indian land affected by the development shall be replaced by not less than four acres selected from unallocated, unoccupied, and unencumbered land. The Canadian Government is responsible for water quality, while Hydro is responsible for providing funds for protection of cemeteries and objects of cultural significance from flooding. Residents' lives and health are provided for by a group insurance program.

The arbitrator for resolving disputes is chosen from a composite list of five names submitted by each party. Any individual named unanimously is appointed arbitrator; failing this, any individual receiving majority support is appointed. The arbitrator may be removed if any three of the four parties desire. The arbitrator's authority and responsibility is to make awards and remedies to area inhabitants under the general guideline that such awards will at a minimum place that person in no worse position than he or she would have been in without the adverse effect. Remedial and/or mitigatory measures are also viewed in the agreements as superior to strictly financial compensation. The arbitrator determines party liability, appropriate remedy or compensation, and the time frame for addressing the problem (Northern Flood 1977).

One of the most significant aspects of the agreement is that the "onus shall be on Hydro to establish that the Projects did not cause nor contribute to an adverse effect, where any claim arises by virtue of an actual or purported adverse effect of the project" (Northern Flood 1977, p. 57). This is in marked contrast to many state statutes in the United States which place the burden of proof of damage on the claimant (Faas 1980).

Aside from an initial delay of two years in deciding upon a mutually agreeable arbitrator, the Northern Flood Agreement has performed well. One of the major results of the agreement is that parties have become more amenable to settling disputes through negotiation rather than resorting to arbitration or litigation. The process for appealing the arbitrator's decisions has been untested as of mid-1983.

Another important aspect of the agreement is that it provides more flexibility than is provided by the court system. The arbitrator is readily accessible, and most claims are resolved in three to four months. As a result, few "frivolous" or unjustified claims have arisen (Sigurdson 1983).

Two major claims have been settled under the agreement. The first pertains to a case of mercury contamination of area waters by the project. Although no settlement has been decided yet, the ruling has been made in favor of the claimant. The second ruling confirms the claim that Cross Lake had been, in effect, destroyed in terms of its quality of recreation and aesthetics. Hydro has been ordered to build a $3 million recreation arena as an interim measure and conduct an environmental impact study to determine whether the area's river and lake system should be reregulated (Sigurdson 1983).

The above examples illustrate that compensation, monitoring, and arbitration agreements can be successfully implemented with numerous benefits for the siting area. However, several additional issues, particularly as they relate to the developer, have not been adequately addressed. Below, we address the two major questions of why developers may wish to become involved in such agreements and when such involvement is likely to be most effective.

In situations such as the Deserado Mine project where the county possessed sufficient leverage to require socioeconomic impact assistance from the developer, the most obvious benefit the utility received from negotiation and compensation was the permit to proceed with the project. In addition to this type of return for negotiation and compensation, however, the developer may experience at least three other benefits.

First, legally negotiated impact agreements may cede to the developer the intervenor's right to challenge the project through litigation. Court delays can prove extremely costly to a developer, and may even lead to a project's cancellation (Morell and Magorian 1982). Thus, in the case of the proposed Sherco 3 plant, the utilities involved made significant concessions to DEPD and MPIRG in return for nonintervention in further proceedings. A similar surrender of rights was obtained by Quebec Hydro in the James Bay Agreements, wherein the impacted natives agreed to "cede, release, surrender, and convey all their Native claims, rights, titles, and interests, whatever they may be, in and to land in the Territory and in Quebec, and Quebec and Canada accept such surrender" (James Bay-Northern Quebec 1976). In return, the affected Natives were granted certain environmental, economic, social, and cultural provisions by the agreement.

A second type of benefit is the avoidance of what Sanderson (1979) has called "demoralization costs." These are possible reductions in future benefits resulting from a decision made in the present which increases the risk associated with a future choice. In other words, if a precedent is set for not compensating groups or individuals negatively impacted by a facility, it may become more difficult or impossible to site additional facilities in the future.

A third benefit is essentially the reverse side of demoralization costs. Through negotiation and compensation programs, a company may acquire a reputation which makes future siting attempts easier. For example, the perception that Basin Electric was a "good company to work with" in terms of being responsible for and responsive to community needs during construction of its Laramie River Power Station (Williams 1982) may have aided future projects initiated by Basin Electric. Similarly, the siting process employed by Wes-Con in establishing a hazardous waste disposal facility made it easier for the company to site a second facility nearby (O'Hare et al. 1983).

The question of when and under what conditions a developer should enter a compensation agreement is a difficult one to address. Several authors have provided some general guidance, however. O'Hare et al. (1983), for example, have identified eight characteristics of disputes which they believe may create ideal conditions for compensation:

1. There are few parties to the dispute.
2. The opponents are geographically defined. This is especially important if the opposition corresponds with some local governmental jurisdiction, yielding an entity with which to negotiate.
3. Opponents are well organized.
4. Mutually acceptable outcomes exist.

5. Impacts are clearly traceable to the project.
6. Recreation of the status quo is possible.
7. The parties involved are capable of offering a binding agreement. For example, some environmental groups are unable to assure agreement or compliance of their members.
8. There is an absence of initial hostility. The way in which a developer approaches the community will strongly influence local acceptance of the proposed project.

In the case of a particularly disagreeable facility, incentives or rewards may be necessary to lessen opposition. Carnes et al. (1982) have identified some criteria to judge the applicability of these payments:[3]

1. What is absolutely necessary? Preconditions for introduction and use of incentives include: safeguards for health and safety (especially for hazardous waste facilities), control-authority arrangements, and negotiations among affected parties. Absence of these conditions may result in siting failure due to withdrawal of key local support or local demand for extreme levels of compensation and assurance.
2. Will it work? Objectives of an incentive include certainty, constancy, adequacy, and ease of administration.
3. Can it be understood? The community must be aware of and understand the incentive; it also must be relevant to their concerns. Failure to meet this criterion can result in failure of the incentive and possibly credibility damage due to bribery charges.
4. What are the consequences? This concerns distributional effects, effects of the program on local consensus, and hopefully resolution of some of the adverse consequences of the facility.

If compensation or incentive payments seem worthwhile after these considerations, O'Hare et al. (1983) have offered some "advice to developers" in implementation. These suggestions focus on developing an intimate knowledge of the potential host community inhabitants' needs and preferences, and of the distributional effects of the project on the inhabitants. They also emphasize the importance of straightforwardness in negotiation and public information. Some of the other suggestions include (1) Focus on bargaining rather than gift giving. Concentrate on what each party has to offer the other; (2) Presume mistrust. Industry and government are often viewed with suspicion in these situations; avoid actions that may be construed as deceptive or threatening; (3) Be sensitive to people's fears. Perceived dangers often effect the same responses as real ones; (4) Think creatively about ways to make people whole. Prevent anticipated damages from occurring, and develop methods to correct unavoidable damages. Also be prepared to negotiate compensation levels; and (5) Suggest ways to resolve future disputes. The arbitration procedures detailed earlier in this chapter may be useful in these cases (O'Hare et al. 1983).

O'Hare et al. (1983) also suggest certain principles for local groups negotiating with the developer. These include not adopting a "no-compromise" position from which it is impossible to accept some modification of the developer's proposal, and building credibility with the developer by maintaining rational and professional relations. The developer must be convinced that it is in his best interest to negotiate. Finally, once an agreement has been reached, the community should be willing to support the developer, subject to specific provisions as to the nature and timing of that support.

In sum, then, compensation, arbitration, and similar agreements may, in fact, be useful for developers as well as for siting areas' residents. They may prevent costly project delays and lay the groundwork for further developments. They must be entered into only when certain conditions exist, however. They must be negotiated in an atmosphere in which information is freely shared and where there are realistic expectations between all the parties concerned. Under such circumstances, these agreements can provide a mechanism that insures that both the unique needs of siting areas and the need of the developer for timely and efficient decision-making can be met.

CONCLUSIONS AND IMPLICATIONS

Institutional mechanisms such as legal agreements, siting acts, and taxation policies affect socioeconomic impact management at the community level. These include (1) state (or provincial) and federal legislation, such as the siting acts of various states and provinces; (2) revenue collection systems, such as severance taxes, that return part of the proceeds to the impacted community; and (3) community-developer agreements providing for monitoring, compensation, and arbitration. All of these institutional arrangements have a common purpose: to insure that development pays the price of the socioeconomic costs it imposes. The absence of such mechanisms may lead to uncompensated losses to impacted communities. Conversely, excessive taxation or permitting requirements may lead to overcompensation of certain groups or failure to site necessary facilities.

Although many communities have possessed sufficient leverage and expertise to negotiate effectively with the developer, it may be necessary for higher levels of government (state, provincial) to take part in the management process--either actively through trust funds, severance taxes, and siting acts, or passively through observation and regulation of community-developer interactions.

Perhaps the ideal program should allow development while assuring controlled, orderly growth. Some flexibility is essential so that local jursidictions are not completely bound by state or federal regulations. In this way, allowances may be made for unique area characteristics. Although regulations vary among states and provinces, there are generally three levels of governmental control: federal, state (or provincial), and local. Federal control provides a loose framework for impact assessment and management, while state and provincial regulations provide more stringent controls which tailor the process to the specific region and project. Finally, the local government(s) in the project's host community provides input and management to see that specific area needs are addressed. As Figure 5.1 illustrates,

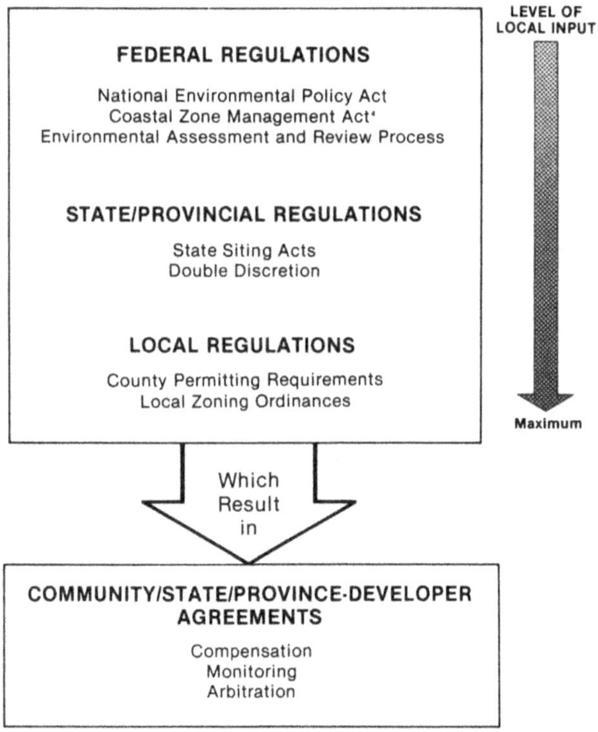

Figure 5.1. Regulation structure of legal mechanisms in impact management

local input increases at each successive level of governmental control. The outputs of this "filtering" process of regulation are the types of community- or state-developer agreements on compensation, monitoring, and arbitration discussed in this chapter.

Institutional mechanisms thus provide another set of factors that must be addressed in the impact management process and another category of means for controlling the impact process. No matter what level of government they involve or the form (e.g., siting or tax legislation or special agreements) they take, they provide numerous opportunities for both the developer and decision-makers in siting areas to insure that a necessary project can be sited and sited in a manner that is beneficial to, or at least is minimally disruptive of, the existing socioeconomic environment in the siting area. As with the other types of noninstitutional mechanisms described in the chapters which follow, institutional means of impact management should be seen as potentially flexible ways of maximizing the benefits and minimizing the costs of developments for both developers and the residents of siting areas.

NOTES

1. For example, see James Bay (1976) or Northern Flood (1977).
2. "Mine-mouth" value is the value of the coal at the mine before processing and transportation.
3. The authors stress that these incentives need not necessarily be monetary.
4. This act, which delineated responsibilities of the state, local, and federal governments for funding impact management, has not received renewed funding from the U.S. Congress.

6
Project Management Measures to Reduce Inmigration

Local socioeconomic impacts of large-scale development projects tend to be closely associated with the relocation (inmigration) of project workers and their families to communities near the project site. Projects requiring large numbers of inmigrating workers may lead to substantial local population growth, extensive demands on local services and infrastructure, severe fiscal problems for local governments, and to increased problems of social assimilation (Murdock and Leistritz 1979). These problems may be exacerbated by the fluctuations in work force size during various phases of major projects. For instance, an electric power plant or synthetic fuel facility may require a work force of 2,000 workers or more within two or three years after construction begins, but this work force will decrease rapidly after construction and be replaced by an operation and maintenance force of only a few hundred within five or six years after the project is initiated (Leistritz and Maki 1981). Construction of a large hydroelectric facility may require a similarly large construction force but involve only a few dozen operating employees. In such situations, local officials face very difficult choices; if they build facilities to meet the population-related requirements of the project's construction phase, they face the possibility of having substantial excess capacity just a few years later. On the other hand, failure to provide needed facilities and services can lead to severe problems during the peak of the construction-phase population influx.

One approach to lessening the project-related demands on nearby communities is to reduce the number of relocating workers (and dependents) associated with project development. This approach may include such specific measures as altering the project site, design, or construction schedule, increasing the proportion of the work force that is hired locally, or encouraging long-distance commuting by construction workers.

Impact management measures that focus on reducing inmigration are often attractive to both communities and developers. They may allow developers and local officials to partially avoid the problems of planning for--and costs inherent in providing--housing and community services for a large but temporary population. In addition, recruitment and training measures aimed at increasing the proportion of project jobs filled by local workers often enhance local support for a project. Such measures are thus important considerations in the impact management process and deserve careful analysis.

The remainder of this chapter is organized into three major sections. First, salient characteristics of work forces associated with large-scale development projects are summarized. Second, alternative measures which can be utilized to reduce the inmigration of project-related workers and dependents are identified and evaluated in terms of their potential effectiveness in addressing socioeconomic impact problems, their administrative feasibility, and the costs likely to be associated with their implementation. Examples of the use of these approaches are examined in order to gain insights regarding the usefulness and limitations of alternative measures. Finally, conclusions and implications concerning the potential usefulness and limitations of each approach are presented.

WORK FORCE CHARACTERISTICS

The socioeconomic effects of a project depend in large measure on the number and characteristics of inmigrating workers and their families. Attributes examined here include the number of workers typically associated with energy development projects of various kinds, the proportion hired locally, and workers' demographic characteristics. These characteristics are examined with respect to three classes of project-related workers: (1) construction workers, (2) permanent facility operation-and-maintenance workers, and (3) those workers who fill the new jobs in the trade and service sectors of the local economy which are created indirectly as a result of the project. These jobs are often termed *secondary* employment or *indirect* and *induced* employment.

Work Force Magnitude

Labor force requirements, including the total size of the work force as well as the skill levels of the workers, vary with the type of project. The direct employment requirements of a large-scale development project typically occur in two phases: (1) construction of the facility and (2) its subsequent operation. The construction work force for many types of facilities is several times larger than the operational work force but remains at the site for only a few years, whereas the operational work force may be quite small but will be required for the life of the facility.

Although the employment levels required by specific projects may vary widely depending on such factors as facility design and the specific technology being utilized, some general patterns can be discerned by examining typical sites. Examples of the work forces of some typical energy facilities utilizing different forms of technology are presented in Table 6.1. These data indicate that large construction work forces may be expected for electric-generating, synfuel, and oil-shale-processing plants, and that synthetic gasification plants and oil-shale-processing facilities may have 1,000 or more permanent operating employees. Clearly, such facilities would be likely to result in substantial socioeconomic effects if located in remote, sparsely populated rural areas.

The secondary employment effects of a large-scale project also may be quite substantial. Estimating the amount of secondary employment that will result from project development is therefore essential to any attempt toward comprehensive socioeconomic impact assessment and management. The amount of secondary employment likely to result from development of a project is often estimated by an employment *multiplier*, which expresses the change in total project-related employment (primary plus secondary) as a multiple of the original change in project employment.

Two major forces influence the magnitude of the employment multipliers associated with new development projects--characteristics of the project and characteristics of the site area. Project features of key importance include the wage and salary levels of project employees, the propensity of these direct workers to purchase goods and services in local communities, and the extent to which the developer purchases supplies and services from local firms. Because salary levels of project workers often are relatively high, the employment multipliers for a new project could potentially be quite substantial. The nature of the site area, however, also affects the magnitude of secondary employment effects. If communities near the project site have poorly developed shopping facilities, project workers may travel to distant trade and service centers to acquire many goods and services. Similarly, the developer's ability to purchase supplies and services locally will be affected by the size and diversity of local trade and service firms. If local firms cannot supply needed inputs, the developer will acquire them elsewhere. These factors, which reduce the level of local expenditures resulting from a project, will also tend to reduce its multiplier effects at the local level. During the construction phase of major projects, when many construction workers may commute long distances to the site, the secondary employment effects experienced by small communities nearby may be quite modest.

The secondary employment effects of large-scale projects have been difficult for researchers to measure with precision. Secondary employment multipliers derived from four recent analyses are summarized in Table 6.2. In all cases the construction-phase multipliers are smaller than the corresponding operation-phase multipliers. It also will be noted that the first three studies indicate multiplier values which are somewhat larger than those from the fourth analysis. This difference can be attributed in part to definitional inconsistencies between studies. The analysis by Gilmore et al. (1982) used only the inmigrating

TABLE 6.1.
Energy facility employment characteristics[a]

Type of Facility	Size	Construction Period (Years)	Peak Construction Work Force (Number)	Operating Work Force (Number)
Surface coal mine	9 million tons/year	2-3	200	475
Underground coal mine	2 million tons/year	3	325	830
Electric-generating plant (includes surface coal mine)	700 megawatts	5	1,050	250
	2,250 megawatts	6-8	3,000	650
Synthetic gasification plant (includes surface coal mine)	250 million cubic feet/day	3-4	4,000	1,300
Oil-shale-processing facility (includes mining)	50,000 barrels/ day	3-4	2,400	1,450
Uranium mining and milling	1,000 tons U_3O_8 concentrate/ day	1-3	250	250
Nuclear waste repository:				
in salt	reference site	3-5	1,700	870
in basalt	reference site	3-5	5,000	1,100

SOURCE: Adapted from Murdock et al. 1983.

[a]Employment figures are estimates for general planning purposes only. Actual employment for any particular facility will depend on size, type of equipment utilized, mining conditions, construction schedule, and numerous other factors.

TABLE 6.2.
Employment multiplier values from selected studies

Study	Construction Phase	Operation Phase
Murdock and Leistritz (1979):		
Average Value	1.51	2.03
Range	1.2-2.1	1.75-2.5
Briscoe, Maphis, Murray, Lamont, Inc. (1978):	1.6	2.50
Murphy and Williams (1978):	1.63	2.42
Gilmore et al. (1982):[a]		
Rural, sparsely populated, no large trade center within impact area	1.2-1.3	1.3-1.5
More urbanized impact areas, population densities moderate	1.3-1.4	1.4-1.6
On the fringe of a metropolitan area	1.4-1.5	1.6-1.8

Note: All values are expressed in the following form:

$$\frac{\text{total employment (direct + secondary)}}{\text{direct employment}}$$

[a]These values are computed using only the inmigrating component of the direct work force and thus are not directly comparable to those of other studies. In addition, these multipliers reflect only secondary employment in the site county.

portion of the project work force in computing multipliers and also considered only secondary employment created in the site county whereas the other three studies considered the entire project work force and estimated secondary employment for the complete area of project influence (impact area), which often included several counties.

Two other recent studies address the secondary employment effects of power plant projects. In a retrospective analysis of 12 nuclear power plants in the United States, Pijawka and Chalmers (1983) estimate that the average local employment multiplier was 1.16 during construction and 1.23 during operation of the facilities. Fookes (1981a) developed a similar estimate of the local employment multiplier (1.125) for the construction of the Huntly Power Project in New Zealand. Pijawka and Chalmers attribute the small multiplier values to substantial leakages of purchasing power resulting from (1) a high percentage of the construction workers commuting daily from nearby metropolitan areas and (2) the developers purchasing few goods and services within the impact area. Fookes cites both of these factors but also indicates that a major effect of the Huntly project was to increase productivity (i.e., sales per worker) within existing firms rather than to stimulate creation of new firms or new jobs within existing firms. While both of these analyses point out the importance of considering leakages when estimating secondary employment effects, it also should be noted that their multiplier estimates are influenced by their definition of the relevant impact area. Fookes' estimate is for the site community (Huntly) only, while Pijawka and Chalmers' estimates are for either the site county or a sub-county area. Had the impact areas been defined more broadly (to include the cities where many of the workers resided), the multiplier estimates might have been considerably larger. (For additional discussion of employment multipliers, see Gordon and Mulkey 1978; Leistritz and Murdock 1981; Isard 1960; Lamphear and Emerson 1975; and Leistritz, Murdock, and Leholm 1982.)

Although the precise magnitude of secondary employment effects is difficult to estimate, it is obvious that secondary jobs can add significantly to the overall employment impacts of a major project. Suppose, for example, that one were evaluating the impacts of a large electric-generating facility with a peak construction work force of 2,200 and a permanent operating work force of 500. Using even relatively conservative secondary employment multipliers of 1.3 for the construction phase and 1.6 for the operation phase results in secondary employment estimates of 660 and 300 workers for construction and operation, respectively. The effect of this secondary employment growth on the level of population influx likely to occur in the local area is illustrated in Figure 6.1.

In conclusion, both direct and secondary employment requirements of large-scale development projects may be substantial. A major factor determining the effect of these project-related employment opportunities on population growth in the site area is, therefore, the percentage of the project workers who are recruited from the local labor force and, conversely, the proportion who are inmigrants to the area.

Local Hiring

An examination of the characteristics of work forces associated with large-scale development projects reveals substantial differences between construction work forces and permanent operations-and-maintenance work forces. For example, a study of workers at coal mine and power plant projects in the northern Great Plains states revealed that the construction work forces were dominated by craftsmen with highly specialized skills who were geographically mobile in response to new job

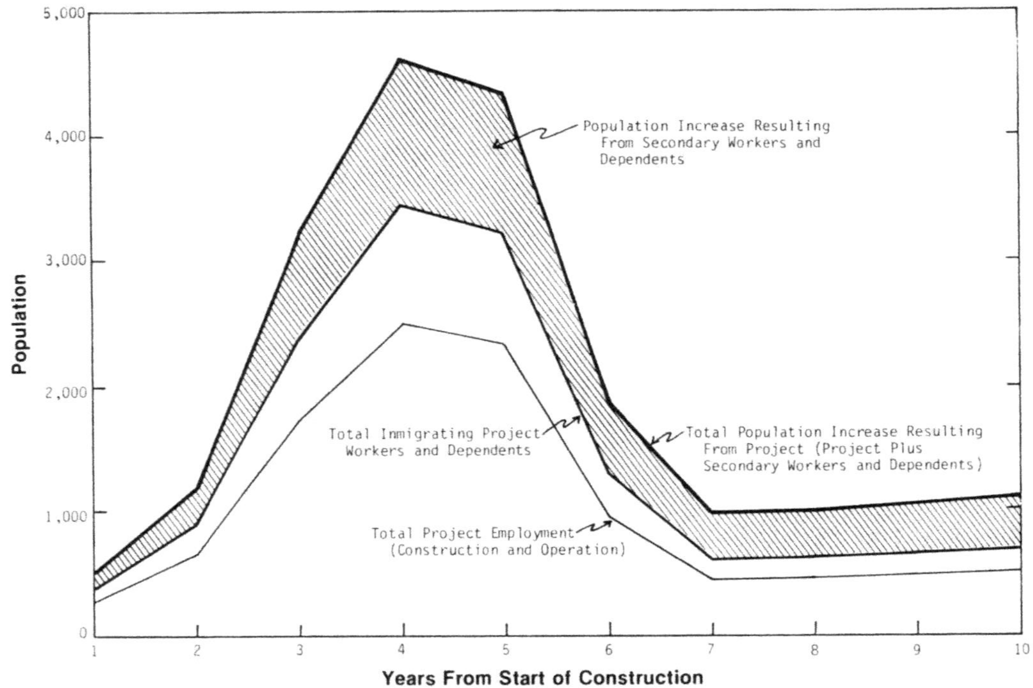

Figure 6.1 Typical patterns of local employment and population growth associated with electric power plant construction

opportunities. Employment of a given craft at an individual project was temporary; average job tenure was about two years (Wieland et al. 1979). Training and apprenticeship periods for many crafts were relatively long, and labor unions played a major role in allocating workers to project sites.

Because of these factors, many construction jobs were filled by relocating workers. A survey of workers at 14 energy-project construction sites in the northern Great Plains indicated that relocating workers made up 60 percent of these work forces. The rate of local hiring appeared to be affected by a number of factors, including the size of the local labor force, the status of other construction projects in the area, and the union referral system. Local (i.e., nonrelocating) workers were most prevalent in the less-skilled job categories; more than half of the laborers were local workers. Local hiring also was more frequent in the more populous site areas (Mountain West Research 1975).

More recent surveys of construction work forces at other types of projects reflect the same general characteristics. For example, a survey of workers at 12 water development projects in the western states revealed that nonlocal workers made up 53 percent of these work forces (Chalmers 1977). The fact that these projects generally had smaller work force requirements than the energy projects described previously may have been partially responsible for the higher rate of local hiring they experienced. In contrast, a U.S. Army Corps of Engineers survey of workers at 55 construction projects indicated that only 31 percent of these workers were nonlocal (Dunning 1981). Most of the Corps' projects were relatively small and were located in more populous areas which probably explains their higher rate of local recruitment.

High rates of local hiring can be achieved even for large projects when the local labor pool is substantial. A survey of construction workers at 6 Tennessee Valley Authority (TVA) power plant projects revealed that 71 percent of these workers were local residents (DeVeney 1977). Similarly, a survey of 13 nuclear power plant sites indicated that local workers made up at least half of the construction work forces in all cases and generally more than two-thirds. Substantial variability was noted in this study, however, with local worker percentages ranging from 50 to 86 percent (Malhotra and Manninen 1980).

The high rates of local recruitment achieved in areas with substantial local labor pools result in large measure from extensive daily commuting by construction craftsmen. Because of the nature of construction manpower requirements, which are both site-specific and highly variable over time, commuting and/or migration to sites where their skills are in demand have become accepted practices for construction workers. Car pooling is frequent when commuting distances are substantial, and buses and van pools have been utilized at some sites (Metz 1982b). In general, it appears that some construction workers are willing to commute 60 to 90 minutes one way to job sites. For example, about one-third of the construction work force of the Great Plains Gasification Project in western North Dakota commuted daily from towns at least 60 miles away (Pearson 1984).

At extremely remote sites such as mines or oil development regions in northern Canada and the North Slope of Alaska, air transport often is utilized to facilitate workers' commuting. In such circumstances, a commuter-rotation system may be implemented whereby workers spend from one to seven weeks at the project site followed by a leave period of one to four weeks. The workers are transported (in most cases, via airplane) at company expense between the project and one or more communities designated as pick-up points. The commuter-rotation system often appears to be an attractive alternative to developing family housing and public service infrastructure at a remote site. It has been noted, however, that long rotation periods often are associated with increased worker turnover rates (DePape 1983).

The operations-and-maintenance work forces at many resource development projects are dominated by heavy equipment operators, craftsmen-technicians, and mechanics. Wages paid are generally higher than those in other rural area jobs, and many firms appear to emphasize local hiring in order to build a stable work force (Leistritz, Murdock, and Leholm 1982). For example, a survey of workers at 14 power plants and coal mines in the northern Great Plains indicated that local workers made up 62 percent of these work forces (Wieland et al. 1977). However, substantial variations in the rates of local hiring were found among the various projects; rates generally were higher for smaller projects and those located in more populous areas. On-the-job training and internal promotion were used to fill skilled positions at these facilities, although a small nucleus of experienced workers was sometimes transferred from other mines or plants when a new project began operation.

More recent surveys of operations work forces indicate rates of local hiring similar to those cited above. For example, a survey of workers at two coal mines near Sheridan, Wyoming, indicated that about 60 percent of the work forces had been recruited locally (Hooper and Branch 1983). Similar results were reported from a survey at the Jim Bridger power plant in southwestern Wyoming (Browne, Bortz, and Coddington 1981). Large-scale development projects may absorb almost the entire local labor supply, however. For instance, a survey of 15 companies developing coal mines in Campbell County, Wyoming, indicated that only 40 percent of the 523 workers hired during 1981 had lived in the county for six months or more prior to their employment by the energy firm (Browne, Bortz, and Coddington 1982).

Although numerous studies have addressed the origins of the project's construction and operations workers, much less attention has been given to the workers who fill the secondary jobs (i.e., in the local trade and service sector and in supplier's firms) resulting from project development. Past impact assessments have frequently incorporated the assumption that most of these new jobs will be filled either by local residents or by spouses of the inmigrating project workers (Berkey et al. 1977; Denver Research Institute 1979). A recent study, however, suggests that this assumption may not be tenable. A survey of local trade and service firms was conducted in nine cities of four western states which had experienced substantial levels of energy-related growth. (In several of these towns, population had more than doubled since 1970). The results indicated that 56 percent of the employees had relocated to these counties since project development began. Of these recently inmigrating workers, only 18 percent had an immediate family member employed at one of the energy facilities. Overall, then, almost half of the local trade and service sector workers in these communities were recent inmigrants and were not at all associated with relocating energy-project workers. Since each worker had an average of 1.74 associated family members, these inmigrating secondary workers constituted a significant source of local population growth (Halstead and Leistritz 1983b).

Demographic Characteristics

Analyses of construction and operations work forces at large-scale development projects reveal both similarities and differences between these two groups. The median age for both groups is generally between 30 and 35, and most of the workers are between the ages of 25 and 40 (Wieland et al. 1979; Browne, Bortz, and Coddington 1982; Browne, Bortz, and Coddington 1981; Hooper and Branch 1983). Exceptions to this norm sometimes occur when a development agency has, by accident or design, established what is in effect a "career" group of construction workers. These workers may tend to move from one of the developer's projects to the next, and in time an older-than-normal construction work force may result. Examples of this phenomenon have been noted in connection with Army Corps of Engineers water projects in the Pacific Northwest (Harnisch 1978), dam construction projects sponsored by British Columbia Hydro in Canada (Vincent 1981), energy projects in New Zealand (Fookes 1981a), and pipeline construction projects throughout North America (Mountain West Research 1979).

The average age of inmigrating secondary workers appears to be somewhat less than for the construction and project operations workers. Surveys of such workers in six energy development areas in the western United States revealed average ages ranging from 27 to 31 years (Halstead and Leistritz 1983b). This might be expected because many secondary jobs are entry level positions with lower requirements for training and experience than are typical for project jobs.

The marital status of workers appears to differ somewhat among job types, with shorter-term, transitory jobs being more attractive to single workers. Surveys of operations-and-maintenance workers generally indicate that 70 to 80 percent are married; similar percentages of married workers often are found at large construction sites (Wieland et al. 1979; Browne, Bortz, and Coddington 1982). Somewhat lower percentages of married workers have been reported for oil field development and pipeline construction workers (Chase and Leistritz 1983; Mountain West Research 1979); these activities often entail a job duration in a given area which is uncertain but generally expected to be quite temporary. For secondary workers, the proportion married is about two-thirds, which appears consistent with the younger average age of these individuals (Halstead and Leistritz 1983b).

Much more variable than the percentage of workers who are married, however, is the proportion of nonlocal married workers who bring their families with them to the site area. It is typical for a substantial percentage of the nonlocal construction workers who are married to come to the project site area unaccompanied by their dependents. These workers then seek single-status accommodations during the workweek and, whenever feasible, return to their permanent residence on weekends. The percentage of married nonlocal workers who were not accompanied by their families has ranged from 25 to 50 percent in surveys of power plant and water project construction work forces (Dunning 1981; Chalmers 1977; Leholm et al. 1976; Malhotra and Manninen 1980). Factors which appear to influence the percentage of nonlocal workers who will be accompanied by dependents include the project's work schedule, the availability of single-status accommodations, and the availability of family-status housing. In order to encourage workers not to bring their families to the area, some projects have established 4-day work schedules (10 to 12 hours per day) which facilitated the workers' returning home on weekends (Metz 1982a). Other project sponsors have established single-status housing (often subsidized) for their workers. The availability of such facilities appears to increase the percentage of workers who will not be accompanied (Rapp 1980). Finally, if family-status housing is in short supply in the area, more workers may choose not to relocate their families.

For pipeline construction workers, whose job duration at a given location ranges from a few weeks to a few months, the percentage of nonaccompanied married workers is even higher, averaging 75 percent in a survey of four pipeline projects (Mountain West Research 1979). The phenomenon of nonaccompaniment does not appear to be significant for operations-and-maintenance and secondary workers because these jobs are generally perceived as being long-term.

Family sizes appear to be quite similar for nonlocal construction, operations, and secondary workers. Family sizes for married workers of all three types generally range from 3.2 to 3.7 persons, including the worker. The age structure of these workers also leads to a substantial percentage (30 to 40 percent) of their children being in the preschool age group.

To summarize, the number of inmigrating workers associated with a project and the characteristics of these workers and their dependents are important determinants of the project's socioeconomic impacts. Key factors affecting the number of workers and dependents who move to the site area include the size of the project's work force, the magnitude of secondary employment effects, the proportion of the jobs that are filled by local workers (including daily commuters), the extent to which nonlocal project workers are accompanied by their families, and the size of those families. Measures aimed at reducing inmigration involve attempts to alter one or more of these factors.

IDENTIFICATION AND EVALUATION OF MITIGATION ALTERNATIVES

Approaches to reducing inmigration fall into two general categories: (1) alterations in facility design or construction schedule, and (2) work force policies geared to reducing the proportion of the project workers who will relocate to the site area.

Alterations in facility design or construction schedule which could be considered as a means of reducing the demands imposed on the site area include

1. Choice of a more urban site or one located within commuting distance of a major metropolitan area
2. Lengthening the project construction schedule to reduce the peak work force requirements
3. Fabrication of components elsewhere in order to reduce on-site labor requirements
4. Phasing of multiple project or unit construction schedules to stabilize combined work force requirements (reduce peak requirements)

Once the facility's location and construction schedule have been determined, several work force policy measures can be adopted which may reduce the percentage of the project workers who inmigrate to the area with their families. These measures include

1. Increasing the percentage of the work force that is hired locally through special contract provisions and/or training programs for area workers
2. Encouraging long-distance commuting as an alternative to relocation for nonlocal workers. Mechanisms for encouraging commuting beyond normal daily commuting distances include company-subsidized buses and van pools (and sometimes even aircraft at remote sites), provision of single-status housing for workers at the site, and provision of liberal travel allowances (Metz 1982a)

Each of these measures may prove useful in reducing demands for housing and community services in the site area. However, in some cases, the goal of reducing inmigration and resultant demands on local services may conflict with other goals, such as minimizing overall project development costs. The advantages and limitations of each of these measures are discussed in the following section and summarized in Table 6.3.

The initial choice of a project site and design will in large measure determine the nature and extent of impact management efforts that will subsequently be required. If the project's work force requirements are modest and the site area is heavily populated with an abundant supply of skilled construction workers, the local impacts are likely to be negligible and consist primarily of increased traffic on local roads (Gilmore et al.

TABLE 6.3.
Measures to reduce inmigration

Option	Method	Advantages	Disadvantages/Limitations
1) Alterations in facility design or construction schedule	1) Site selection close to metropolitan area	--reduces number of inmigrants --reduces need for new infrastructure	--may not be possible for most energy resource projects because of resource location
	2) Lengthening construction period	--reduces peak work force requirements --reduces number of relocating workers	--increases project cost
	3) Off-site component fabrication	--increases construction efficiency --eases needs for craftsmen and engineers on-site	--may be limited by union-employer contractual agreements and/or capability to transport large components
	4) Scheduling of multiple units	--reduces peak work force requirements	--is applicable only to projects with multiple units or when several projects are planned for the same area
2) Reducing the percentage of inmigrating project workers and families	1) Increasing local hiring a) local hiring preference	--increases percentage of economic benefits accruing to local residents --enhances stability of work force	--may violate union-labor agreements --may be viewed as discriminatory --increases competition for local labor with area businesses --success depends on current employment situation in area
	b) training programs	--may reduce projects' competition with local employers --is popular with local residents --increases number of workers hired locally	--may not increase local hiring due to union-labor contractual agreements --requires careful initiation; lead-time consideration
	2) Increasing commuting a) measures to reduce travel costs b) provision of temporary housing	--increases ease of labor force recruitment --increases productivity --reduces number of relocating workers	--may aggravate local traffic problems --induces payroll leakages from local community --may lead to higher turnover

1982; Shurcliff 1977). If, on the other hand, work force requirements are large relative to the local labor supply, if the site area has very limited population and service bases, and if the area is remote from large urban centers, then impacts may be substantial. A mitigation program of major proportions may be required in such cases (Metz 1980; Murdock and Leistritz 1979). One possibility for lessening demands on local services and facilities is for the developer to change some of the construction aspects of the project.

Altering Construction Parameters

Site selection. While the importance of site selection in determining subsequent impact problems and mitigation needs is widely recognized (Metz 1982a; Santini, Stenehjem, and Meguire 1978), there are only a few cases in which socioeconomic impact considerations are known to have played a significant role in site selection.[1] Sites for major resource development projects are typically selected on the basis of several criteria; resource availability and transportation and market factors are usually among the most important. For example, the location of mines is governed primarily by the location of economically recoverable mineral reserves. Energy conversion facilities are somewhat more flexible in their siting; the principal criteria are availability and cost of feedstock (e.g., coal), availability of adequate water supplies, proximity to major market areas and environmental considerations. Thus, if no sites satisfy all criteria, a choice may be made between siting (1) at mine-mouth, (2) near the major demand centers, or (3) at an intermediate location which offers adequate water supplies and favorable transportation access. In recent years, however, environmental considerations (especially air pollution) have become a more important factor in the site selection process and appear to encourage siting in areas remote from major urban centers.

The influence of socioeconomic impact considerations on site selection is likely to be manifested primarily through concerns regarding work force recruitment and siting permit approval. Successful development of a major project will require recruitment and retention of a productive work force. If the site is located in a remote area with limited infrastructure and amenities, the developer may be forced to offer higher levels of compensation or to make expenditures to provide quality housing and infrastructure in order to attract and retain a productive work force (Metz 1982a; Cummings and Schulze 1978). Similarly, socioeconomic impact considerations may lead to more stringent requirements for site approval. In recent years, federal, state, and local regulatory bodies have increasingly required developers to undertake specific mitigation activities as a condition of their licenses and siting permits (Watson 1977; Peelle 1979).

Even though developers are of necessity becoming more aware of socioeconomic impact issues and of the need for mitigation activities (Metz 1979a; Gilmore 1980), this awareness does not appear to lead to greater interest in sites near urban areas. Rather, the trend in siting energy extraction and conversion facilities points toward an increase in remote siting (Santini, South, and Stenehjem 1979). If this trend continues, it will be important for developing firms and agencies to give greater attention to socioeconomic impact issues early in the site selection process (Gilmore et al. 1982). Although the explicit consideration of potential impact problems and mitigation requirements during the project feasibility and site selection phase may not alter the site selection decision which emerges, such preliminary analyses should prove valuable in enabling project managers to incorporate mitigation costs directly into project development budgets and to initiate early planning to manage impact problems effectively (Luke 1980).

Lengthening the Construction Period. Once a site has been selected and the facility design has been established, the next possibility for lessening the requirements on local services is establishing the project construction schedule. A decision to lengthen the construction schedule will usually lead to a reduction in peak work force requirements and thus to a reduction in the proportion of the construction jobs which must be filled by relocating workers. A few instances have been reported in which project construction activities were constrained as a result of impact concerns. For example, the Missouri Basin Power Project agreed to a construction work force ceiling of 2,250 workers at its Laramie River Station near Wheatland, Wyoming (West 1977).[2] However, limiting the construction work force in order to lessen impact problems has not been widely practiced, because of the cost implications resulting from lengthening the construction schedule (Gilmore et al. 1982; Metz 1982a).

Schedule delays during the construction of large energy facilities can cost the developer several hundred thousand dollars per day, primarily in increased interest charges. Thus, there is a substantial incentive to keep the project on schedule. Rather than limiting the on-site work force in order to alleviate local impacts, the more typical experience at large power plant construction projects has been for the actual work force to exceed greatly the estimates on which impact projections (and mitigation plans) had been based (Gilmore 1980; Braid 1980). In many cases, factors such as regulatory delays, labor disputes, unfavorable weather, or supplier problems caused the construction activity to fall behind schedule. The work force was then increased (often by double-shifting) in an effort to make up lost time (Gilmore et al. 1982). Such occurrences increase the difficulties inherent in mitigation planning and indicate the need for a well-designed impact-monitoring system as an integral part of any mitigation plan (see Chapter 5).

Off-Site Fabrication of Components. Another possible means of reducing on-site labor requirements and lessening demands on local systems is increased fabrication of facility components at other locations. An incentive for using off-site fabrication as much as possible is the greater efficiency typically associated with shop fabrication as opposed to field assembly (U.S.

Department of Energy 1981). Although this approach has also been suggested as a means of easing potential shortages of construction craftsmen and engineers in the event of a major effort to increase synthetic fuels production (Federal Energy Administration 1974), it has not been widely practiced (Metz 1982a). Off-site fabrication does not appear likely to become a major factor influencing work force requirements in the near future because of the limitations of present transportation facilities and highway systems for moving large components. In addition, use of this mitigation alternative may be limited by union-employer contractual agreements which may specify what equipment must be field assembled (U.S. Department of Energy 1981).

One way that off-site fabrication has been successfully utilized to reduce inmigration to areas near major project sites, however, has been through use of prefabricated housing units. In Mercer County, North Dakota, for instance, manufactured (prefabricated) homes have accounted for a substantial percentage of new permanent housing units (Halstead and Leistritz 1983a). Use of such manufactured units can significantly reduce the work force requirements and inmigration associated with housing development.

Scheduling of Multiple Units. When the proposed facility involves multiple units or when several major projects will affect the same area, a possible means of lessening local impacts is to stagger the unit or project construction schedules. Sequential phasing of multiple projects or units can result in substantial reductions in combined peak labor requirements, with commensurate reductions in demands for housing, public services, and infrastructure (Santini, Stenehjem, and Meguire 1978; Wernette 1980). This approach will be most effective if construction labor requirements substantially exceed those for project operation. When sequential unit or project phasing is compatible with other goals of the developer, such a strategy can ease problems of work force recruitment as well as reduce requirements for investment in local infrastructure.[3] These benefits must, however, be weighed against other objectives of the developer and against the added costs which a delay in construction may impose. In general, it appears that the projected demand for the facility's output will be the primary factor determining multiple-unit construction schedules.

To summarize, the mitigation approaches involving alteration of project construction parameters offer an obvious means of reducing local impacts. The effects on overall project development costs of implementing such measures may be substantial, however. The trade-offs between the benefits of impact alleviation and the additional development costs associated with these measures must be carefully evaluated. In general, it appears that alternative mitigation strategies will usually be more cost-effective than altering construction parameters, and hence are more likely to be adopted.

Reducing Inmigrating Worker Populations

Once the project site and construction parameters have been established, the principal means for lessening local impacts is to reduce the proportion of the project workers who inmigrate to the site area. As noted above, this objective can be achieved through measures which either (1) increase the proportion of project jobs which are filled by local workers, or (2) encourage nonlocal workers to commute from relatively great distances rather than relocate to the site area. These results may be achieved by a number of specific measures that are discussed in the sections which follow.

Increasing Local Hiring. Greater utilization of local workers is generally expected to lead to reduced inmigration and consequently to fewer problems typically associated with inmigration and rapid population growth. In addition, programs to increase the proportion of project jobs which are filled by local workers will enhance the positive local employment benefits of the project. Energy facility employers generally offer higher wages than are typical in other local industries, and the job opportunities associated with a new project are thus usually regarded as one of its major local benefits (Murdock and Leistritz 1979). Measures designed to increase local workers' participation in these new job opportunities also may be important in gaining community acceptance for a new project (Luke 1980). Furthermore, in some settings (e.g., some Canadian provinces) specified levels of local employment participation may be required as conditions of granting mining leases or siting approvals (Storey 1982).

Programs to increase local hiring typically have two major components (1) a policy of preferential hiring of local workers, and (2) a training program to ensure that local workers possess the necessary skills to fill project-related jobs. These measures may be employed individually or in combination to increase the proportion of a project's work force which is recruited from the local area.

Local-Hiring Preference. Programs aimed at increasing the proportion of workers hired locally usually include a policy, formal or informal, of giving preference to area residents in the hiring process. Such policies may be implemented through specific provisions in contracts between the project sponsor and the general contractor, and between the general contractor and subcontractors. Although the specifics of local-preference measures may differ, they generally include target levels (percentages) of local hiring which are to be achieved and/or provisions that qualified local workers will receive first preference in hiring (Storey 1982). Formal agreements of this type have been implemented at several new mines in northern Canada (DePape 1982). More informal approaches for implementing a local-preference policy are also possible, and more frequently practiced.

Hiring measures favoring local workers have two major advantages from the standpoint of the developer and the affected community. First, these policies tend to result in a higher percentage of project-related benefits (i.e., attractive jobs) accruing to local residents. As noted above, local leaders typically view the new jobs associated with a proposed project as one of its major positive aspects, so they tend to view as favorable any program which will enhance local residents' participation in these job opportunities. Such views may be particularly strong in areas where new job opportunities have been limited and unemployment and underemployment rates traditionally have been high (DePape 1981; Murdock and Leistritz 1979).

A second advantage of local hiring from the viewpoint of the developer is that emphasis on the recruitment of local workers may enhance the future stability of the work force. Work force stability is important, particularly during the project operation phase, because the developer typically incurs a substantial training cost for each new worker that is hired.[4] For this reason, firms which operate facilities such as coal mines and electric power plants rely heavily on internal promotion (often formalized through a "job bidding" process) to fill job vacancies above the entry level (Baker 1977). By recruiting local residents with a commitment to the area, developers hope to minimize turnover in entry-level jobs and thus to ensure a dependable supply of experienced workers for promotion to the more skilled positions (Wieland et al. 1977; Baker 1977).

Local-preference programs are not without their problems, however. Several factors may limit the implementation of such hiring programs; the most important of which is usually union labor agreements.[5] Union practices are especially important during the construction phase of a project when the union referral network is often the principal vehicle for dissemination of job information (Baker 1977; Lovejoy 1983). Under this system, the prime contractor develops estimates of the magnitude and timing of project labor needs by craft. This information is presented to representatives of the appropriate union locals who then may contact other state locals, regional locals, or their international organization, depending on the relationship of estimated requirements to available supply. When labor is actually required on the site, the prime contractor makes a formal request to the appropriate local. Jobs are then filled with first preference given to local members, then to members of other locals in an order determined by the union's established practices. If labor requirements cannot be provided by the union within a specified time period, sometimes 48 hours, the project may be allowed to hire nonunion workers to satisfy unmet requirements.

The union referral system is generally regarded as an efficient method of information dissemination and manpower allocation in the construction industry where skills are often specialized and where labor demand may fluctuate substantially in both time and space, thus implying the need for high rates of short-term job turnover. Because the life of most construction projects is limited, migration and commuting, as opposed to training, have been the principal means of meeting qualitative manpower requirements (Baker 1977). This system, however, may place substantial constraints on the implementation of a local-preference program.

The constraint imposed by union labor agreements is that established union members are to be given preference in hiring and nonunion workers are utilized only when the pool of union members, including those available from other areas, has been exhausted. Further, even though a large number of workers may be supplied by the union "locals," this does not necessarily mean that these workers will be residents of the project's local impact area (Braid and Kyles 1977). Rather, the geographical area of a given union local's jurisdiction may be quite large, and most of the "local" members may reside in cities far from the project site. These workers may be required to relocate or to commute very long distances to work at the site. In addition, some developers, such as Britsh Columbia Hydro, have substantial pools of experienced construction workers who have participated in several previous projects. These workers typically will commute or temporarily relocate in order to work at a new project (Vincent 1981).

The key role of unions in providing skilled labor at major construction projects has several implications for impact assessment and mitigation planning. First, union officials constitute a valuable source of information in evaluating the potential impact of a project. When provided with estimates of the labor requirements of the project, they should be able to estimate the proportion of the jobs which could be filled by members of their local. Based on experience with past projects, they should also be able to estimate the response of workers at other locals to the project's needs (although the response will depend on the overall regional demand for workers of that craft, and such demands are often rather volatile in the construction industry). In addition, information concerning the areas where most of the union local's members reside can be valuable to the impact analyst in determining the likely extent and configuration of the project's impact area. Finally, implementation of a local-preference program will almost certainly require negotiation with union officials.[6]

Other factors also may limit the implementation of local-hiring programs. Thus, such programs may be deemed to be discriminatory in the United States (i.e., against inmigrants) and hence illegal.[7] These legal implications may limit the ability of the developing firm or agency to give preference to area workers; for example, established affirmative action programs of development firms or agencies may limit the ability of these entities to implement local-hiring efforts. It may be possible, however, to focus job information and recruitment efforts on the local impact area and/or to devise techniques which make it easier and more economical to hire area residents rather than import labor from elsewhere (Braid and Kyles 1977).[8]

Another limitation on local recruitment efforts is that such activities will tend to increase the project's competition with other employers for the area's labor resources. Local businesses and public sector entities may then be forced to substantially increase their levels of compensation or risk losing their most experienced workers (Gilmore et al. 1977; U.S. Department of Housing and Urban Development 1976). These employers may resent this competition and, as a result, develop negative attitudes concerning the project. Since these individuals often represent some of the area's dominant economic sectors, their opposition can be detrimental to the project. In addition, increased competition for local labor may contribute to inflation in the site area as local trade and service firms raise their prices to compensate for increased labor costs (Leistritz and Maki 1981; Gilmore et al. 1982).

Local interests occasionally attempt to restrict a project's employment of local workers in order to lessen its effects on the area's labor market. During construction of a large oil terminal at Sullom Voe (Shetland Islands) in Scotland, for example, attempts were made to restrict the employment of local men. This policy proved difficult to sustain, however, in the face of local pressures for access to the highly paid jobs (Sewel 1983).

Yet another limitation to the implementation of local recruitment strategies concerns their effectiveness as a means of reducing project-related inmigration. If the workers who are hired locally were previously unemployed or are new entrants to the labor force, then it is reasonable to assume that each additional local worker will result in a net reduction of one relocating worker associated with the project. On the other hand, if many of the workers hired locally were previously employed and if their jobs are refilled (as seems likely), then the net effect of local hiring on inmigration is uncertain and will depend upon the characteristics of the replacement workers. If these workers are primarily inmigrants, there may be little or no net reduction in project-related inmigration because of the local-hiring strategy (Gilmore et al. 1982). But if the replacement workers are local and consist primarily of the previously unemployed and new labor force entrants, the project's local-hiring strategy may be quite effective in reducing inmigration. More information concerning the labor market dynamics associated with large increases in basic employment will be needed before firm conclusions can be drawn.[9] One recent study, however, suggests that inmigrants may fill a substantial proportion of the vacancies (or new positions) in the local trade and service sector (Halstead and Leistritz 1983b).

Training Programs for Local Workers. Local hiring of workers for the construction and operation of major resource development projects may be severely constrained if area workers lack needed skills. Job training programs for area residents may thus be necessary if local recruitment goals are to be achieved. The advantages and limitations of special training programs as a means of increasing local hiring and reducing project-related inmigration are discussed in this section.

Job training programs have several advantages as a mechanism to enhance local hiring for large-scale projects. First, such training efforts may be a necessary adjunct to a policy of local hiring if local workers lack needed skills. Special training to prepare workers for jobs in the facility may be conducted either by local and regional vocational-technical institutions, often with support from state or federal government and/or developers, or by the development firm or agency itself (i.e., on-the-job training). Institutional training is seldom a complete substitute for on-the-job training, however, because a part of the necessary training for new workers involves familiarization with the development company's operating procedures and orientation to specialized equipment. Further, the procedural job allocation rules employed by many companies and unions effectively exclude well-trained but inexperienced workers from all but entry-level positions (Baker 1977).

Traditional systems involving on-the-job training and internal promotion appear to be an adequate source of skilled manpower for many resource development industries when the industry is expanding at a moderate rate (Baker 1977). When industry expansion is rapid, however, the traditional systems may not be satisfactory, and there may be a need for special manpower development efforts. The rapid expansion of coal mining and electric power plant development in the western United States provides an example of the training efforts that may be undertaken under such circumstances. Institutional training programs have grown rapidly at vocational-technical schools and colleges located in energy-rich areas. At the same time, energy companies have expanded their own training activities.[10] For example, it has become a frequent practice for firms constructing power plants in remote areas to provide several months of special training for their new workers before the plant begins operation.

A second advantage of special training programs is that they may reduce the project's competition with other local employers. By increasing the number of local workers possessing the skills required for development-related jobs, training programs may at least partially alleviate the labor market problems often reported in rapid-development areas (e.g., rapid wage rate increases, high turnover rates, worker "pirating"). The shortages of skilled workers may not be confined to the occupations required in the new facility, however. The secondary economic effects of a major project often lead to increased requirements for skilled personnel in the trade and service sectors of the local economy. Some observers believe that, in areas undergoing rapid energy development, the potential occupational bottlenecks are greater in these sectors than in the energy industries themselves (Hannah and Mosier 1977). Manpower planners should consider the potential needs for trained personnel in the local trade and service sectors as well as in the primary development industry in planning training programs.

A final advantage of job training and manpower development programs as a mitigation strategy is that they are very popular with local residents. Such programs not only offer a means for local residents to obtain a greater share of project benefits but also offer them an opportunity to acquire valuable skills which can potentially be utilized in other employment when (if) the project terminates. Such programs may thus be valuable in building local support for the project.

While training programs for local residents have obvious advantages, there are also a number of limitations to their utilization which must be carefully considered in planning such programs. First, there is the possibility that institutional training may have little effect on the ability of local workers to obtain employment at the project. Union labor agreements must be evaluated to ensure the compatibility of their provisions with the goals of the training program. Likewise, the developer's hiring policies should be evaluated to ensure that graduates of the training program will have adequate opportunities to obtain work at the project (Braid and Kyles 1977). Obtaining advice from the developer concerning the structure of the program may contribute to this end.[11]

A second consideration concerns timely initiation of training efforts. Adequate lead time is particularly important if training is aimed at increasing the pool of local workers who can participate in project construction. Yet early initiation of training programs may be discouraged by the uncertainty associated with many resource development projects. If such programs are undertaken and development is delayed or cancelled, the trainees may find little opportunity to utilize their new skills. For example, the Province of Newfoundland instituted training programs to prepare its work force for employment opportunities expected to result from offshore petroleum development. Repeated delays in development activity have been a major disappointment to recently trained individuals (Fuchs 1982).

A third factor which must be carefully considered before a major training program for local residents is initiated is the potential duration of demand for the acquired skills within the project area. If the project construction period is expected to be relatively brief and few projects requiring similar skills are anticipated, local workers trained in construction trade skills could be confronted with a difficult decision. Once project construction is completed, such individuals may be forced to choose between remaining in their home community, typically at jobs with substantially reduced wages, or leaving the area for work elsewhere (Gilmore et al. 1982; Braid and Kyles 1977). This problem has recently become evident in the Tennessee Valley region in the wake of the cancellation of several TVA power plant construction projects (O'Connor 1983). A possible solution could be to concentrate construction training efforts on skills which could be readily transferred to jobs in the project's operational phase or to other employment opportunities in the local area (DePape 1981).

The final considerations with respect to the implementation of training programs relate to procedures for establishing such programs, financial responsibility for their support, and the process for selecting participants. The first question often relates to the selection of the entity which will actually conduct the training program. Area vocational-technical schools often provide training in basic skills, and industry provides more specialized training and orientation as part of its initial work experience at the project. The second question concerns financial support for training activities. The basic skills training programs provided by local schools generally depend heavily on federal and state support, with industry sometimes providing special equipment and/or access to specialized facilities (Baker 1977).[12] The firm-specific on-the-job training is financed by the company, and trainees are generally paid throughout the training period. Training in skills required for jobs in the local trade and service sectors is almost invariably a public sector responsibility. The third question deals with determining who qualifies to enter the training program. When the number of applicants greatly exceeds the number of training positions available, this can be a difficult problem (Braid and Kyles 1977).

A Case Study in Local Employment Participation. Increasing the participation of area workers in project-related job opportunities is most effectively accomplished through a comprehensive program involving local-hiring preference, active recruitment of area workers, training and orientation programs for new employees, and counseling activities aimed at increasing worker retention. An excellent example of such a program is offered by the Cluff Lake Project, a uranium mine and mill operation in northern Saskatchewan. The project site is very remote, and most area residents are Native Americans. Because the region has historically experienced very high rates of unemployment, the Board of Inquiry which reviewed the project recommended that measures be taken to ensure that area residents would derive substantial benefits from development. The surface lease agreement between the developer and the Province of Saskatchewan incorporated measures and targets which the company was expected to implement and achieve in order to maximize northern (i.e., local) employment and business participation in the project (Amok/Cluff Mining Ltd. 1981).

Because most area residents lack the necessary skills and experience for mine or mill work, a comprehensive program for recruiting, hiring, training, orienting, and counseling has been established. The program is directed toward persons who have lived in the area for 15 years or half of their life, whichever is less. Two native coordinators, employed by the company, organize and conduct most of the recruiting activities. They work closely with Canada Manpower officials and community leaders to identify and assess potential candidates. When a position becomes available, Canada Manpower offices throughout northern Saskatchewan are notified and given six days to submit a list of candidates. The position is given to an area resident if a suitable candidate is available.

More than ten technical training programs are conducted by the company. Most of these courses have been approved under government skills training or apprenticeship programs. Courses typically are conducted in three stages: (1) classroom instruction, (2) practice in a demonstration setting, and (3) practice on-the-job. Pay increases accompany completion of each step, which usually takes about six months. Most of the training is conducted at the Cluff Lake site by five professional trainers on the project staff.

In addition to the on-site programs, a pre-employment mill operator training course is offered in various area communities. This program is undertaken jointly by the developer and the area's community college. Participants who successfully complete the several-week course are guaranteed a mill operator job at Cluff Lake and a higher starting salary (Amok/Cluff Mining Ltd. 1981).

Because of the remote location of the project, the standard work schedule is seven days on-site, during which the workers are provided with single-status housing, food, and recreational facilities, and seven days off. Air transportation between the site and the workers' home communities is provided by the company. Worker orientation and counseling activities are designed to assist new employees in adjusting to an industrial work environment. A four-day orientation course for new employees provides an introduction to camp life and work routines, safety instruction, and company policies.

The Cluff Lake program has been quite successful in achieving target levels of employment for northern (area) residents. During the period 1979-1980 about half of the operations work force consisted of northern workers. This percentage is much higher than that generally associated with Canadian and Alaskan resource development projects in predominantly native areas (DePape 1982; Schaeffer 1983). During the construction phase, northern workers accounted for about 25 percent of the labor force, and most of these workers were employed by locally based contractors.

Personnel who were actively involved in the implementation of the Cluff Lake program feel that several lessons can be learned from this effort. They indicate that during the operations phase of a project it is important to utilize professional trainers and to separate training responsibility from production responsibility. In addition, an active recruitment program utilizing persons with local backgrounds is essential. During project construction, the most effective approach for increasing local employment participation is to utilize local contractors whenever possible (DePape 1981).

To summarize, programs to increase local hiring through preference policies and training programs have substantial potential as a means of both reducing project-related inmigration and also building local support for the project. However, these programs appear to have greater potential with respect to the project's operation phase labor requirements than for the construction phase labor force. The relatively short duration of the construction period and the key role of the union referral system in project staffing are the major factors which limit the potential for substantially affecting local-hiring rates during the construction period. In order to reduce construction phase inmigration and associated demands, therefore, it may be necessary to examine measures aimed at encouraging commuting as an alternative to relocation.

Increasing Commuting. If the developer desires to encourage long-distance commuting as an alternative to relocation for the project work force, a number of implementation measures are available. These measures are generally aimed at either reducing workers' travel costs or providing convenient workweek accommodations for workers who commute weekly. The advantages and limitations of these methods for encouraging commuting as an alternative to relocation are discussed in this section.

Measures to Reduce Travel Costs. Measures to reduce workers' travel costs include provision of bus or van pool transportation for workers or provision of travel allowances to offset the workers' commuting expenses. In addition to reducing the magnitude of worker relocation and thus lessening impacts on local communities, bus or van-pool programs offer other potential benefits to project developers. These include (1) increased ease of labor force recruitment, (2) reductions in worker turnover and absenteeism, (3) increased worker punctuality and productivity, (4) reduced traffic congestion on roads leading to the site, and (5) reduced costs for providing parking for workers (Metz 1981).

A number of utility companies have provided bus or van transportation to workers at their power plant construction sites. Perhaps the most extensive program of this kind to date was the one initiated by the Tennessee Valley Authority (TVA) at its Hartsville (Tennessee) nuclear power plant construction project. TVA purchased 31 buses and 150 vans at a total cost of $3.5 million. About 56 percent of the work force utilized these vehicles.

This transportation program is credited with reducing worker relocation and increasing the minority share of the work force (Metz 1980). There were more than three times more blacks at Hartsville than at other TVA construction sites, and over 50 percent utilized the TVA transportation program, as compared to 36 percent of white employees (Metz 1981). Another benefit of the TVA transportation program was reduced parking costs. It is estimated that each van at TVA construction sites reduced parking needs by seven spaces, and each parking space is estimated to cost $500 for construction plus annual maintenance costs of $100 (Metz 1981). TVA has also established similar programs at its Phipps Bend (Tennessee) and Yellow Creek (Mississippi) nuclear construction sites.

A number of other utility firms have also utilized bus or van transportation (Metz 1982b). Pacific Power and Light Company used about 40 buses at its Jim Bridger project in southwestern Wyoming. The buses transported workers from the towns of Rock Springs and Green River, located about 35 and 55 miles from the site, respectively.[13] At the Palo Verde nuclear site in Arizona, buses carried about 1,000 nonmanual workers on a 130-mile round trip from Phoenix. The use of air-conditioned buses was credited with reducing the extremely high turnover rates which had previously occurred during the summer months (Metz 1980). At the South Texas Nuclear Project, 129 vans were used to transport about 1,250 workers from distances up to 100 miles. The van pools were operated on a break-even basis and were credited with reducing worker turnover and absenteeism and with increasing the number of local workers at the site (Metz 1980, 1981).

A variety of options exist for operating a transportation program. Major decisions include choice of vehicle type (buses, vans, or a combination), vehicle features, administrative responsibility (in-house vs. contractor operated), and operational procedures.[14] The costs of operating a transportation program will be influenced by all of these choices as well as by the number of workers using the system, the distances traveled, terrain, condition of area road systems, and other site-specific factors.

Typical costs for a van pool program and two alternative bus programs are presented in Table 6.4. Costs of each system were estimated assuming an average of 600 riders (a level consistent with the work force requirements of a variety of large-scale energy projects). Because of the numerous factors affecting costs of worker transportation and the wide variations observed in the cost of such programs at existing energy project sites, the cost estimates are presented in ranges. The cost estimates do not include contributions from riders, which could partially or completely cover program costs.

At some sites, the workers themselves have initiated mass transportation arrangements. At the Susquehanna, Pennsylvania, power plant site, for example, 15 worker-hired buses were operating at the peak of project construction. Likewise, workers constructing power plants and a coal gasification facility in Mercer County, North Dakota organized bus and van pools to minimize the inconvenience of their 75-mile trip from Bismarck (Halstead and Leistritz 1983a). Worker-initiated car pools are common at many sites, and utilities have encouraged multiple ridership by setting aside special parking areas for car pools and vans (Metz 1980).

Travel allowances for workers who commute from a significant distance have become a common feature in construction labor agreements. The magnitude of the allowance differs from project to project with a rate of $11 per day reported for the Palo Verde site (Metz 1980); rates of $3 to $5 per day were typical at sites in the eastern United States (Metz 1979b). Such allowances are becoming more common in other countries also. At the Wagerup alumina refinery in Australia, a graduated scale was instituted, and construction workers who commuted more than 42 miles one way received $20.40 per day (in Australian currency). A similar graduated scale was used at the Huntly Power Project in New Zealand where workers traveling more than 12 miles one way were paid for 80 minutes at 1.5 times their regular rate plus $3 per day (Brealey and Newton 1981; Fookes 1981c). By offsetting some or all commuting costs, travel allowances appear likely to encourage commuting as an alternative to relocation. Such allowances, however, may also reduce workers' incentive to participate in multiple-ridership arrangements (Metz 1979b) or to utilize the company's single-status quarters. Careful attention to the interactive effects of different program components is thus essential in devising a strategy to encourage commuting.

TABLE 6.4.
Estimated costs of alternative worker transportation programs (1981 prices)

Number of Riders	Vehicle	Number of Vehicles	Average Round Trip (miles)	Total Program Costs (Month)	Per Vehicle Mile Cost	Total Vehicle Cost (Million)
600	Van	80[a]	73	$41,000-70,000	$0.35-0.60	$0.75-1.00
600	Bus	15[b]	73	$28,000-52,000	$1.30-2.50	$0.50-2.25
600	Bus	15[b]	125	$48,000-92,000	$1.30-2.50	$0.50-2.25

SOURCE: Metz 1981.

[a]Assuming an average of 8 passengers in a 12-seat van with five spare vans.
[b]Assuming an average of 45 passengers in a 52-seat bus with two spare buses.

Temporary Housing Alternatives. When the project site is quite remote from major population centers, daily commuting may be infeasible for a large proportion of the project's work force. Many construction workers, however, appear willing to commute from homes at distant locations on a weekly basis if adequate accommodations are available in the site area. One example of such weekly commuting is the nearly 90 construction workers who return home on weekends to the Iron Range in northeastern Minnesota from the coal gasification plant in west central North Dakota, a round trip of over 1,000 miles via bus (Schmickle 1983). (These workers are frequently termed "weekly commuters" or "travelers.") Early surveys of construction work forces in remote areas revealed that many of these workers were accommodated in local motels or rented sleeping rooms while others lived in recreational vehicles during the workweek (Leholm et al. 1976; Wieland and Leistritz 1978). In response to the need for workweek accommodations, a number of firms engaged in constructing large projects in the western United States and Canada have developed single-status quarters and/or recreational vehicle parks near their sites. These facilities serve to encourage weekly commuting as an alternative to relocation. Because the factors relevant to decisions concerning such facilities are closely related to those associated with development of other forms of housing, temporary housing alternatives are discussed in greater detail in Chapter 7.

<u>Evaluation of Increased Commuting as a Mitigation Strategy</u>. Encouragement of long-distance commuting as an impact mitigation strategy is most applicable to the construction phase of a major project located in a remote area. Its advantages during this period lie in the substantial reduction in demands for local housing and support services which may result. Reductions in these demands during the construction period may be particularly advantageous to nearby communities because local service and fiscal problems are usually most severe during construction. In addition, because the housing and service requirements of construction workers often differ substantially from those of the permanent work force, both in magnitude and in nature (e.g., mobile homes vs. permanent housing), a reduction in construction phase demands may also alleviate problems of potential excess capacity once construction has been completed.

Commuting is less likely to be encouraged during the operational phase of a project. In fact, many firms encourage their permanent workers to live near the project site so that they will be readily available should an emergency develop (Leistritz and Maki 1981; Fookes 1981c). Company-subsidized housing has been provided to workers at some remote mines in the western United States as an inducement to reside close to the facility. Increased worker productivity and reduced turnover are frequently cited as advantages of these arrangements (Metz 1982a).

Despite the obvious advantages associated with a high level of worker commuting during the construction phase, this approach to mitigation also has some associated problems. First, increased commuting may aggravate traffic problems on local roads, although an increase in multiple-ridership, through increased use of vans and buses, offers a means of alleviating this difficulty. A second problem which may be perceived by local interests is that increased commuting will almost certainly lead to increased leakages of the project's payroll from the local area. Thus, the secondary benefits of the project to the local trade and service sector may be greatly reduced if commuters make up a large proportion of the work force (Tweeten and Brinkman 1976).

A final problem is that high levels of commuting may lead to higher worker turnover rates and a general volatility of the work force in some cases. This problem has been experienced most frequently at sites where weekly commuters (travelers) made up a high percentage of the work force. Apparently, workers who have few ties to the area may be especially prone to change jobs, particularly if favorable opportunities appear in their home areas. For example, at the Laramie River Station in Wyoming, the rumor of an impending strike which circulated just before the Fourth of July weekend led to substantial employee turnover even though the strike never occurred. This site also experienced high turnover rates during the winter months, with most losses being workers from southern states (Gilmore et al. 1982). Likewise, Holmes and Narver (1981) report, based on their case studies of several remote construction projects, that single-status workers generally have significantly higher turnover rates than workers whose dependents are living with them in the site area.

CONCLUSIONS AND IMPLICATIONS

Mitigation measures which reduce the demands imposed on local systems have a special appeal. These measures concentrate on avoiding the problems associated with overtaxed local economic, governmental, and social systems by reducing the number of inmigrants associated with a project. Such measures can thus be characterized as an attempt to avoid impact problems rather than to solve them after they occur. Some of these measures, particularly local hiring and training programs, also appeal to local residents because they tend to increase the share of project benefits which is retained within the communities near the site. Such measures can thus be valuable in maximizing local project-related benefits and in gaining local acceptance of a project.

Methods for reducing demands on local systems fall into two general categories: (1) alterations in facility design or construction schedule, and (2) work force policies to reduce inmigration. As discussed earlier, certain advantages and problems are associated with each of these measures.

Decisions regarding site selection, facility design, and construction scheduling are very important in determining the nature and magnitude of socioeconomic impacts that will be associated with project development. Greater attention should be given to socioeconomic impact considerations during the project feasibility study and site selection process. Because socioeconomic impact implications are only one of the many factors which must be considered, it is probably not reasonable to expect that site selection and facility design decisions generally will be altered substantially in order to avoid socioeconomic impact problems. In fact, a number of factors appear to support a trend toward increased siting of certain types of facilities in remote areas, where socioeconomic impact problems are likely to be more severe.

Labor force policies can be a valuable tool for alleviating potential impact problems as well as for achieving other project objectives. Determining the best labor force strategy to adopt and the most effective implementation measures to utilize requires detailed analysis of local and regional labor markets. In general, however, programs to increase rates of local labor recruitment will be most effective with respect to the project's permanent (operational) work force. On the other hand, during the construction phase of a project, implementing measures which encourage workers to commute rather than relocate to the area may prove to be a very cost-effective mitigation alternative.

NOTES

1. There is at least one recent case in which socioeconomic impact factors appear to have influenced site selection. In selecting a site for a new power plant, Montana Power Company chose a location near a city (Great Falls) with substantial infrastructure capacity and available local labor in preference to a mine-mouth site in a remote, sparsely populated region (Owens 1983). Further, while this conclusion appears to hold with respect to most natural resource development projects, the adequacy of the local labor force and public service infrastructure appears to be a more important consideration in siting decisions for other types of industrial facilities which may consider locating in rural areas (Summers et al. 1976; Lonsdale and Seyler 1979).

2. The work force ceiling was incorporated as a condition of the project's siting permit. The developer subsequently requested that the work force ceiling be raised to 2,650 workers, with the justification that the community infrastructure which was in place or being developed would adequately accommodate the additional workers. This request was granted, and the project's construction work force subsequently peaked at slightly over 2,600 (Rafferty 1981).

3. For example, the ability to achieve relative stability in construction work force requirements is cited as a significant advantage of the energy park (or energy center) concept (General Electric Company 1975). Similarly, staging the construction of multiple facilities to stabilize work force requirements is being considered as a major impact mitigation strategy in connection with a large hydroelectric project in northern Manitoba. This approach is expected to provide enhanced opportunities for local

business participation and local employment, as well as decreasing demands on local infrastructure (DePape 1981).

4. For example, Metz (1982a) estimates that "every new underground coal or uranium miner can cost a company approximately $30,000 for the first 90 days, all unproductive, for salary, benefits, training, and recruitment." Similarly, Huesflon (1981) indicates that power plant operators pass through six levels of training during their first seven or eight years with the company and that the total cost of this training exceeds $50,000.

5. At project sites which are quite remote from urban areas and have a very limited local population base, very few potential workers may be available within a reasonable commuting distance. In such situations, of course, the potential for implementing a local-hiring program will also be quite limited.

6. Some examples of successful implementation of local-preference hiring programs in cooperation with construction craft unions do exist. For instance, at a large hydroelectric project in northern Manitoba, the national manpower agency was given 48 hours to locate qualified northern (local) workers to fill any new job openings. Only if the agency was unsuccessful would the union initiate a call for workers from outside the region (DePape 1981).

7. For example, the state of Alaska enacted legislation that contained a requirement that firms developing petroleum resources under state leases give preference in hiring to qualified Alaska residents (Alaska Statute, Title 38, Chapter 40, "Local Hire Under State Lease"). In 1978, the U.S. Supreme Court held the statute unconstitutional in that it discriminated against nonresidents and violated the privileges and immunities clauses of the United States Constitution (U.S. Department of the Interior 1982).

8. Individuals experienced in designing and implementing local-hiring programs suggest that some of the most important factors influencing the success of a local-hiring effort are (1) concentration of recruiting activity in the target area, (2) location of the hiring site in the area, and (3) utilization of persons with local backgrounds in the recruiting effort (DePape 1981).

9. It should also be noted that inmigration of replacement workers may pose special problems in implementing a mitigation program. The relocation of such workers is inherently difficult both to predict and to monitor. In addition, while a developer may be willing to accept responsibility for community impacts which can be attributed directly to the project's work force, impacts associated with the relocation of secondary and replacement workers are less likely to be included in mitigation planning.

10. For example, Bismarck (North Dakota) Junior College, located in an area where substantial development of coal-fired power plants is taking place, has developed a 13-month course in "Power Plant Technology." Students learn basic principles of power plant operation but generally must complete a substantial training and orientation program if hired by a power company. Graduates of the course have a better chance of obtaining power

plant jobs, however, and some students are offered power plant positions prior to graduation (Huesflon 1981).

11. For example, if representatives of the development firm(s) are invited to serve on the curriculum committee of the local training institution (e.g., area vocational-technical school), the probability that the program will be compatible with industry needs will be enhanced (DePape 1981).

12. The current trend toward austerity in federal government activities may significantly affect the amount of public support available for training programs.

13. It should be noted that the primary purpose of the Jim Bridger busing program apparently was not to reduce inmigration; most of the workers at the project had relocated to Rock Springs and Green River from outside the area. Rather, the principal objective was to improve worker retention as the trona mines which were competing for the Jim Bridger project workers' services were offering transportation to their work sites.

14. For a detailed discussion of these options and their implications, see Metz (1981).

7
Planning for Growth: Increasing Community Infrastructure Capacity

Development of an effective impact management program requires that planning start well in advance of actual construction, and that roles and expectations of the various actors be clearly defined. Rather than focusing mitigation efforts solely on the construction and operation phases, initial efforts should be directed toward eliminating or reducing adverse impacts before they occur. One means of accomplishing this goal is to reduce the size of the population relocating into the affected community. Appropriate techniques toward this end were discussed in Chapter 6. A second method of softening development impacts is to take steps to insure that needed public services and capital facilities are in place before peak construction employment occurs, so that demand for these services does not exceed supply. Measures to increase this local infrastructure capacity are the subject of this chapter.

This chapter is divided into three sections. The first section discusses methods of organizing the community and enhancing local planning skills to deal with developing and financing impact management programs. The second section deals with provision of housing in rapid-growth communities. This is often problematic, since the private sector is sometimes unwilling or unable to supply housing in sufficient quantities. In addition, supply often lags behind demand. Methods for alleviating these problems include direct industry involvement through provision of permanent and temporary housing facilities, and stimulation of the housing market through mortgage assistance and landlord subsidy programs. The final section examines impacts on local public sector systems. These include transportation, education, utilities, medical services, law enforcement and fire protection, and social services.

ORGANIZING THE COMMUNITY

In order to achieve the goals of advanced planning, the community must be organized to insure that the expertise to manage growth impacts is in place. The residents of communities with small, stable, or declining populations often lack the background to manage the impacts of large-scale developments (Greene and Curry 1977). Assistance from the developer or higher levels of government may therefore be necessary to help the community acquire this planning expertise.

Developing Administrative Capacity

Since a great deal of money may be needed to develop an effective mitigation program, adequate administrative expertise is necessary to provide a channel for the funds or to insure that the funds are not misdirected. For example, officials in Custer County, Idaho, (pop. 3,385; area 5,000 sq. miles) were faced with the responsibility of handling $450,000 in prepaid taxes from the Cyprus Creek mine. Half of these funds, which were to be spent over a five-year period, were used the first year, causing some local citizens and officials to question the county's management of these funds (Accola 1983). Adequate administrative capacity gives the community the ability to design and carry out planning duties, personnel management, and fiscal administration (Federal Energy Administration 1976).

Many small communities lack the personnel needed to mobilize and inform the community and other members of the concerned public, and build the needed administrative structure to manage growth. Briscoe et al. (1978) have recommended that the community hire a professional administrator to perform these tasks. A competent professional can be a great asset to the area by developing needed policies, supervising their administration, and negotiating with higher levels of government for financial assistance. In a study of rapid-growth communities in the southwestern United States, ROMCOE (1982) found that local officials strongly advocated hiring professional planners and administrators. Howell et al. (1983) also recommend the hiring of a professional community development specialist. Thus, while it is important that the local community assume much of the burden for organization and planning, the infusion of outside expertise or financial support can be a great asset during this phase of impact management.

Company-Sponsored Planning Assistance

Effective action by these administrators and community initiators can help promote controlled, orderly growth, which benefits both the impacted communities and the developer. The planning phase of the growth impact management task (although a continual process) is probably of greatest value during the predevelopment stage. Generally, this phase begins as soon as the community learns of the project. Often it is best for the community to be involved in the research and feasibility study period, before an official announcement is made. Timing is an important factor, since more planning lead time for the community generally can result in more successful mitigation efforts. The developer can facilitate these planning efforts by providing technical assistance and funding for planning efforts, as demonstrated in the following example in Colorado.

A number of companies engaged in oil shale development in Rio Blanco County, Colorado, contributed $80,000 to the county, to be used in a planning program. In addition, the companies hired a consultant and a planning firm to conduct studies for towns in the county. The money contributed to the county was used for hiring an attorney and for the planning effort which resulted in a comprehensive plan adopted and certified by the communities. These planning efforts continue to involve communities and counties in Colorado directly with the companies and higher levels of government (Quality Development Associates, Inc. 1978).

Although many communities have administrators on their staffs, these administrators' efforts are not always directed exclusively toward planning. A number of companies have helped facilitate local planning efforts in impacted communities by providing advice and financial assistance. Three of these efforts are summarized below.

The Tennessee Valley Authority (TVA) provides funds to offset planning staff costs and provides TVA staff assistance in preparing plans or drawing necessary ordinances. It is the basic policy of TVA to encourage the formation of planning commissions to deal with impacts induced by energy projects (Metz 1980).

The Gillette Subcommittee of the Wyoming Mining Association has assisted the city by providing funding for the first year's salary of a city-county planner and by helping to specify his role in the growth management process. The Southwest Wyoming Industrial Association (SWIA) has also contributed funds to Sweetwater County for planning efforts (Metz 1980).

In Uinta and Lincoln counties, Wyoming, the Overthrust Industrial Association (OIA) had provided more than $250,000 as of 1982 for planning staff and assistance. The OIA, composed of oil and gas companies operating in the Overthrust Belt, has sponsored road, land use, water, sewer, and master plans in these and other Wyoming counties (OIA 1982).

Government Planning Assistance

Another source of assistance in the total planning process is government--local, regional, state or provincial, and federal. The state government, because it retains control over the authority and limitations of local governments, may be the most appropriate level of governmental assistance. Specific arrangements will depend primarily on state leadership. State staff are often needed to design Areawide Planning Organizations (APO) appropriate to the geographic, economic, and political scale of the area's growth (Houstoun 1977).

Houstoun (1977) argues that initial state and federal investments should be directed toward planning and management assistance, rather than nonspecific grants. This directed assistance will help insure that policies will be produced which minimize immediate adverse impacts and long-term costs. The single, unified APO would be financially supported by all municipalities, counties, and special districts involved in the impacted areas. These jurisdictions would be required to participate in areawide planning and to submit all applications for aid, budgets, zoning and building codes, and plans produced under state enabling legislation to the APO for review and comment as to their conformity with areawide growth management policies.

These APOs, established by state law, are usually required to produce policies and growth management objectives that participating jurisdictions can use. These policies would include considerations of costs, revenues, bonding positions, and service levels of alternative growth options, and would also be required by law to be a basis for all development-related planning performed by state or substate planning districts (such as transportation, housing, and economic development) (Houstoun 1977).

Colorado utilizes several aspects of the APO method. The state Department of Local Affairs (Division of Mineral and Energy Impact) has field personnel who help establish local impact teams, assist in the preparation of funding requests, provide administration for assistance contracts, and monitor work projects (TOSCO Foundation 1980). The field personnel also expedite various kinds of state assistance and keep local communities updated as to the current status of assistance programs.

The Colorado Joint Review Process (JRP) is designed to coordinate regulatory and administrative reviews by the federal, state, and local governments concerning major energy and mineral resource development projects (TOSCO Foundation 1980). Government and industry voluntarily enter the JRP, which encourages increased public and industry involvement in the review process. Basically a management system, the JRP involves all parties in the decision-making process, and its success is highly dependent on communication, cooperation, and compromise. However, one problem noted in this approach has been that involvement of too many actors in the planning process may be counterproductive (Halstead and Leistritz 1983a).

MEETING HOUSING DEMAND

One of the most serious problems often encountered by a community experiencing rapid growth is a lack of adequate housing for inmigrating workers and their families. Local builders may be unable or unwilling to handle the increased demand for new housing if the future of a project is uncertain. Developers from outside the impact area may move in, though this may take several years (Denver Research Institute 1979). Consequently, state and local governments and the project developer may need to become involved to insure that the housing supply is sufficient to meet local demand. Housing strategies generally focus on two areas: first, direct stimulation through construction of new units and revitalization of existing housing; and second, indirect stimulation of the market through mortgage assistance, employee buy-back guarantees, and landlord subsidies.

Direct Housing Market Stimulation

Direct housing assistance by energy companies can be roughly divided into three categories: (1) new towns and rebuilt existing towns; (2) temporary housing; and (3) permanent subdivision development (Metz 1982a). The method chosen depends upon such factors as size and duration of project and population of the surrounding area; often, two or more approaches are used conjunctively.

Construction of an Entire Community. Construction of self-contained communities, or company towns, is not a new idea. Such activity was a common occurrence in coal, copper, iron, and lumber development areas of the western U.S. and Canada, where several thousand towns were constructed between 1850 and 1950 (Metz 1979a; Betz 1980). These company towns were needed in remote areas where little or no housing and services existed previously. Although many of these old towns have been abandoned, some energy companies have determined that the best solution to impact problems is still the development of an entire new town, especially in remote areas of Canada and Australia (Berkey et al. 1977; DePape 1983; Neil 1982). Key considerations affecting the final decision are project location, worker productivity and turnover, and the developers' willingness to subsidize the town. Some of these towns in the United States are described in Table 7.1.

These resource towns vary in size, ownership, government, and even expected lifespan. In some cases, the sponsoring company may choose to divest itself of ownership and governing responsibilities once the town is established and functioning. In extremely remote regions, plans may be made for dismantling and removal of town facilities once the local ore body is depleted, or the project completed.

One frequently cited example of a modern company town is Colstrip, Montana. Originally founded by a railroad in the 1920s for its employees, the town currently houses employees of Montana Power Company's nearby mine and power plant. The company financed water and sewer systems, recreational facilities, streets, and fire protection, as well as organizing and financing housing development and construction. Future plans for Colstrip include its incorporation, self-government, and eventual transfer of ownership to its residents (Myhra 1975b).

A more recent example of a western U.S. town is Atlantic Richfield Company's (ARCO) Wright, Wyoming, constructed to house employees of its local coal mining operations. Managed by Housing Services, Inc. (a wholly owned subsidiary of ARCO), housing in Wright is constructed by private home builders on lots purchased from Housing Services. Eventually, the town will be incorporated

TABLE 7.1.
Examples of company provision of housing services

Town (Company)	Housing Units	Services	Remarks
Hiawatha, Utah (United States Fuel Company)	60 single-family houses	Privately run general store and post office Owner operates town sewer and water system, maintaining local streets and recreational areas, and conducts general upkeep on all dwellings	Owner contributes about $50,000 a year to support this town, but considers it an asset due to low worker turnover and having personnel readily available at the remote mine
Sunnyside Mine, Utah (Utah Fuel Company, 1960: Kaiser Steel Corporation)	240 single-family houses of 7 basic designs with numerous variations in porches and trim	An estimated $2 million was spent for land, sewer, and water systems, recreation facilities, a community center, and single-family houses	Kaiser Steel Corporation divested itself of its company town in the 1970s on the condition that the town would be in optimal condition, solvent, and self-sufficient at its release
Wright, Wyoming (Atlantic Richfield Company ARCO) (City being developed by Housing Services Inc. a subsidiary of ARCO)	311 unit mobile home park with recreational vehicle spaces, bachelor quarters, several dozen single-family houses with plans for 52, 40 units of garden apartments, and 19 units of town houses	Four churches, a commercial mall, and a community center	The company will eventually extricate itself from the town, recouping part of its investment through land and housing sales
Shirley Basin, Wyoming (Joint effort by: Pathfinder Mines; Kerr-McGee Corporation; Getty Oil Corporation; and Petrotomics.)	Developed trailer pads with about 200 individually-owned trailers	Joint investment (1969) of approximately a half million dollars; the roads, sewer and water systems, commercial areas, trailer pads, street lights, and parks have been developed	Pathfinder Mines became sole operator when others sold out and continues to subsidize the town on the basis of low employee turnover and less absenteeism
Federal-American Partners' Village, Wyoming (FAP)	92 trailer pads with individually-owned trailers	Trailer pad rental is $20.00 per month which includes all utilities	Company employees have the choice between renting trailer pads or receiving $3.00 a day inconvenience pay for commuting daily from larger cities
Pathfinder Mines' Village, Wyoming (Pathfinder Mines)	40 trailer pads (employee owns trailer) and 7 single-family houses with 3 bedrooms	Rentals for trailer pads ($25/month) and houses ($50/month), includes all utilities	Company has chosen to subsidize a bus system instead of expanding the village

SOURCE: Adapted from Metz (1979).

and directed by resident-elected officials (Housing Services, Inc. 1981).

In Canada, where remote resource towns are currently more prevalent than in the United States, one example of a company town is Elkford in British Columbia. Founded in 1971 by the Fording Coal Company, the town currently has a population of about 1,700 housed in single-family homes, mobile homes, and apartments, as well as a temporary construction camp slated for phased removal. Elkford features a mix of company-constructed and privately constructed housing, with the coal company managing about 1,000 housing units. Rental units are subsidized below cost, and home ownership is encouraged by provision of a $20,000 interest-free, nonforgiveable second mortgage. The company, however, retains a 20-year option to purchase and the right of first refusal to repurchase any property acquired with company assistance (Pinfield and Etherington 1982).

Since the company town approach to impact management requires a major financial commitment, the developer bears a substantial risk in the event of project cancellation. Cancellation of Exxon's Colony Oil Shale project in Colorado in 1982 resulted in indefinite postponement of development of Battlement Mesa, the model town planned to accommodate project employees and support personnel, after considerable investment had already been made. Thus, these risks, as well as the costs of developing and maintaining the town, must be weighed against benefits of higher worker productivity and lower worker turnover.

Although there is sometimes no alternative to construction of entire communities in remote areas to accommodate project-related population, serious problems may arise from this strategy. Detomasi (1982a) has noted short-term shortages and supply lags for provision of noncompany resident housing, inappropriate unit and residential design, and lack of choice in housing units as difficulties experienced by residents of remote Canadian resource towns. Brealey and Newton (1981) have identified disadvantages of single-industry towns in remote areas of Australia which are applicable to North America, including a general lack of services and amenities due to the town's small population and a lack of diversity in employment opportunities. Social problems may also result from outmigration of young people and the lack of opportunity for contact with anyone but other company employees. This permeation of company influence through virtually all aspects of residents' lives may restrict the town's ability to function as an autonomous unit. Thus, previous experience is useful in pointing out problems to be avoided by developers facing the prospect of utilizing the company town approach.

Revitalization of Existing Housing. An alternative to providing new housing units for inmigrants to the community is to revitalize under-utilized buildings. The revitalization process may simply include renovating existing hotels or motels, or may include a moderate amount of interior remodeling to convert various buildings into boarding houses or hotel-like facilities. It has been estimated that over half of the single-member households anticipated at the Clinch River Breeder Reactor Plant in the Oak Ridge-Knoxville, Tennessee, area could be housed in existing or revitalized hotel-motel complexes in the immediate impact area (Braid and Kyles 1977).

These motel units are beneficial for single-member households for several reasons:

1. The accommodations at these motels generally include restaurant facilities which could supply lunches for noon meals.
2. Maid and laundry services are readily available.
3. These facilities are generally located on major highways, thus allowing decreased commuting times and good routes to neighboring facilities.
4. The concentration of larger numbers of workers in these units enhances car and van pooling, which eases traffic problems and transportation costs for workers.

An added benefit to the developer is that the use of existing facilities, even if they are subsidized, will be much less costly than constructing new facilities.

A number of other existing structures could also be converted into housing units. Although a more extensive revitalization or remodeling process would be needed, older housing units and even nonhousing structures could be converted into multifamily units. Large single-family housing units can be converted into duplexes or three and four unit complexes. The same type of remodeling could be applied to vacant business structures or underutilized buildings to convert them into apartment or multifamily units.

Temporary Housing. Provision of temporary housing in the form of single-status facilities and leased or rented mobile homes can be an effective means of accommodating a project's construction work force, which is generally larger than the operation work force and has less permanent housing requirements. Demand for this type of housing is affected by site accessibility, local labor availability, and project schedule (Metz 1982a). Temporary housing techniques are also useful as a proactive mitigation measure (see Chapter 6).

Temporary facilities vary in size and amenities. The modular single-status facilities, often called bachelor quarters or mancamps, each have about 20 units per module, with one or two workers per unit (Metz 1980). Total camp occupancy generally ranges from 100 to 800. These camps usually feature a mess hall, recreation center, and sometimes even a laundry (Halstead, Leistritz, and Chase 1983). A mancamp with average facilities requires an initial investment of about \$10,000-\$14,000 per resident, while more luxurious facilities may run as high as \$18,000 per resident (Metz 1982a). The residents usually pay a flat weekly fee that includes room and board. These mancamps can be designed so that infrastructure and roads can be used later by single-family units, or constructed so that the units can be removed and the landscape returned to its original appearance. A survey of some of these temporary housing facilities is provided in Table 7.2.

TABLE 7.2.
Selected single-status housing facilities, western United States

Project/Owner	Location	Peak Work Force	Construction Years	Population Centers (Distance)	Size (Maximum Occupants)	Construction Type	Quality (as stated by housing service company)	Percent of Work Force Housed
Laramie River Power Station/Missouri Basin Power Project	Wheatland, Wyo.	2,609	1974-1982	Wheatland, Wyo. (12 mi) Laramie, Wyo. (118 mi) Cheyenne, Wyo. (60 mi)	200	Modular	Excellent	6
Colstrip Units 3 & 4/ Montana Power Co.	Colstrip, Mon.	3,000	1979-1984	Miles City, Mon. (69 mi) Sheridan, Wyo. (137 mi) Billings, Mon. (110 mi)	312	Modular	Excellent	10
Spring Creek Mine/ Northern Energy Resources Co.	35 Miles North of Sheridan, Wyo.	500	1979-1981	Sheridan, Wyo. (35 mi) Billings, Mon. (66 mi)	144	Modular	Excellent	29
Yampa Project/ Colorado Ute Electric Association, Inc.	Craig, Col.	693	1969-1984	Craig, Col. (6 mi) Grand Junction, Col. (133 mi)	200	Modular	Fair	29
Soda Ash Plant/ Tenneco Oil Co.	Sweetwater County, Wyo.	835	1980-1982	Rock Springs, Wyo. (45 mi) Rawlings, Wyo. (106 mi)	400	Modular	Fair	48
Amoco Gas Sweetening Plant/AMOCO	Evanston, Wyo.	750	1980-1982	Evanston, Wyo. (12 mi) Ogden, Ut. (87 mi)	750	Modular	Fair	100
Cyprus Creek Molybdenum Mines/ Cyprus Creek-AMOCO	Challis, Id.	500	1981-1983	Challis, Id. (35 mi) Clayton, Id. (3 mi)	588*	Modular	Excellent	*

SOURCE: Burtco, Inc. (n.d.); Mather (1983); Sattaltheite (1983).

*Percent of work force housed at Cyprus Creek is proprietary information.

Metz (1982a) maintains that there is a direct correlation between mancamp quality and problems such as worker turnover, vandalism, and worker-management confrontation. For example, Arizona Public Service had problems with its mancamp at the Cholla construction site which resulted in management problems and eventually in closure of the camp. Sites such as Holleran Services' high-quality Cyprus Creek camp in Challis, Idaho with numerous amenities and professional security, are credited with promoting worker satisfaction and minimizing turnover (Sattalthite 1983). Parkinson et al. (1980), after studying the impacts of construction camps (mancamps) on the Canadian town of Fort McMurray, Alberta, concluded that there are six essential features a camp should possess to minimize negative impacts on the local community and to enhance worker productivity and well-being. These factors are (1) a good camp facility, (2) good food in quantity and quality, (3) security and policing which are forceful without being officious, (4) good pay with opportunities for overtime, (5) regular breaks to get out of camp, and (6) varied and well-organized recreational and leisure-time activities programs.

Recreational vehicle (RV) parks also play an important role in absorbing excess housing demand. Many construction workers at remote sites sleep in their RVs during the workweek, and sometimes commute home on weekends (Leholm et al. 1976; Wieland et al. 1979). Costs per pad range between $3,000 and $4,500 each (Metz 1982a). Often, these parks are built adjacent to mancamp facilities and have recreation, shower, and laundry services on the site.

Finally, some companies have invested in mobile homes to rent or lease to their employees. For example, Basin Electric leases 36 mobile homes in Beulah, North Dakota, to workers at its nearby Antelope Valley Station (Halstead and Leistritz 1983a).

Table 7.3 presents cost figures for a hypothetical 440-bed mancamp and 210-pad RV/MH park. Cavanagh (1980) has estimated that 25 percent of a construction work force at a remote project site will desire single-status housing, 10 percent will require RV parking facilities, and only 3 percent will need temporary family-status housing such as rental mobile homes or apartments. Although these facilities can be costly--Arizona Public Service spent nearly $7 million on its 500-worker Palo Verde, Arizona, facility--cost reductions from decreased turnover can be significant. It has been estimated that a 1 percent increase in turnover can result in increased costs of $1 million on a 1,000-Mw power project, while an increase of 1 percent in the absenteeism rate can cost the developer about $2 million (Cavanagh and Geiger 1982). In addition, delay issues related to the work force can cost the developer substantial amounts in interest, contract extension penalties, and inflation. For example, a month's interruption in construction of a 2,200-Mw power plant can cost the developer up to $25 million, and the cost of construction delays on a $1 billion project (due to inflation) has been estimated to be between $25,000 and $35,000 per hour (Metz 1982a). High work force turnover, high absenteeism (25 percent per day),

TABLE 7.3.
Estimated costs of constructing and operating a hypothetical 440-bed single-status dormitory and 210-pad RV/MH park (1981 prices)

Construction	Dollars
Land purchase and site preparation	$ 325,000
Infrastructure (utilities)	1,000,000
Dormitory (440) and MH (50) units	3,700,000
Landscaping (landscaping and paving)	640,000
Auxiliary facilities	1,100,000
TOTAL	$6,765,000
Operation (annual)	
Service costs (peak)	$2,050,000
Miscellaneous (utilities and community assistance)	470,000
TOTAL	$2,520,000
Per Worker Costs	
Mancamp construction (total)	$13,000.00
RV/MH park construction (total)	$ 4,000.00
Average mancamp service costs (daily)	16.60
Average RV/MH service costs (daily)	4.00
Average utility costs (daily)	1.40

and low productivity were estimated to have caused a $50 million cost overrun at the Jim Bridger Power Plant site in Wyoming (Metz 1982a). Provision of acceptable temporary housing can help to minimize these losses.

Permanent Subdivision Development. Many energy companies have entered the housing market through construction and maintenance of entire subdivisions in energy-impacted areas. These subdivisions vary in terms of location (within or outside of town limits), occupancy (company employees only or open to local residents), ownership (company owned or sold to occupants), and type (mobile home or single-family units).

Mobile home parks provide several distinct advantages to the developer. The park can be rapidly developed and expanded, simplifying installation and removal. The parks can also be easily modified to accommodate worker RVs. In addition, workers can generally finance a mobile home more easily than a single-family unit (especially if mortgage rates are high). Parks can also be designed to eventually use the installed roads and utilities to service single-family units which may replace the mobile homes (Metz 1982a; Halstead, Leistritz, and Chase 1983).

These positive features must be weighed against several disadvantages, some of which can be overcome through careful planning. A major complaint against mobile homes and mobile home parks is that they are sometimes visually unattractive. In some situations, they may even devalue adjacent properties (ROMCOE 1982). Through the use of careful zoning, parks can be structured attractively to achieve the aesthetic qualities of permanent housing in the area. A second complaint is that mobile homes usually provide only a fraction of the tax revenue to local government that permanent housing does, yet their occupants have many of the same utility and public service requirements (Chapter 8). Steps can be taken to address the effects on tax revenues, however. The town of Hazen, North Dakota, which is experiencing substantial growth resulting from the construction of several large energy projects, has attempted to alleviate this situation by passing an ordinance to allow taxation of new mobile home parks and other mobile homes as permanent housing on private land. As of 1984, results of this ordinance were uncertain; however, the expected change in Hazen's tax revenue was not expected to be large (Frovarp 1984).

Subdivisions of single-family units are generally constructed for the benefit of operating employees and management. For example, Great Plains Gasification Associates is building a single-family subdivision for its employees in Beulah, North Dakota (Halstead and Leistritz 1983a). This type of subdivision may cause problems for the company, however, if careful attention is not given to access, landscaping, land use, prices, and the life styles of prospective inhabitants. Amoco/ Cyprus Creek built 260 single-family homes at their Challis, Idaho, molybdenum mine site; the homes, however, have suffered from a low occupancy rate due to failure to address aesthetic preferences and financial capacities of the company's employees (Halstead, Leistritz, and Chase 1983).

A final potential problem is that concentration of units in one section of the community combined with excluding noncompany personnel from occupancy may foster a lack of interaction between town residents and newcomers, and create an "us-them" relationship (ROMCOE 1982; Metz 1982a). This can be avoided by the process of "infilling" where companies purchase and develop lots scattered throughout the community, rather than concentrate development in one area (Metz 1982a). In Leeman, Australia, where employees of Western Titanium Company are housed in a single enclave, 72 percent of town residents responding to a household survey indicated that they would have preferred having the units scattered throughout the town rather than concentrated in one area (Brealey and Newton 1981).

Indirect Housing Market Stimulation

Although some companies have become directly involved in permanent housing provision, many lack the expertise or capability to become long-term landlords. In addition, inmigrants may have trouble financing new homes due to credit problems or high mortgage rates. In these situations, stimulation of the private market can be helpful in alleviating housing problems.

This option is an attractive impact management strategy for developers for two principal reasons. First, it is less costly, since the bulk of the expenses for construction and purchase will be borne by the home buyer, with the sponsor (developer or government) concentrating instead on making home construction and purchase attractive and affordable. Second, in the case of mortgage subsidies and loans, a developer bears less risk of a major financial loss than if he were to take the initiative for constructing and selling company housing.

Applications of this strategy vary widely by eligibility for assistance (general population or company personnel only), restrictions on type of housing purchased (for example, some assistance programs set a mandatory ceiling price on the housing that can be purchased), and type of subsidy/assistance. Four general types of assistance are available:

1. Outright subsidy. In the form of a forgivable loan, interest differential payment, or landlord subsidy (in return for maintaining reasonable rents).
2. Purchase of previous residence. In the event that an employee cannot sell his previous residence, the developer may purchase it from him.
3. Housing buy-back guarantee. The developer may agree to repurchase an employee's home in the event of premature facility closure.
4. Guaranteed purchase of new homes constructed by private developers. In return for constructing new housing in a community, a developer may issue guarantees to private construction firms that the new housing will be sold within a specified time period, or the developer himself will purchase it. For example, in Wheatland, Wyoming, the Missouri Basin Power Project contracted with a local developer to construct 19 single-family homes, with the guarantee that any homes not purchased within six months would be purchased by the project. This agreement resulted in Missouri Basin purchasing 17 of the homes, 14 of which were later sold on the open market (Western Research Corporation 1983).

The essence of these measures is that they attempt to spread the risk and cost of expansion of the housing market among the developer, private contractors, home buyers, and sometimes local, state, or federal government agencies. As noted, private housing construction firms may be reluctant to enter an energy-impacted community due to uncertainty as to the stability of the project. Likewise, individuals interested in purchasing a house may be concerned over project stability, financing problems,or both. These market stimulating measures provide both groups with stability, while assuring an adequate supply of housing at a lower cost than if the developer engaged in construction and management of housing properties.

Various federal, state, and private agencies may become involved in the process, as well as the developer himself. Federal agencies such as the Federal Housing Administration (FHA) and the Farmers' Home Administration (FmHA) may provide funding sources for financing housing market improvements in impacted communities; however, federal funds are usually in demand in many communities throughout the country. Therefore, subnational governments and the developer may provide the best sources of funding, with the developer usually taking the dominant role (Pinfield and Etherington 1982). Four examples of such programs --one state-run and the others industry initiated--are described below.

The Wyoming Community Development Authority (WCDA), created in 1975, is an independent subdivision of state government. WCDA is authorized to sell revenue bonds worth $750 million to provide funds for housing mortgages. The Authority has sold tax exempt securities worth $369.9 million on the national bond market and used the money in-state to finance mortgages. As of June 30, 1981, WCDA had purchased 5,136 loans for $276.8 million. The authority offers lower-than-market mortgage rates, ranging from 7.6 to 13 percent, to longtime and new residents.

Wyoming also provides authority to the state treasurer to invest up to $100 million of the Permanent Mineral Trust Fund for use in real estate mortgages, about 75 percent of which has been available to state financial institutions. The 12.9 percent mortgages can be used to finance up to 95 percent of a single-family home with a value of $80,000 or less (Ellis 1982).

Some companies involved in energy development have adopted housing assistance programs for their employees. For example, Basin Electric (BE) has adopted a three-faceted assistance program for operating employees at its Antelope Valley Station near Beulah, North Dakota, consisting of the following provisions:

1. Mortgage assistance for those operating employees who cannot qualify for loans from more conventional sources such as FHA.
2. Home purchase guarantees. In some situations where a prospective employee cannot sell his or her home to move to Mercer County, BE will purchase the employee's previous residence.

3. Mortgage interest differential payments. BE will pay the difference between an operating employee's old mortgage and the new higher mortgage rate for three years (Pearson 1983).

In Idaho, the Amoco/Cyprus Creek operation has instituted a similar program for employees at its Challis mine. However, these housing assistance actions are directed mainly toward selling some of the single-family homes which the company has built in Challis. Cyprus Creek's plan contains the following measures:

1. A forgiveable loan (up to $6,000) for down payment
2. Subsidizing interest payments on employees' conventional mortgages
3. Housing buy-back guarantees. In the event that the mines close prematurely or cut back severely, the company will repurchase the employee's house (Sattalthite 1983)

At the Salt River Project in St. Johns, Arizona, the utility paid landlords a fixed monthly subsidy in return for signing an agreement to rent housing to construction workers at reasonable prices (Metz 1980). This method could also be used for elderly, low-income, or handicapped citizens in the community.

Thus, a number of options exist for alleviating housing shortages in the project area. The cases discussed indicate that it is possible for both the developer and units of local government to become actively involved in the housing market without resorting to large-scale subsidization and construction. While there will undoubtedly be many situations where the local housing market will accommodate increased housing demand without this involvement, knowledge of these methods of market stimulation can prove valuable in assuring that local housing supply (both in quantity and in cost) keeps pace with demand.

Housing Provision for Fixed Income Groups

One phenomenon which sometimes occurs in rapid-growth communities is a general inflation of prices in area markets (Haynes 1983). This inflation can be especially acute in the housing sector, since there may be considerable lag time before supply adjusts to demand. While project employees and other local workers may be financially capable of weathering these costs, those groups living on small fixed incomes (such as low income and elderly) may suffer inordinately. Some provisions therefore may be in order to assist these groups in finding adequate shelter.

Reese and Cummings (1979) have suggested that the local government form a housing authority through which state and federal housing programs can be channeled into the community, a policy which proved effective in Wheatland, Wyoming, during nearby power plant development (Western Research Corporation 1983). In Wright, Wyoming, the developer of this planned community took steps to insure that a sufficient supply of housing for low and moderate income groups would exist (Housing Services, Inc. 1981). In Mercer County, North Dakota, funds from the Federal Department of Housing and Urban Development's Section 8 Housing Assistance Payments Program were used to construct an apartment complex for the elderly (Halstead and Leistritz 1983a).

While these housing shortages may indeed prove severe and should be monitored, several studies have found communities' elderly population to be less vulnerable than expected (Moen et al. 1981; Freudenburg 1982). Because many older, longtime residents may own their own homes, they are not affected by escalating rents, though tax and maintenance expenses may increase (Haynes 1983; Davenport and Davenport 1980).

PUBLIC SERVICE IMPACTS

The increased size and diversity of population which may result from energy development also may require increases in quantity and quality of services, such as transportation, education, utilities, medical services, police and fire protection, social services, and recreation. Some of these inmigrants may differ from longtime residents in the type or quantity of public services demanded. For example, a former city dweller may expect more of certain recreational or educational services than a rural resident (Schwarzweller 1979). However, a recent study has indicated that newcomers are not generally more dissatisfied with services in nonmetropolitan communities than longtime residents, although it was found that younger residents tend to expect higher levels of public service provision than older ones (Lovejoy et al. 1983).

This section contains a discussion of some of the major services which may be affected by rapid growth. The additional demand on these services will depend in part on other issues addressed in this book, namely, the extent of efforts to reduce the demand on local services, the proximity to large population centers, workers' commuting patterns, and the types of families and housing units brought into the community.

Figure 7.1 illustrates the population changes which might be expected in a small community undergoing energy development. Peak demand for services, such as law enforcement, education, and health care provision will probably occur at the time of peak population. Expansion of private sector areas such as secondary businesses may be greatest during the operating (stability) phase of the project, when employment multipliers are generally higher than construction phase multipliers. The curve illustrates one of the dilemmas of planning for service provision in impacted communities; that is, whether to expand services (especially capital facilities) to accommodate peak growth populations and be faced with excess capacity during the stability period, or to weather shortages during the construction period and plan for the more stable population occurring during the operating phase. In some situations, provision of temporary facilities (such as mobile

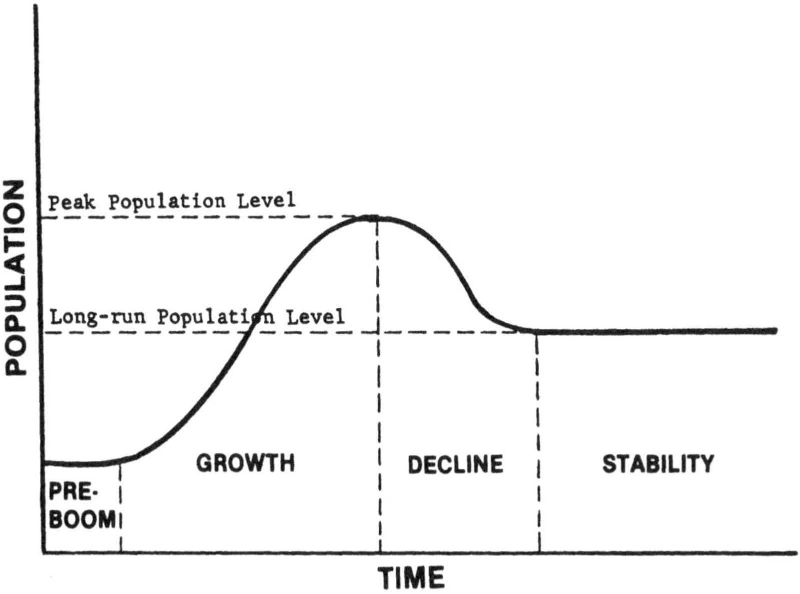

Figure 7.1. Stages in resource community development

classrooms) may provide the solution to dealing with large, temporary demand increases.

The increase in supply capabilities of local public and private services may come about through four basic efforts. First, existing services may only need to be improved, revitalized, or expanded. Second, new facilities may have to be constructed or new services acquired. Third, the community, county, or state could make arrangements to share services and facilities. Finally, the community could contract with outside sources, such as county, state, or private agencies, to provide these services. Principal methods of financing these options are discussed in Chapter 8. Seven major services which may be affected are transportation, education, utilities, medical services, law enforcement and fire protection, social services, and recreation.

Demand for certain services, such as utilities, will affect both industrial and residential sectors. Provision of services, such as electricity, waste disposal, and water and sewer, are often handled by both private and public sector suppliers. Services such as fire protection are generally provided by the local community; however, in some cases the developer may provide equipment and personnel for the construction site, which may be shared with the community. Thus, although these and other services are usually termed public services, they may actually be provided by private or quasi-public entities (such as public utilities or private waste disposal firms) or by the developer, as well as by the public sector. A detailed discussion of providing any of these seven affected services is beyond the scope of this book. A brief overview of some of the options and difficulties of providing these services (transportation, education, medical services, law enforcement, social services, and recreation) follows.

Transportation

Transportation impacts in rapid-growth communities result from movement of equipment to the facility, general construction trade traffic, and worker traffic to and from the site. The two major expense categories are road maintenance and road construction. The financial costs may place burdens on the local (i.e., city or township), county, state, or federal government, depending on the type of road. In some instances, developers have assisted with road construction (Halstead and Leistritz 1983a; ROMCOE 1982). The length of time needed to construct new roads complicates expansion of the road system.

Assuming there is an adequate highway or road system already in place, the key to reducing traffic congestion is organization. Local measures (such as control of road access) can be useful in promoting orderly traffic flows. In addition, the developer could greatly decrease traffic congestion by setting up staggered working hours; only a portion of the work force would then be accessing the transportation network at one time. However, since decreasing traffic itself may be the most desirable alternative, the community may desire to set up a transportation coordinating committee to plan and oversee these operations.

Education

The school system can be one of the most seriously impacted areas of the community due to the costs and logistics of accommodating the influx of new students. Lack of qualified instructors and available classrooms can be major problems, further complicated by the uncertainty of the number and age of the new children who will be attending school in the community. Overbuilding may be just as detrimental as underbuilding, since the community often pays for new facilities through bond issues or loans. A reliable estimate of class size is essential before impacts can be mitigated.

To alleviate overcrowded classrooms and high student-to-teacher ratios, a number of measures can be considered. Mobile classrooms and existing community buildings could be employed temporarily to offer additional space (Doricht 1982). Double or extended sessions may also be utilized to service more students with the same classrooms and instructors (ROMCOE 1982); however, since this will place greater demands on the instructors, the quality of education may decrease due to increased workloads and less student-to-teacher contact.

An additional demand on the educational facilities may come from the adult population. Newcomers may expect adult education classes, expanded library facilities, nursery schools and day care centers, recreational and sporting events, and facilities for meetings of special interest groups. New or larger facilities and more professional staff may be needed in the event of this type of demand.

Other problems may result from an area's particular situation. Problems with discipline and consistency have been noted due to construction workers' highly transient lifestyle, which hampers students' ability to adjust (Cortese 1982; Halstead and Leistritz 1983a). Difficulties may also arise between newcomers and longtime residents, who may feel that the newcomers are to blame for teacher and classroom shortages (Pietens 1979; Cortese 1982). Providing housing for new teachers in tight housing situations has also been a problem in some energy-impacted communities. Finally, although some state agencies, such as North Dakota's Energy Impact Office, may do an ample job of providing capital facilities, it has been noted that there have been deficiencies in providing funding for teachers and social services staff (Halstead and Leistritz 1983a).

Medical Services

Since large hospitals staffed with many different specialists are seldom constructed in remote areas, medical service provision may be of acute importance to rapidly growing communities. There is already a large volume of literature dealing with health care delivery (Schmidt et al. 1978; Newhouse et al. 1982; Miller 1982; Copp 1982; Hassinger 1982); therefore, we will not attempt to address this issue in depth in this volume. However, a brief discussion of some of the concerns and problems associated with these services is presented.

Two basic problems in service delivery are a lack of facilities and difficulty attracting competent physicians. Since construction of a major medical facility in a rural area may not be justified, routine health care may be provided by a local clinic, while transportation arrangements to larger facilities (for example, vans, ambulances, and even airplanes) can provide for obtainment of emergency or other major medical health care provision.

However, it may be unrealistic to expect to recruit competent, primary care physicians into small, remote communities, since most physicians prefer to live in metropolitan areas with access to medical facilities and in proximity to other professionals in their field (Kennedy 1979). Physician assistants, nurses, or emergency medical technicians can provide many health care services without direct physician involvement, which can lessen demand for a resident doctor.

Impact management planners can utilize a variety of resources when planning for health care. Generally, the state university system can provide faculty and staff capable of providing assistance in organizing and improving local health care, and can also provide access to additional expertise throughout the country. Professional organizations of physicians, nurses, and other health professionals can also provide assistance. Finally, many states have developed health systems agencies to provide assistance in service distribution (Kennedy 1979).

Law Enforcement

Rapid population growth will cause additional strains on local police forces. As the population increases, the number of crimes are also likely to increase, resulting in both increased workload for officials and overcrowded jails and facilities. Additional law enforcement personnel will have to be hired and more equipment and larger facilities acquired, although assistance from county or state law enforcement departments could help handle the increased demands. The developer could hire a private agency to patrol the construction site and housing developments and assist local officials in providing the community with more comprehensive security.

The quality of this site security force is more important than the actual size; some developers recruit retired law enforcement personnel for their force. Emphasis is placed on professional training and physique of workers (Parkinson et al. 1980; Mather 1983). In the case of the UPA/CPA Coal Creek Power Station in North Dakota, the utility contracted with the local sheriff's department to provide site security. This policy also had the effect of reducing competition for qualified security personnel (Leistritz and Maki 1981).

Social Services

Some researchers have found that rapid growth can sometimes cause stress and mental health problems among newcomers and longtime area residents alike (Weisz 1979; Dixon 1978). Area social service staffs are often overburdened by administering support programs and aiding in newcomers' adjustment. Results of a recent study indicate that human service programs in rapid-growth communities (annual growth rate greater than 6 percent) experience a five-year lag in keeping pace with population growth (Uhlman and Olson 1984).

In some situations, a development may attract workers to an area who, after drawing a short term of employment, remain in the area in hopes of being rehired. This may lead to an increased number of persons with no substantial means of support and for which no particular organization claims responsibility. Increases in reports of child abuse and neglect have also been noted (Halstead and Leistritz 1983a; Leistritz and Maki 1981). The resolution of these problems has been compounded by budget cuts in federal programs that fund social service operations. In addition, state impact management organizations often do not provide funding for social service personnel due to statutory limitations (Halstead, Leistritz, and Chase 1983).

Impacts on an area's elderly residents may also be substantial. Increases in traffic, noise, and crime which accompany large population increases may pose special problems for older residents (Moen et al. 1981). These residents may become more isolated and find their usual network of resources and support disrupted (Haynes 1983; Brown 1977).

One program to offset these stress and isolation problems is the REACHOUT program in Garfield County, Colorado. Funded by the Colorado Division of Impact Assistance, REACHOUT's goal was to anticipate and prevent social stresses associated with the oil shale boom. The program's structure included several professionals who recruited volunteers (both newcomers and longtime residents) from the community. After a 20-hour training session to enhance volunteers' skills and acquaint them with the problems which newcomers face, the volunteers distributed information (both formal and informal) on available services, activities, and resources (McHugh 1982). Since the cancellation of the area's Colony Oil Shale Project, REACHOUT has also served as a support group for the unemployed (Ludwig 1983).

There is considerable disagreement as to the level of effort which should be directed towards social service provision in impact management. For example, the North Dakota Energy Impact Office specifically forbids the use of EIO funds for financing social service staff. This problem stems partly from difficulty in quantifying some of these social impacts, and from sometimes hazy cause-effect relationships. There is also a lack of consensus in the literature dealing with energy development as to the type and magnitude of the social service impacts to be expected (Davenport and Davenport 1979; Wilkinson et al. 1982; Finsterbusch 1982; Murdock and Leistritz 1982), as well as some uncertainty as to the best mitigatory measures. Weisz (1979), for example, stresses that simply providing more services is like "fingers thrust into a bursting dike," and that primary prevention programs are a necessity in helping community residents adjust to the stresses of rapid growth. In any event, statistics often do document increases in the number (if not the rate) of social service caseloads and demand for programs such as AFDC in rapid-growth communities, as well as in other service areas. Impact management planners thus need to examine the potential range of these impacts and possible preventive or reactionary measures to deal with them.

Recreation

Increased demands on recreational facilities may be overlooked by the community when it is struggling with the provision of utilities, law enforcement, or medical facilities. Recreation, in fact, may appear to be a luxury and may not be considered at all. However, lack of recreational facilities may tend to increase boredom, which in turn could result in increased drug abuse, alcoholism, crime rates, and employee turnover (ROMCOE 1982). A recent survey of residents of seven energy boom towns found that lack of recreational opportunities was among the most serious problems experienced by local youths, families, and single adults (Uhlman and Olson 1984).

Many recreational facilities could be shared with the school system, which likely has the greatest demands for these facilities. Indoor and outdoor facilities could result from community projects or from donations of money, time, and/or equipment from the developer. For example, Atlantic Richfield and Kerr-McGee donated $450,000 for a community recreation center in Campbell County, Wyoming, and Western Energy Company has provided for several park and recreation facilities in Colstrip, Montana. Colstrip's parks are maintained by a private company which derives its income from property owners and the operating companies (U.S. Department of Interior 1983). Outdoor facilities, such as parks and football and baseball fields, may be constructed quite easily by the developer by using some of the heavy equipment from the construction site. In Wright, Wyoming, Atlantic Richfield and Thunderbasin Coal Company provided land, labor, and equipment for construction of outdoor recreational facilities (U.S. Department of Interior 1983).

Preimpact planning and zoning laws could once again play an important role in providing needed services by causing the developer to address socioeconomic impacts. A local tax base for recreation should be considered early in the development to help finance these facilities; Rangeley, Colorado used $1.5 million of tax revenues from nearby oil shale developments to finance a recreation complex. Federal aid could be requested for various recreational facilities as well as for state or national parks.

CONCLUSIONS AND IMPLICATIONS

Preconstruction measures to equip and expand the host community's capacity to deal with the project's population effects can help soften impacts, as well as enhance positive benefits. In addition, these measures can benefit the developer by increasing worker productivity and reducing worker turnover and absenteeism.

Measures to expand the community's capacity to handle growth are primarily directed at four areas: (1) community organization, to assemble an effective planning and administrative capacity; (2) housing for project-related inmigrants and displaced locals (such as elderly and low-income groups); and (3) public services.

The major problem often encountered in rapid-growth areas is that of insufficient housing for the new population. A number of options are available to deal with this, from total developer subsidization of housing projects to stimulation of the private housing market. Housing options include provision of mobile home parks or permanent housing and revitalization of existing housing. Which technique is most cost-effective will depend upon the final site chosen.

The amount of investment in permanent capital structures--new schools, firehouses, etc.--should generally be based on the size of the population which is expected to settle in an area permanently. Similarly, this consideration should affect the housing sector. If a development has a construction period of only a few years, it may be unwise to construct housing and service facilities which are unused or underused when the project is completed. Likewise, if an area's inmigrating population for a project's construction phase is double that for the operating phase, it would be imprudent to construct permanent facilities for the temporary population. In these cases, after the proactive tools discussed in Chapter 6 have been used to reduce inmigration, measures which are essentially reversible could be employed to reduce possible overbuilding. These include temporary worker housing and mobile home parks rather than permanent housing subdivisions, and mobile classrooms to absorb the temporary overflow of students.

The primary goal of these strategies is to insure ordered, balanced growth of needed facilities and services. An essential element is close coordination between the developer and the community to help identify excess capacity, revenue and service shortfalls, and population needs. By planning for community needs and taking steps to offset potential negative impacts, many of the undesirable effects of rapid growth can be avoided. The end result can be a healthy, dynamic community (both socially and economically) that experiences expanded employment and business opportunities, and a developer that benefits through greater worker productivity and reduced worker turnover.

8
Financing Development in Rapid-Growth Communities

A recent study reported that rapid-growth communities in the western United States required financial capital early in the development process to cope with new demands for public facilities and services. Unfortunately, monies to finance additional service requirements are often unavailable to these communities until after growth is well underway (ROMCOE 1982). Such a mismatch of available revenues and required expenditures is all too common for these rapidly growing communities. In another study of rapid community growth, survey results revealed that half of the respondents would leave Sweetwater County, Wyoming, if the housing situation were not improved while a third would leave if the retail service selection were not improved (Gilmore and Duff 1975a). Although the area's local governments were experiencing fiscal stress, insufficient financial capital was also seriously hampering the provision of needed private goods and services.

These examples illustrate that large-scale resource and industrial projects have important implications for the financing of development in both the public and private sectors. The projects directly and indirectly create demand for public facilities and services and concomitantly enhance the base of public revenues. The specific nature of the demands depends primarily on the characteristics of the incoming population and new businesses. Such heightened economic activity will also increase demand for financial capital to support private sector development, particularly in housing and commercial business.

In this chapter, we will discuss the effect of large-scale resource projects on the availability of capital required for both public and private sector development. The financial effects of rapid growth are first addressed with regard to the public sector. Particular emphasis is given to the principal problematic issues influencing fiscal distress and the fiscal responses and financial mechanisms available for public sector readjustment. The discussion then turns to the private sector and considers the impact of insufficient financial capital on secondary economic activity. Capital requirements and availability in rapid-growth communities are reviewed as well as the options for improving private capital availability.

ADDRESSING FISCAL REALITIES IN PUBLIC FACILITIES AND SERVICES PROVISION

In sparsely populated areas, public facilities and services in preimpact communities are limited. Given the long history of population decline and aging in many of these rural communities, local governments seldom offer the full complement of services to their residents. Public facilities may have been constructed with minimal excess capacity, that is, if they were built at all. The provision of most services in these rural centers has often been deemed deficient by urban standards. With the level of public facility and service provision a reflection of residents' priorities, many communities are simply unprepared for the rapid tempo of change (Murdock and Leistritz 1979).

Given such a setting[1] and the substantial magnitude of potential population change, it is hardly surprising that the provision of public infrastructure and services has become such a prominent topic. And yet, this provision problem begs further questions which are primarily financial. How much revenue will accompany the population increase and the associated structural economic change? When will the additional revenues be available to the local governments? Who should pay for the expanded services? And what financial mechanisms are available to local governments? Such questions illustrate that the fiscal stress and financial difficulties accompanying rapid growth are often due to cash flow problems.

Key Problematic Issues in Financing Development

In looking at the problem of financing public infrastructure and services, there are a number of interrelated issues to consider. Among these issues are uncertainty surrounding the project, intertemporal gaps of revenues and expenditures, jurisdictional mismatches, demand determination and fluctuating demand levels, existing service capacities, and delineation of responsibilities.

Uncertainty. Probably the foremost problem one encounters in financing public infrastructure and services is uncertainty. Though the nature of uncertainty varies from one impacted community to the next, uncertainty forms the common backdrop in addressing the financing issue (Branch et al. 1982). There are many sources of uncertainty with one of the principal sources being the inherent volatility associated with the causal agent, namely the resource development project itself. Not only is there uncertainty concerning the initiation and location of the project, but even after project construction commences, uncertainty remains that the project might later be substantially modified (e.g., Intermountain Power Project coal conversion development in Utah) or even abandoned as infeasible (e.g., Cold Lake heavy oil facility in Alberta, Colony oil shale project in Colorado). Such factors affect the behavior of many actors within these communities, including both borrowers and lenders in the financial markets. For example, within the municipal bonds market, underwriters and rating services are often quite reluctant to participate in and approve issues where significant uncertainty exists (Gilmore et al. 1976). Such reluctance has undoubtedly been accentuated by such events as the unprecedented default on $2.25 billion of municipal bonds by the Washington Public Power Supply System (*Business Week* July 11, 1983).

Intertemporal Gaps. Variations in both revenues and expenditures throughout the period of rapid growth cannot be overlooked (Leistritz and Murdock 1981; Murdock and Leistritz 1979). Often when growth is occurring, additional revenues may not keep pace with increasing expenditure requirements. In fact, the revenue resulting from development generally occurs well after development-induced spending. This is partially due to lags in the receipt of property tax revenues--the schedule for assessment, levy, and collection might take upwards of 18 to 24 months. The fiscal situation in many locales is further complicated by the timing of the property tax assessment--the new facility is usually not placed on the tax rolls until it is completed and ready to use, often several years after construction was initiated. Such a lagged situation of costs exceeding revenues--often referred to as the "front-end financing" problem--may be inconsequential for large cities but can cause significant fiscal problems for small communities. The financial predicament becomes especially serious when large capital expenditures are required. The community's ability to respond in a timely fashion is hampered by institutional and technological restrictions. Bond issues cannot be prepared and sold overnight, and construction of the needed capital improvements may take several months.

Demand Determination. Related to the timing issue is the fluctuating nature of demand levels for public infrastructure and services. Estimation of the magnitude of population influx over time is extremely difficult. Take, for example, the unpredictable nature of workforce peaks and valleys that inevitably occur in the construction and operation phases. Recent ex-post studies indicate that construction workforce projections have often been inaccurate (Leistritz and Maki 1981; Gilmore et al. 1982; Chalmers et al. 1982; Malhotra and Manninen 1980). Even if relatively reliable estimates of the labor force required to construct and operate the facility are available, the magnitude of additional inmigration induced by development (e.g., job seekers for either the primary facility or secondary and tertiary activities) may be difficult to calculate. Critical to these demand estimates are distinguishing between temporary and permanent demand levels and determining the development pace over time. The demand for services changes with the transition from a construction work force to a more permanent worker population. With each group comes a different service demand level, income level, and ability to pay.

Perhaps intuitively obvious but nevertheless central to demand estimation is the notion that population magnitude is the determining factor in service provision. Prior empirical analyses have clearly shown that the likelihood of provision for a particular service in a community is largely a function of population size (Muller and Soble 1982). For each service, there exists a population threshold beyond which there is a better than even chance that the community will provide the service. Figure 8.1 arrays graphically the population thresholds at which small communities initiate expenditures and then employ personnel for various selected public services. For a small community the figure indicates which services would normally be provided, and what additional services would be required if the community increases to a higher population level.

Once demand levels for public infrastructure and services are determined, an equally difficult issue must be addressed: how many of these demands should be satisfied by the impacted local government? Unfortunately, there are no cost-free solutions to the provision of local services. Investment strategies selected by local government officials become important to the timing and magnitude of project-related costs. There is a range of alternatives available to local decision-makers to choose the most efficient and equitable way of providing services. At one extreme, the community could attempt to meet the infrastructure and service demands of the peak population during construction, only to face the possibility of substantial overcapacity at the beginning of the facility's operation. Conversely, local officials could plan provision levels to meet the expected needs of the long-run stable population. This alternative, however, could imply a substantial deterioration in the quality and/or availability of public facilities and services during the short-run growth period of construction. Thus, the problem becomes one of selecting the optimal level of investment that balances the potential for long-run idle capacity against a potential short-run deterioration of services (Cummings and Mehr 1977; Cummings and Schulze 1978; Henry 1980).

Interjurisdictional Differences. Benefits and costs of large-scale projects are also often not uniformly distributed across local jurisdictions. Sometimes, the communities most affected by large-scale projects are not the jurisdictions where the development is actually sited, but instead the communities better able to accommodate the new wave of inmigrating population. As such, these communities will likely find their revenues insufficient to provide the services and facilities needed by the new population. Such jurisdictional mismatches occur frequently in the United States. Rarely are resource developments located within the corporate limits of cities. Frequently they will be situated just across school district, county, or even state boundaries from where the new population will reside. For example, most of the local government revenues generated from a large-scale coal extraction facility (located near Decker in southeastern Montana) are paid to its site county of Big Horn while much of the project-induced population growth and associated public service costs are occurring in the city of Sheridan, Wyoming--20 miles south of the development (Murdock and Leistritz 1979). In such a case, Big Horn County, Montana, experiences a

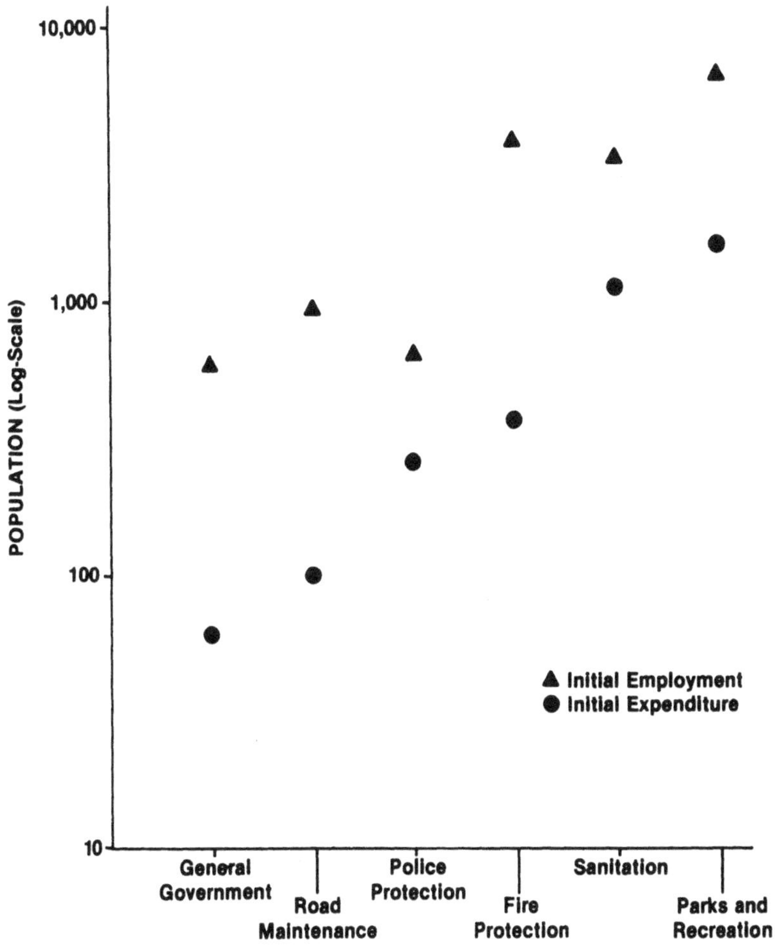

Figure 8.1. Population thresholds for initial municipal expenditures and employment for selected local public services

SOURCE: Muller and Soble 1982

tax windfall while Sheridan, Wyoming, is faced with severe fiscal stress.

Existing Service Capacity. The capacity of the community's existing service delivery system is a major determinant of the impact of population growth on local government expenditures (Stinson 1981). A rapid-growth community with substantial excess capacity will be able to absorb many new residents with only a small increment in expenditures. If, on the other hand, existing facilities and personnel are already fully utilized, even a marginal increase in population can substantially increase local expenditures. Given such supply constraints, small rural communities may require extensive expansion and replacement of existing facilities. Existing service capacity is different for each community. While some services may be incrementally expanded as the need arises, the "lumpiness" (i.e., available only in distinct sizes) of many capital items necessitates major expenditures. These capital items, such as schools, water treatment plants, streets, and police cars have economies of scale where it is cost effective to anticipate future growth or meet existing needs. Such services are the most likely to face capacity constraints in rapid-growth situations.

Delineation of Responsibility. If local public infrastructure and services require expansion, institutional arrangements will play an important role in the assignment of responsibilities, that is, who is responsible for what, when, and under what circumstances (Branch et al. 1982). Although the local community is generally considered the beneficiary of economic development, it also assumes responsibility for providing community services. With large-scale developments, the sheer magnitude and pace of additional service and facility requirements make it impossible for many impacted communities to adequately respond. Under such circumstances, the assignment of responsibility becomes open to debate. This is an extremely difficult political issue which has yet to be resolved in North America. Community leaders and residents want to ensure that the quality of community services does not deteriorate, while maintaining control over infrastructure and service-related decisions. State and provincial officials want to ensure that an adequate standard of living is maintained in impacted communities, but unless they can obtain revenues from the developmental activity, there is a general reluctance to commit state (or provincial) resources to the effort. In most cases, unconventional institutional arrangements between the state (or provincial) government and local units of government are necessary to accommodate the revenue problems, particularly bond powers, and mechanisms of distribution and timing of tax revenues. Indebtedness statutes, aid formulas, and other structures to alleviate local fiscal stress may require reformulation by state governments (Bronder et al. 1977).

Corporate officials, who want to get their project "on-line" and to operate it efficiently, have become more cognizant of the need for good community relations and the prerequisites of high worker productivity. As with other actors, corporate entities have vested interests--conducting business with a positive company-community relationship will be advantageous for the company whether that be in the form of decreased operating costs, shorter project completion schedules, or prompt government approval of project plans and permits (Roberts et al. 1980; Johannesson and Plesuk 1982). While companies remain quite sensitive to dispensing corporate funds without justification (e.g., rate of return), it is evident that industry-community relationships have evolved, such that many companies are now actively engaged in various kinds of impact mitigation activities.

Fiscal Consequences of Rapid Growth

The resultant effects of rapid growth on the public sector have been well-publicized and extensively analyzed (Gilmore 1976; ROMCOE 1982; Murray and Weber 1982; Murdock and Leistritz 1979). Indeed, such communities as Colstrip (Montana), Rock Springs (Wyoming), Craig (Colorado), Grants (New Mexico), Fort McMurray (Alberta), Tuktoyaktuk (Northwest Territories), Huntly (New Zealand), Gladstone (Australia), and Peterhead (Scotland) have become bywords in the social impact assessment lexicon for severe social, economic, and fiscal problems due to construction and operation of large-scale projects. Analyses of such cases indicate that the problems of financing public sector development can be grouped into three general categories: capital market failures; shortfalls in public facilities and services; and structural fiscal distress (Gilmore 1983; Bradbury 1982, 1983).

Capital Market Failure. For our purposes, capital markets are defined as that web of institutions and mechanisms by which financial resources are saved, investment opportunities are identified, and savings channeled to borrowers (individuals, businesses, and governments) for their productive use (Daniels and Kieschnick 1979). A capital market fails when that market does not adequately respond to the appropriate signals and/or does not allocate capital to its most productive use. Simply stated, capital market failure occurs when capital is effectively unavailable, whether that unavailability means having to pay an unnecessarily high price (i.e., interest rate) or there is a nonexistent supply at any price (Shaffer 1983). In rapid-growth situations, the capital market fails when the sudden increase in local demand for public capital is not met by existing market mechanisms or institutions at any acceptable price because of risk premiums in pricing or lack of supply. Many times, this capital shortage indicates either inadequacies or breakdowns in exogenous institutions (Gilmore 1983). Examples include response failures in state school assistance programs, government impact assistance programs, secondary capital markets, and public bond markets.

Shortfalls in Public Provision. Although covered in the previous chapter, this topic requires additional discussion. Shortfalls may occur either when the local government lacks fiscal resources, expertise, experience, and access in providing the services and infrastructure needed to accommodate a growing population, or where the government is simply unwilling to make the investments necessary to provide them (Gilmore 1983). Such shortfalls are often complicated by uncertainty resulting from problems associated with technology, markets, project management, project sponsor's cash flow, regulation, or lack of credible information on project employment and schedules.

Structural Fiscal Distress. Although there is a lack of widely accepted measures of fiscal distress, some local governments face enormous difficulties in providing services and raising revenues to support infrastructure and development. These fiscal difficulties facing communities are exacerbated in rapid-growth situations. Bradbury (1982) discusses two broad types of fiscal distress: budgetary fiscal distress and citizen fiscal distress. Budgetary distress refers to a local government's short-run difficulty in balancing its budget. Citizen distress occurs when the local government poorly performs its dual function of providing a package of local public services and collecting taxes and other revenues to pay for them. Indications of citizen distress are either high tax rates and/or low public service levels. Community residents suffer from such distress when they are unable to obtain a "reasonable" level of services at a "reasonable" monetary sacrifice. For instance, residents are generally not well served when taxes at an acceptable level will only finance municipal services of low or meager quality or when tax rates to support adequate services are exorbitant.

Underlying either of these two types of distress are structural economic and fiscal conditions, specifically the long-term imbalance between local government responsibilities and its potential revenue-raising ability. In the short run, an impacted city can avert impending cash flow problems by either raising taxes or reducing expenditures. This traditional short-term trade-off belies the problem's complexity in the long term. A local government's ability to achieve a long-term balance between revenues and expenditures depends on various structural factors, i.e., those factors that are part of the institutional and economic structure facing the local governments and, as such, largely outside their control (Bradbury 1983). Some of these factors are (1) size of tax bases; (2) amount of intergovernmental aid; (3) overlying government tax collections from local residents; (4) range of local government's service responsibilities; (5) local input prices and production costs; (6) local service needs (actual and projected); and (7) externally imposed limitations on local tax rates, tax bases, revenues, or expenditures. Structural fiscal distress results from the unfavorable combinations of these structural factors, specifically when there is "more" of factors 3 through 7 and "less" of factors 1 and 2. A recent study (Bradbury 1983) analyzed the likely determinants of long-term imbalance and later incorporated these factors into an index of structural fiscal distress for comparing the structural conditions of large U.S. cities in the early 1970s. Other than isolated case studies (Lamont et al. 1974; Gilmore et al. 1976), no comparable study is available for assessing the structural fiscal distress of small, rapid-growth communities. Reasons for this paucity of empirical research on nonmetropolitan fiscal stress are the lack of accurate, timely, and readily available data from rural local governments and insufficient conceptual development in modeling and monitoring rural fiscal conditions (Reeder 1984).

These fiscal consequences of rapid growth are not unique to impacted communities, rather many municipalities experience structural fiscal distress, shortfalls in facility and service provision, and lack access to financial capital markets. However, in rapid-growth situations, local governments face sudden increases in demand for public services and infrastructure with limited revenue capacity in a substantially compressed time period.

Mechanisms of Response

A new industrial or energy resource development raises questions regarding the impacts on local revenues and expenditures. If local officials are to plan effectively for providing additional services required by industrial and population growth, they will need sound estimates of both revenues and costs. Although a number of fiscal impact studies (i.e., assessing the differences between new revenues and new expenditures) have been conducted (Barrows and Charlier 1982; Murray and Weber 1982; Detomasi 1982b; Burchell and Listokin 1978; Leistritz and Murdock 1981), estimation problems for both revenues and expenditures remain. Smaller cities have an especially difficult time determining accurate and useful estimates of local impacts of growth--the major obstacle is that estimation techniques have been typically designed for larger cities (Stinson 1981).

Although we will primarily focus on the revenue side of the ledger, a brief discussion of expenditures is warranted. In spite of recent developments in fiscal impact analysis, estimation techniques for expenditures are less advanced than for revenues (Leistritz and Murdock 1981). Seldom is there a clear-cut basis for accurately estimating the effects that population changes have on expenditures.[2] In developing estimates, local officials need to be cognizant of several factors that influence the cost of service provision and delivery. First, economies of size (i.e., expenditures per capita decrease as population increases) can be achieved by local governments in delivering some public services. Second, population growth implies change in demographic composition and as such, may result in increased per capita costs for maintaining the same quality of service. In addition, changes in social conditions can contribute to demand changes (e.g., residents may prefer a different mix of services, or changes in service quality). Third, population growth may also alter the techniques of service production. Lower per capita costs may result from more efficient use of existing facilities and/or personnel or by adopting new cost-saving technology. A final, and perhaps most important determinant, is the community's existing service capacity. Whether a community's predevelopment service capacity is excessive or deficient will affect the expenditure level of local governments during development.

In addressing the what, when, and how of public service provision, local officials need to evaluate their set of alternatives by such criteria as efficiency (i.e., Will the service be provided at the lowest per unit cost?), effectiveness (i.e., Will the desired outcome be achieved?), responsiveness (i.e., Will the provided service be able to adjust to changes in public demand?), and equity (i.e., Will service delivery deny access to any resident groups?).

Communities can benefit from selecting among alternatives the most efficient and effective way to provide services. Examples of these techniques are private contracting for provision of specific public services; joint construction of common community-industry facilities; direct provision of local services by the project developer, nonprofit corporations, or by other public entities (whether overlying governments or nearby localities); and demand limitation of certain services. State-mandated limitations on revenues and outlays and citizens' resistance to increasing taxes have helped to generate interest in private sector provision of local services traditionally delivered by public entities. Lovejoy and associates (1982) contend that there are several advantages to private contracting including (1) increased set of choices, (2) built-in incentives for private efficiencies, (3) economies of scale achieved, (4) minimization of cost, and (5) increased local government responsiveness to public preferences. In spite of these advantages, private contracting has not yet been widely applied. Reasons behind its limited implementation include (1) the inability (and unwillingness) of private contractors to provide the available range of public services, (2) public resistance to private provision, and (3) legal restrictions by states and localities on the type and scope of service delivery. Nevertheless, a contracting scheme holds promise as one potential method of service provision for improving the quality of life in rapid-growth communities.[3]

Population growth not only significantly affects the demand for public services, but also the amount of local government revenues available to provide a satisfactory level and mix of services. In the face of rapid growth, the primary tasks of local governments are to expand their revenue base, and whenever possible, to shift the added costs of service provision to nonresidents (e.g., commuters and temporary residents) and recent in-migrants who may cause a portion of the growth-induced problems. Although revenue estimates are also fraught with difficulties in rapid-growth communities, of paramount concern are the following questions: (1) How much revenue will accompany the project siting and associated population increase?, (2) From what sources will revenues be obtained?, and (3) How long will it take before that revenue is available for local government purposes?

Local governments obtain additional revenues from growth in four general categories: (1) local property taxes; (2) other taxes, including income, sales, and severance taxes; (3) user fees and charges; and (4) other financing methods, such as tax prepayments.

Property Taxes. Of the above categories, property taxes represent the single most important source of locally generated revenue and the primary means of financing local public education. In 1980, property taxes accounted for nearly 55 percent of all revenues raised by municipalities (U.S. Bureau of the Census 1983). The property tax provides a significant and steady source of revenues which in turn help to determine the level of services and facilities the local government is able to provide.

Since local governments have long been associated with the administration of the property tax, one might assume that the process is conducted with efficiency and equity. There are, however, potential problems associated with the method and timing of local property assessment.

First, in spite of statutes requiring that property assessments be at full market value (or at some specified fraction of full market value), underassessment is widely practiced. One major complaint about the tax concerns the equalization between different parcels similarly classified but not necessarily taxed in like manner.

Another notable problem, called competitive underassessment, involves the deliberate assessment of one jurisdiction's parcels at a lower ratio of assessed to market value compared to a neighboring jurisdiction. The result enables the local government to reduce its state property tax obligations, and where the assessed valuation is a criterion for state assistance, competitive underassessment leads to an increase in the jurisdiction's entitlements.[4]

A third problem relates to the different tax treatment of mobile homes. These mobile homes--substantially relied upon by short-term residents in impacted communities (e.g., construction workers and their families)--require similar services as conventional housing, but the additional property tax revenues may not cover the cost of these needed services. The timeliness of assessments is another problem besetting local communities. Current tax rates are often based on prior assessments which were completed several years ago and thus do not accurately reflect the current market. The community is obviously foregoing revenues if property values have increased since the last assessment. Similarly, there is the time lag between the completion of construction of new taxable property and the due date of the tax payment. Short-term residents, for instance, may have already left the state before taxes on their mobile homes come due. Such a situation obviously allows some residents to receive local services without paying for them. Finally, local governments are vulnerable to tax delinquency. High interest rate penalites have been instituted by most states to combat such abuses.

One suggested method of reforming the property tax assessment system in impacted communities is for these localities to convert their annual real estate tax billing system to a semi-annual billing process. The effect of this twice-a-year billing procedure is that the local government gains a cash flow benefit early in the fiscal year and receives earnings from six-months interest (Muller and Soble 1982). Another mitigative method is for communities to compress the entire assessment, levy, and collection timetable for property taxes. Some western states have already instituted this procedure for mobile homes. In North Dakota, for instance, a special license must be obtained within 30 days after the mobile home enters the county. This license fee is approximately equivalent to the local property taxes due on a conventional dwelling of similar value (Stinson and Voelker 1982). Relatedly, impacted communities should revise their assessment schedules in order that property tax rates more accurately reflect the current real estate market.

Other Taxes. State codes and constitutional limitations on tax rates and revenue collections have made the property tax a less significant source of revenue in impacted communities. Inevitably, concerns of tax burden arise in these communities as to who should pay for these additional public services. In some instances, the reasonable and equitable solution offered is to shift some of the costs of service expansion to the new and temporary residents. Taxes on lodging and meals are probably the most effective tax mechanisms for shifting a portion of the tax burden to new temporary residents (e.g., construction work force). These taxes are directly tied to the consumption of commercial services and, as such, help to offset the costs of service provision.

Another tax levied by local governments in several states is the earnings tax (Muller and Soble 1982). In rapid-growth situations, the earnings tax may be viewed as one fiscal response to the jurisdictional mismatch problem, i.e., between nonresident service consumers and the municipal service provider. Such a tax is assessed on the income or payroll of nonresident commuter workers who consume municipal services in the course of their daily activities. Resident workers are also subject to the earnings tax, though at a different rate than nonresident commuters.

Other indirect revenue sources that are related to the increase in wages and salaries resulting from economic expansion are general sales and excise taxes. The general sales tax is uniformly imposed on most retail transactions while the excise tax is on selected (often luxury) goods or on such so-called "sin" items as alcohol and tobacco products. Both of these taxes are income regressive, affecting the low-income residents more than the higher-paid newcomers. The important consideration in reviewing both the general sales and excise taxes is the means and level of revenue distribution to local governments.

For energy- and mineral-rich states (or provinces), perhaps the most significant sources of revenues are those taxes directly applicable to the extraction and conversion of energy and mineral resources. Many states and provinces levy a severance or production tax on these resources. Severance taxes are assessed against the amount of mineral produced by a mine over a specified time period in accordance with a rate schedule. The rate schedule refers to either the dollar amount of the tax per unit of extracted mineral or a per unit percentage of the sales price of the extracted mineral. Although in recent years these taxes have evoked much controversy,[5] our concern here is whether sufficient revenues are available to meet the needs of state (or provincial) and local governments during periods of rapid growth. Many of these state severance taxes were enacted in part to help finance impact aid programs for rapid-growth communities associated with mineral development. In this light, such taxes are seen as a form of industrial user charge, in that the industry which creates demand (either directly or indirectly) for public services is asked to partially fund these services.

Whether these taxes are effective mitigative instruments that lessen the external costs associated with boom town conditions (e.g., inadequate public facilities and services, inadequate private services and amenities, and potential of a bust or decline following a short-lived boom) is debatable.[6] The key issue, however, is whether the revenues from severance taxes do indeed go for impact mitigation. Commonly, states allocate severance tax revenues to (1) the state general fund; (2) a trust fund; (3) a special fund for impacted jurisdictions; (4) other state special funds; and (5) general funds of local jurisdictions where the mineral is mined. Although 33 states assess some form of severance tax on mineral extraction (Stinson and Temple 1983), revenues in many states take a rather circuitous route (see Table 8.1). New Mexico's coal tax revenues, for instance, go into the state's general fund, while Wyoming's severence tax revenues go to the state's general impact fund for use by communities that need not be near the mine or facility that generated the dollars.

User Fees and Charges. Many local governments have recently found themselves between a fiscal "rock and hard place." Increases in the range of services provided and the cost of meeting service demands have necessitated heavier tax burdens for communities. Concomitantly, local governments are hard pressed by both state-mandated limitations on revenues and outlays and voter dissatisfaction over escalating tax rates and new forms of taxation. These factors have led local officials to examine alternative methods of raising additional revenue. One response that has grown in popularity is the imposition of user fees and charges--charges assessed for the performance of a service or provision of a good. Such a mechanism allows a local jurisdiction to levy fees on a customer receiving a specific service when that service may not be needed by all residents. User fees and charges are most appropriate where individual usage of the service can be measured and where the benefits are mainly enjoyed by the direct users (Muller and Soble 1982). Fees and charges are levied for a wide variety of services including sewage treatment, water consumption, solid waste disposal, building permits, and liquor licenses.

TABLE 8.1.
Severance tax collections and apportionment in selected states, 1981

State	Severance Tax Minerals	Severance Tax Revenues	Percent of Total State Revenues	Distribution of Severance Tax Collections (in percents)							
				State General Fund	State Trust Fund	State Highway Fund	State Education Fund	Local Government General Fund	Local Assistance Impact Fund	Local Highway Fund	Other
Colorado	coal, petroleum natural gas, metallic minerals, molybdenum	$35.9 million	2.5	--	50.0	--	--	7.5	42.5	--	--
Kentucky	petroleum, natural gas, coal	$194.4 million	8.5	50.0	--	--	--	--	50.0	--	--
Louisiana	petroleum, natural gas	$815.2 million	29.1	33.3	46.7	--	--	--	20.0	--	--
Montana	petroleum, natural gas, coal, metallic minerals	$99.2 million	21.3	17.75	50.0	--	5.0	--	18.75	--	8.5
North Dakota*	petroleum, coal, natural gas	$103.4 million	22.9	30.0	15.0	--	--	20.0	35.0	--	--
Oklahoma	petroleum, natural gas	$601.5 million	26.9	78.0	--	--	--	--	--	10.0	12.0
Wyoming*	coal, natural gas, petroleum, uranium, trona	$138.3 million	29.5	19.05	23.8	9.5	--	--	19.05	--	28.6

SOURCES: Stinson and Temple 1983; U.S. Bureau of the Census 1982.

*Distribution of severance tax revenues for coal used.

Under conditions of accelerated growth and fiscal uncertainty, user charges represent an important source of additional revenue for local governments. Fees and charges are generally organized into three categories: licenses and permits; utility charges; and current charges. Licenses and permits provide administrative revenues to governments as part of their regulatory function. These charges for motor vehicle licenses, liquor licenses, dog tags, and so forth tend not to respect the ability-to-pay criterion of equity in taxation due to their imposition of uniform fees. Utility charges are assessed by locally operated public enterprises, such as municipal electricity, natural gas, water, and toll bridges. Although many municipal utilities accumulate surplus revenues, access fees should include the pro-rata share of facility expansion. These charges should be sufficient to meet normal operating repairs and eventual system replacement. Current charges or service fees are imposed on a wide range of services including trash collection, medical care, and recreation facilities. Such fees are helpful in encouraging reductions in service demand, equity in pricing, and improved efficiency in service delivery (Muller and Soble 1982).

In addition to these categories, recent cases of one-time development fees on new housing construction have become a significant source of revenue for local governments, particularly in the southern and western United States and Australia (Nickens 1983; Hargreaves 1982). These development fees generally cover a pro-rata share of the total capital costs for public services within the residential and commercial project. Such one-time, lump sum fees are obviously designed so that growth pays its own way, that is, shifting the costs of additional services to the developer, and ultimately, to the new residents.

<u>Other Financing Methods</u>. There are a variety of other mechanisms that growth-impacted communities can employ, some of which do not involve taxes or user fees. Such methods include the earlier discussed alternatives of private contracting and joint contracting for service provision. These alternatives may provide significant cost savings for the participating communities. Local governments may also take steps which limit the demand for services, thus reducing the outlays needed for service provision. Strategies to reduce demand, such as annexation and control of sewer and water extensions, may be based on existing state statutes or on locally promulgated policies.

Other fiscal tools are primarily tax or fee related. In order to alleviate the front-end problems endemic to rapid-growth communities, some states (e.g., Montana and Wyoming) allow the property tax assessment of the project facility during the construction period on a percentage completed basis. Other states (e.g., Colorado and Utah) allow, or even require, the project's sponsor to prepay a portion of their property taxes to assist local governments. Some states permit local governments to levy a local option sales tax. Evanston, Wyoming, is one community that adopted the local option sales tax to cope with rapid growth associated with petroleum development.

Programs for Assistance

In addition to these numerous revenue-enhancing techniques, rapid-growth communities may benefit from assistance programs available through federal and state (or provincial) governments, industry, or some manner of public-private partnership. State, provincial, and federal aid, for instance, have become leading sources of assistance for many impacted communities. The amount of revenue assistance varies among states (or provinces) and types of governments.[7] Monies are available for a wide variety of purposes and programs including construction of community infrastructure, housing projects, business development, comprehensive planning assistance, education and training, and general government.

Effective programs address varied problems including (1) shortfalls in operating revenues during early stages in the project's development, (2) inability to finance needed capital facilities, and (3) inadequate private capital formation. Policies that provide the needed assistance should be evaluated in terms of their effectiveness of both intended effects and potential side effects (or unintended effects). Evaluative criteria used to measure program or policy effectiveness might include the following (Gilmore et al. 1976):

1. Political feasibility. Any policy and implementation program involving state (or provincial) or local action must be politically palatable in the context of regional traditions, experience, and attitudes. At the state (or provincial) level, there may be political opposition or constitutional limitations on indebtedness. More significant is the potential local opposition by officials and voters toward incurring the cost and risk of authorizing bonds or other general obligation borrowing.

2. Equity. A typical perception of development is that the benefits accrue over a wide region while the costs are imposed locally. Local people are apt to feel that they need not settle for either drastically higher taxes or degraded quality of public services. Thus, the increasingly prevalent view is that beneficiaries should absorb the costs. Ideally, this implies that they should bear the incremental costs of public infrastructure improvements and services. This criterion also implies that risks (associated with the back-out costs of bust) should be shifted towards the beneficiaries of the development.

3. Responsiveness. Assistance mechanisms that are otherwise desirable but would require a lengthy delay in implementation are simply not needed by rapid-growth communities. For these communities, the future is now. Outlays for public infrastructure are actually needed prior to the occurrence of rapid population growth.

4. Efficiency. The level of assistance needed by impacted communities varies greatly depending on how efficiently existing revenue sources are allocated and utilized. Failure to fully utilize existing assistance programs and failure to obtain funds from the additional tax bases to the impacted jurisdictions substantially increases the need for external assistance. On a

theoretical level this involves the issue of whether externalities are internalized within the impacted region. Practically speaking, requirements that existing resources (e.g., federal, state programs, industry assistance) be fully utilized as a condition for receiving special impact assistance may significantly reduce the cost of assistance programs. For instance, local communities may desire outright grants, but such grants may in fact be the least efficient, most costly solution to the problem.

5. Administrative simplicity. The premise that many impacted communities in rural areas lack sophistication and expertise is merely one side of the coin. Often times, substantial bureaucracy and/or a complex set of administrative procedures for implementation impede a program from accomplishing its stated objectives. In general, programs that can be enacted and put into operation within a short period of time and without bureaucratic obtrusiveness are to be preferred.

6. Comprehensiveness. The fiscal problems associated with coal and oil development, as well as hardrock mining communities are varied but nevertheless interrelated. For example, a separate funding program to cover only hardrock mining impacts may duplicate the functions of an existing coal impact program, whereas other developments, like oil and gas, may in fact have no funding program to draw on for impact assistance (Owens 1983). Though a single, unified program is preferable, not all problems unique to any particular development would be addressed. Yet an assistance program should address most of the relevant problems and remain adaptable to differing development situations in order to have its desired effect.

Whatever the characteristics of the selected assistance programs, such programs must address the two sources of financial problems facing rapid-growth communities. These problems are categorized as affecting either the communities' *supply* of funds or their *demand* for funds. Various financial programs, policies, and mechanisms have been instituted by federal and state (or provincial) governments and industry in recent years to aid impacted communities, whether by correcting supply-side deficiencies, or by removing demand-side barriers.

Supply-side Programs. The majority of the existing programs affect the supply of funds by improving the rapid-growth community's cash flow situation and financial resource availabilities. Special funds have been instituted through state (or provincial) and federal legislation or through agreements negotiated with private industry. Several western states and provinces, such as Montana, North Dakota, Wyoming, Colorado, Alberta, and Manitoba, affected by recent energy development use special funds in their respective programs. Funds are in the form of either legislative grants or earmarked receipts from specific resource-related revenue sources (in general, severance taxes). In many states, special impact boards have been created for disbursing these impact funds to local governments to assist them in providing facilities and services needed as a direct result of mineral development. Grants are awarded based upon consideration of such factors as population, need, merit of proposal, and resource-matching ability (see Chapter 5).

Some states (e.g., Alaska), however, prohibit the establishment of dedicated funds for impacted communities. In such instances, an appropriation by the state legislature or the development of a grant (conditional or unconditional) program are more feasible financial mechanisms. The state of Wyoming has established a program to provide both grants and loans to local governments affected by energy development. Under this program, the state will borrow up to $60 million through conventional lending institutions to provide these grants and loans. The state debt in turn is financed through receipts from leasing federal mineral lands (Stuart/Nichols Associates 1979).

In addition, many impacted communities have developed strategies which have enhanced their financial resources through matching grants from private industry. Most of the private industry payments to communities are indirect in the form of state and local taxes (e.g., property, corporate, severance) in which some portion of the receipts are earmarked for local uses. Industries, however, do make direct contributions (monetary and nonmonetary) to communities in such forms as prepayment of property taxes, area planning grants, loans, technical assistance, and underwriting of bonds. Industry as well as impacted communities has begun to recognize the need for cooperative community-developer management planning (Cole et al. 1983).

Demand-Side Programs. Impact assistance programs are crucial for rapid-growth communities to meet their financing obligations for capital improvements and increased operating expenses. Such programs greatly facilitate the construction of needed infrastructure and decrease its overall cost. Grants and other revenue sources, however, are unable to satisfy all of the community's front-end financing requirements. Thus, many impact communities enter capital (bond) markets to meet their unmet financial obligations. Because growth often implies increased ability to support debt, rapid-growth communities might be thought to have easy access to the capital markets. There are, however, market-imposed as well as legal and constitutional limitations that affect impacted communities' access to capital.

With regard to market-imposed limitations, Auger and others (1978) have cited that the impacted community is at a disadvantage in two respects: (1) its ability to obtain financing is bound to the feasibility of the impact agent, i.e., industry or mining company instigating the impact; and (2) it must compete directly with other debtors for the same investor funds. The impacted community's ability to market its bonded debt is inextricably linked with the vitality, stability, and market position of the impacting local industry.[8] For example, a community whose major industry is highly susceptible to business cycles will exhibit considerably less access to capital than a similar community whose major industry (e.g., a utility firm) is more or less insulated from market fluctuations. The hard fact is that financial markets will tend to view the impacting industry and community as a unit. A community's dependence on the industry will essentially result in the evaluation of public impact debt as if it were private project debt. Furthermore, the impact community must compete with other public borrowers for the funds traded on the bond market. Many of these borrowers may be better known to the market and present a less risky profile in many respects, not the least of which is their more diversified economy. The bonds of rapid-growth communities are generally of lesser quality from the market's viewpoint than are bonds of more stable municipal issuers.[9] The result is that most "impact" bonds have found little enthusiasm in the national capital markets; rather they are underwritten by either local banks or financial intermediaries such as the publicly held Bank of North Dakota (Fisher 1983).

Besides capital market failure, there are institutional factors, i.e., the legal and constitutional limitations on impact bonds. All states regulate the issuance of debt by their own municipalities in the interest of avoiding over-extension and subsequent reorganization. Although the effect of these regulations is generally positive on most municipal issuers, many of these regulations become counterproductive in impact situations where the access to capital is limited below what would be economically justified. There are six principal kinds of legal and constitutional restrictions which limit demand for capital in impact communities (Auger et al. 1978):

1. Debt limitation. Most municipalities are required by their state constitutions to limit the debt they issue to a fixed percentage of the assessed valuation in their tax base. In Colorado, for example, the general obligation debt limit is three percent of actual property value (Gulliford 1983). This is a significant problem for small rural communities which are rapidly growing; their tax bases are weak compared with the funds they need to borrow to finance capital improvements as well as operating expenses. By law, the needed funds could not be borrowed.

2. Amortization limitations. Most states limit the amortization schedule for municipal bonds to 20 years or less. Projected cash flows of many projects exhibit substantial surpluses, but require longer amortization schedules.

3. Interest rate limitations. Most states limit the interest rate their substate jurisdictions can pay for public money. In impact situations, however, the market-set rates for public borrowings are often higher due to risk premiums than the rate ceilings set by state law.

4. Limitations in applications of funds. The funds of public corporations can only be applied toward public purposes. Obstacles abound when impacted communities desire to apply public funds for subdivision development and housing, or for commercial and service sector development.

5. Public support required. The need for public support for public debt, whether general or limited obligation bonds, is increasingly ubiquitous. In certain instances, debt approval by bond elections is rather difficult for impacted communities because of risk aversion by preimpact residents.

6. Equity limitations. For most applications, public projects must be structured so that beneficiaries bear the costs of the project and do so prorata as they benefit. In practice, limitations posed by equity requirements in impacted communities are that legal, accessible beneficiaries (i.e., those upon whom the bonding authority may levy) often lack the financial strength to support the investment, while other beneficiaries escape without contribution.

Programs either proposed or in place seek to overcome these barriers of access to capital for impacted communities. A number of programs have been proposed for improving the marketing support of public debt issued by rapid-growth communities including third party (e.g., federal) guarantees of the debt, interest rate subsidies, and bond insurance programs. Marketing support for impact bonds, while a significant contribution to the needs of rapid-growth communities, is largely cosmetic in that it does not change the underlying structural problem of impact finance. Questions about risk, economic viability, and liquidity of public enterprise remain unaddressed. Another series of programs available to impacted communities are termed capital supplements. These schemes are aimed at supplementing local investment programs for public infrastructure in the impacted community. Capital supplements are utilized as a special kind of grant, one used in conjunction with debt finance in such a way to render the debt financing more sound. These supplements could either be used to reduce debt service uniformly throughout the impact period or merely reduce debt service in the early impact stages. Similar to capital supplements are revenue maintenance programs which make up any deficiencies in a given fund for a rapid-growth community. Such programs are also called "revenue guarantees" or "contingency grants," which can provide relief for a community's capital and operating budgets.

In summary, a community's ability to handle growth depends upon several fiscal factors including: (1) level of fiscal stress or the revenue-expenditure gap; (2) financial resource availabilities; (3) accessibility to public bond markets; (4) responsiveness of overlying governments for impact finance; (5) range of responsibilities in service provision; (6) resource or industrial corporate financial assistance; and (7) local financial management and planning expertise. Fiscal policy decision-making in rapid-growth communities would be greatly enhanced if local governments instituted a monitoring program for on-going evaluation of their financial conditions. Various fiscal trends including municipal revenues, expenditures, debt, fiscal capacity and effort, public employment and wages, and cost indices could be analyzed to identify dynamic fiscal problems associated with population growth. However promising, such a system has yet to be developed for small rural communities.

FINANCING PRIVATE SECTOR DEVELOPMENT

Analysis of the private sector effects resulting from resource development projects has been adequately discussed elsewhere (Murdock and Leistritz 1979; Leistritz and Murdock 1981; and Chase et al. 1983). In addition to the employment and income created directly by project construction and operation, resource developments stimulate increased economic activity in various trade and service sectors of the local economy.[10] Discussion of these indirect and induced economic effects typically centers around estimation of the multiplier, i.e., a measure which expresses the total economic change as a multiple of the original or direct project change (see Chapter 6). Although the primary causal agent behind these private sector changes is the project itself, an important (albeit secondary) driving force is the increased population pressure in the local region. The changes resulting from this population influx are principally felt within the housing and services sectors, with new residents demanding a greater supply of residential housing and a more complete selection of retail services.

Critical to this secondary development within the local economy is the availability of financial capital, primarily required for (1) the emergence and/or expansion of businesses, and (2) the purchase of residential housing. The major demand on local financial institutions for housing is mortages, both home mortgage demand for new housing as well as for mortgage refinancing for existing homes. Financial capital is also required for supporting an expanded commercial business sector, wholesale trade sector, service sector, contract construction sector, and manufacturing sector.[11]

In spite of its importance, the financing of private sector development in rapid-growth communities is a neglected research topic and a disregarded topic in the policy arena, but the need for the analysis of such problems is thus evident. In the remainder of this chapter, we will review the financial capital requirements for housing and businesses in rapid-growth areas, along with the availability of capital from traditional financial sources. Our discussion will then turn to a review of the options for improving private capital availability. We will conclude with an assessment of innovative programs, recently implemented in a number of states and provinces for the purposes of capital market intervention.[12]

Private Capital Requirements and Availability

The private financing problem confronting most rapid-growth communities is rather simple in origin. Prior to the advent of the large-scale development project, most communities were generally self-sufficient in providing for their private capital requirements. Loan demands were met by funds supplied from existing financial institutions. Needs for housing mortgage funds were largely met by savings and loan associations (S & L's) and to a lesser extent by commercial banks. Funds for such loans came primarily from local resident and commercial depositors. Commercial banks provided most of the commercial and industrial mortgages, small and medium-sized construction loans, short-term business (e.g., working capital loans) and intermediate business (e.g., equipment loans) credit, and some consumer credit. Using funds from local depositors, credit unions provided much of the consumer credit loans. Equity needs to initiate or participate in new ventures came primarily from retained earnings and savings from previously successful local entities or were generated by existing local development corporations (MacDonnell et al. 1982). Local financial resources were supplemented with access to funds through the correspondent banking system and national financial markets.[13]

As impacted communities experience rapid growth, existing funds from local depositors become insufficient to meet the need for new loans. According to published interviews from the Rocky Mountain Center on the Environment (ROMCOE) Rapid Growth Communities Project (1982), residential housing and commercial businesses are the most affected components of the private sector. Population growth in a community requires the provision of additional housing and commercial businesses to accommodate these increased needs. The capital requirements associated with housing include both contract construction financing and mortgage financing. Local financial institutions face substantial loan demand for mortgages for both new and existing houses (i.e., mortgage refinancing). An expansion of commercial businesses, retail trade, wholesale trade, and services will ensue from the increased population. Capital required to expand these sectors includes funds needed to establish new business enterprises as well as expand existing ones. Capital requirements for this expansion will be greatest in the retail trade category (Payne 1982). For instance, capital requirements for expansion in the retail trade sector in Colorado's oil shale region have been estimated to be $330 million for the period 1981-1990. Assuming that 50 percent is debt-financed, the loan demand on local financial institutions alone would be $165 million (MacDonnell et al. 1982).

Although the demand for funds may indeed be the highest for the retail trade sector, other business sectors will also require substantial funding for expansion. The whole range of services for people and businesses will expand to keep pace with the population growth. Wholesale trade, for instance, will expand in accordance to local retail trade growth. Capital requirements for other sectors (e.g., manufacturing, transportation, utilities, contract construction) will expand as the area grows. Activities directly linked to the resource development project, such as input-supply businesses, will no doubt lead to an increased demand for local funds. The expected project-related growth in capital requirements for these sectors should not diminish the level of traditional demand for funds within the region. Current demand for agricultural lending, for instance, can be expected to remain relatively constant.

In rapid-growth areas, the primary sources of financial capital are commercial banks and S & L's. Other members of the local financial community may include industrial banks, credit unions, mortgage companies, and consumer finance companies. Although commercial banks and S & L's are expected to handle the major share of future loan demand, a shortfall of funds will ensue. Given the substantial gap between locally available capital and the expected growth in capital requirements, these financial institutions are faced with four possibilities (MacDonnell et al. 1982):

1. Raise the cost of available funds by adding origination fees or other points and raising interest rates.
2. Tighten evaluation of credit by making only better-secured loans and less-risky investments (i.e., applying credit rationing).
3. Seek additional local deposits by becoming more aggressive in seeking compensating balances from loan customers, and attempting to obtain large deposits from incoming development firms and/or the state (or provincial) government.
4. Attempt to attract capital from within or outside the region.

All of these options, further classified as either "demand constricting" or "supply expanding," may occur (even simultaneously) and with differing consequences. With regards to restricting the demand for funds, raising the cost of available capital will cause some business ventures to be either canceled or delayed. The effect of the higher cost funds may in fact discourage local businesses from even attempting expansion. As a result, the long-term viability of some of these businesses may be affected.[14] On the other hand, raising the cost of locally available capital may encourage businesses to seek capital from outside the community. Outside financial capital would take some pressure off the local deposit base and may lead toward attracting new competing financial institutions into the community. Obtaining loans from outside financial institutions, however, may be more costly for local business establishments. Outside banks generally lack knowledge about the business manager and/or the establishment. In addition, the inherent economic volatility of many rapid-growth communities creates uncertainty for the outside lender. Businesses within Colorado's energy development region, for instance, have obtained outside financing for expansion, but at additional cost to compensate for risk and uncertainty. Colorado business managers have dubbed this situation the "Craig Factor" after an energy boomtown on the western Colorado slope (ROMCOE 1982).

Raising the mortgage cost makes it difficult for inmigrants to purchase housing in the rapid-growth community. Many project developers, however, usually provide some kind of housing assistance for their employees (see Chapter 7). Though company programs have helped to mitigate rising housing costs, many community residents remain disadvantaged. Groups most vulnerable include secondary workers, elderly, and the like.

The other "demand-constricting" method--credit rationing--will also have a dampening effect on the local community. Available funds are biased toward large well-established businesses or those establishments most likely to succeed within a rapid-growth environment. Smaller, nonstandardized businesses and loan applicants new to the community are unlikely to obtain available credit. Complicating the loan process for these businesses are local bank acquisition and turnover of bank personnel. Small local businesses are especially hurt by this credit squeeze. Entirely dependent upon the local financial institutions, such business establishments are essentially locked-out (ROMCOE 1982).

While the increased population will create additional demand for funds, inmigrants will also deposit funds in local financial institutions that will later become available for loans. Some financial institutions have been successful in obtaining large deposits from the incoming development companies (ROMCOE 1982). The result may be additional funds available locally for financing mortgages and business expansions.

Importing funds is essential for improving private capital availability. Mechanisms for importing at least some portion of the capital are already in place for many commercial banks and S & L's. Commercial banks may have correspondent relationships with larger banks outside the region. S & L's may have existing participation arrangements and access to secondary markets for some of the mortgages they originate. Other financial institutions (e.g., mortgage companies, credit unions, finance companies) also have connections to external sources of capital. Accessing external sources of capital to meet local loan demand inevitably means new risks, a higher average cost of funds, different requirements for lending and borrowing, and a need for improved expertise. Given such pressures, it is not surprising that some local financial institutions in rapid-growth communities have chosen not to undertake the effort and expense of aggressively seeking to import capital. In certain cases, the most effective mechanisms for importing capital have been initiated not by local banks or S & L's but by incoming development companies, newcomer financial institutions, or concerned state (or provincial) officials (MacDonnell et al. 1982).

Options for Improving Private Capital Availability

Given the private capital needs within rapid-growth communities, most efforts to access new sources of financial capital are directed outside the region. In examining the available options for importing capital, four types of private capital requirements are discussed: housing mortgages, long-term commercial and industrial loans, intermediate-term business loans, and equity participation.

Housing Mortgages. As indicated above, the capital requirements for housing far exceed the private capital needs in other sectors of a rapid-growth community. In recent years, it has been increasingly difficult to purchase housing. Reasons, such as the changing structure and competitive environment of financial institutions and high interest rates, are well known. However, these problems are magnified in rapid-growth communities where mortgage demand quickly outstrips savings deposits in S & L's and commercial banks. The volatility of these resource towns in general inhibits the flow of capital into these areas. Offering higher rates of return would attract additional capital, but the results would be far less than encouraging. Higher mortgage costs would prevent a substantial share of employees from purchasing a house. Adjustment problems are further compounded in those areas where the financial community is not well developed, i.e., lacking adequate financial institutions (Shaffer 1983).

Although there are a number of prominent issues concerning the financing of housing in rapid-growth communities,[15] our discussion will be confined to (1) expanding the access to outside capital sources for housing mortgages in a timely and cost-effective manner, and (2) improving the affordability of housing by reducing the cost factors. Options available for increasing the outside supply of financial capital for housing include government-organized secondary mortgage institutions (e.g., Canada Mortgage and Housing Corporation, Federal National Mortgage Association, Federal Home Loan Mortgage Corporation), private secondary market arrangements, mortgage companies, and mortgage-backed securities. Federal government involvement (at least in the U.S.) in the development of secondary mortgages has been substantial. One shortcoming of such involvement, however, is that financial institutions in small communities generally have no need to access funds through secondary markets. When rapid development begins, these financial institutions lack the necessary expertise to take advantage of these government-sponsored programs. Arrangements with individual buyers from capital-surplus areas are limited by untimeliness, sporadic nation- or region-wide liquidity squeezes, and perceived instability of rapid-growth areas. Mortgage companies, however valuable in selling all originated mortgages, have a limited function for many boomtowns because of their nonexistence prior to the advent of rapid growth. Finally, a variety of publicly and privately insured mortgage-backed securities are available. These mortgage-backed securities have recently attracted increasing attention. One popular alternative is the placement of these securities with public and private pension fund buyers. A major initiative in this regard was undertaken in 1981 when a consortium of trade associations formed the Mortgage Corporation of Colorado (MCC). Such a mechanism could be important in improving the availability of mortgage funds in high demand areas (MacDonnell et al. 1982).

Improving housing affordability in rapid-growth communities occurs through resource development corporation subsidies, public sector mortgage subsidies, and mortgage subsidy bond issues. Developers have devised a variety of mechanisms to reduce housing costs for their employees. The basic approach is to sell (or rent) at market levels with a number of different forms of subsidy ranging from low-interest or interest-free loans, below-market or below-cost purchase agreements, buy-back provisions, and rent-buy options (Detomasi 1982b).[16] No matter which approach is taken, if the program is confined to employees of the resource development company, it will lead to the creation of a segmented housing market in the community. There still would be an inadequate supply of unsubsidized housing for service sector employees (Rabnett 1978; Brealey and Newton 1978). Public sector mortgage subsidies have also become commonplace in rapid-growth communities. The Wyoming Community Development Authority (WCDA) for example, has had a significant influence in the mortgage market of several rapid-growth areas in Wyoming. The Authority initially sells tax exempt bonds, then in turn sells the proceeds to local financial institutions at below market rates. These institutions then loan funds to qualified households. In effect, the WCDA functions as a specialized secondary mortgage market mechanism channeling funds to communities in rapid-growth areas. Its ability to offer mortgage funds at a lower interest rate (usually 3-4 points below conventional rates) is due to the tax exempt status of its bonds. Tax exempt financing is also utilized by selling mortgage subsidy bond issues. Substantial portions of required mortgage funds can be raised by utilizing this mechanism.

Long-Term Business Loans. Businesses need long-term financing for such items as land acquisition, facility construction, and equipment. Although the demand for such funds is relatively small in impacted communities, loan requests may rapidly exceed locally available resources. In some communities, such as Rock Springs and Wheatland, Wyoming, the impact of such a credit squeeze fell primarily on local business people. Without well-timed credit for expansion during the rapid-growth period, many small businesses were edged out by new outside competitors (ROMCOE 1982). Viable mechanisms for improving the availability of funds are categorized as either traditional, government-supported, indirect, or new mechanisms. The traditional method for providing commercial and industrial loans from outside the community has been through external loan participation, the most common being correspondent banking. Participation has not been very effective in rapid-growth communities with many loan requests being rejected by the correspondent (MacDonnell et al. 1982). Government-sponsored mechanisms have generally improved the availability of long-term credit for businesses. The Small Business Administration (SBA) Section 502 loan guarantee program and industrial revenue bonds (IRBs) have been utilized effectively in many communities. The use of IRBs, however, has elicited much controversy because they provide subsidized financing to attract new businesses (and new competition according to opponents). An indirect approach is for the resource development company to make deposits in local financial institutions. The Wyoming Industrial Siting Council requires companies to make such deposits as conditional upon receiving a siting permit. This approach has had limited effectiveness due to limited funds and insufficient stipulations as to their targeted use(s) (MacDonnell et al. 1982). Mechanisms used more recently have centered around expanding the potential pool of lenders, namely pension funds and secondary marketing for commercial mortgages.

Intermediate-Term Business Credit. Intermediate-term loans are often made for equipment purchases and expansion of existing businesses. Under this category, the leasing of equipment has become an increasingly attractive and viable alternative to equipment purchases. The attractiveness of leasing has been further improved in the United States by the Economic Recovery Act of 1981. One aspect of the act established a new system of depreciation known as the Accelerated Cost Recovery System (ACRS) which has the effect of speeding up the recovery of taxable investments. For companies engaged in leasing, the ACRS allows the sale of the improved cost recovery allowance and investment tax credits. Though the costs of leasing are reduced, most beneficiaries tend to be large, publicly held corporations.

In numerous states, business development corporations (BDCs) have been established to make intermediate-term credit available either to targeted types of businesses (e.g., high risk businesses, disadvantaged small businesses) or targeted geographical areas (e.g., high unemployment areas, rapid-growth areas). The majority of these BDCs have been initiated either by a group of banks, often in response to the U.S. Community Reinvestment Act (Hayden and Swanson 1980), or by states under an economic development mandate. The more aggressive BDCs, such as that established by the Economic Growth Council in Great Falls, Montana, have gone beyond simply lending money to offering business counseling and taking equity participation. The intent of many of these public-private arrangements is to ensure the promotion of sound economic development within their borders.

Equity Participation. Business development requires a substantial amount of equity funds, especially in the case of new businesses and smaller, less established businesses. Traditionally, much of equity support comes from informal sources such as personal savings, family, and friends. There are also formal sources potentially available to businesses in rapid-growth areas including venture capitalists and traditional debt lenders increasingly interested in taking equity positions (e.g., insurance companies). Most of the venture capitalists operate out of the eastern United States with a distinct investment bias toward innovative businesses (e.g., distinctive product, potential national market) that have the potential for substantial profit return in five to seven years (MacDonnell et al. 1982). Because much of the capital invested has been in high-technology-related firms, few businesses in rapidly growing resource development areas would be of interest to private venture capitalists (U.S. General Accounting Office 1982). In the United States, the use of federal funds to broaden and strengthen the private sector has been accepted public policy for nearly 30 years. Since the mid-1950s federal programs have supported privately held venture investment firms known as Small Business Investment Corporations (SBICs) and Minority Small Business Investment Corporations (MESBICs). Currently, there are nearly 500 private firms that are licensed as either SBICs or MESBICs by the federal government (U.S. Small Business Administration 1983). These investment corporations are organized to provide access to low cost funds from the SBA. In turn, these firms are generally restricted as to the types and sizes of loans they may make. Clearly, SBICs offer some potential as a source of long-term debt and equity for business in rapidly growing areas. Another possible equity source for business development is Community Development Corporations (CDCs). Established in the 1960s, CDCs are designed to develop revenue-generating businesses that are controlled through community ownership and to promote the economic and social development of the community (Deaton 1975).

Although capital requirements in rapid-growth communities exceed locally available capital, there are many options available to attract capital for housing and commercial/industrial development. For housing, the secondary market for home mortgages seems to be the best source of extended capital. Public and private sale of mortgage-backed securities is another option which holds promise. Reducing the cost of housing by offering subsidies is perhaps most effectively utilized by resource development companies and by state and local governments issuing tax-exempt housing bonds. Capital requirements for commercial/industrial development, especially involving new and small businesses, are another matter. Risks tend to be greater and institutional incentives fewer for commercial lending. Efforts being made to expand the potential pool of lenders hold much promise in this area. Innovative mechanisms and policies have been instituted in many resource-rich states to provide the private sector incentives for expanding and diversifying economic development in rapid-growth areas. In the next section, a number of these programs are described.

Institutional Innovations in Public-Private Partnerships in Financing Development

In recent years, a growing array of new public-private partnerships has been formed in the arena of economic development. Cooperative partnerships encompass a variety of arrangements and relationships including government incentives for business development, improvement of government effectiveness in assisting private development, public economic development agencies, private spending for public purposes, business expertise applied to government, and contracting public services to private firms. In spite of the recent spate of literature (e.g., Bearse 1982; Fosler and Berger 1982) and the popularity of the public-private partnership concept, cooperation between the public and private sectors has occurred throughout political economic history. Indeed, such a relationship lies at the very core of all economic development activities. The purpose of this final section is to describe a variety of institutional innovations which have arisen on several levels to help mobilize and allocate financial capital for economic development. While some of these innovations have been implemented in resource-rich states (or provinces), others developed elsewhere provide potentially relevant examples for rapid-growth areas.

State (Or Provincial) Involvement. States and provinces together with the private financial community are pursuing innovative programs to refine the way capital is allocated to improve access for economic development. Basically, five different forms of state (or provincial) involvement have been utilized in the capital allocation process (Ide and Siegel 1983; Daniels et al. 1981):

1. Role of observer. The underlying principle in the state's acting as observer is that the private sector, acting in its own self-interest, can more efficiently correct any imperfections in the capital market. This role is basically one in which the state is not at all involved in the capital allocation process. Nevertheless, the state may be able to influence private financing methods simply by promoting activities that enhance efficiency and equity. Examples that illustrate this laissez-faire scenario include private sector initiatives such as Control Data Corporation's Venture Development program or the Community Reinvestment Revolving Loan Fund. These programs target funds and technical assistance to both disadvantaged businesses and geographical areas. By and large, resource development companies have not yet instituted long-term venture investment programs in rapid-growth areas.

2. Role of catalyst. In this case, the state helps establish new privately funded and managed financial institutions. Public sector involvement is minimal, with the only costs being for start-up administrative costs. Once the financial institution is formed and chartered, the state steps back and allows the private market to operate. One example of such a catalytic role is the British Columbia Central Credit Union, a provincial chartered reserve bank for British Columbia's 178 credit unions. Formed on the direct initiative of the provincial government, the bank provides member credit unions with access to national capital markets and a wide range of financial services which they cannot provide for themselves (MacDonnell et al. 1982). Another example is the Business and Industrial Development Corporation (BIDCO). These BIDCOs have been established in a number of states primarily for the purpose of accessing federal matching and guarantee programs for disadvantaged businesses.

3. Role as manager. A state (or province) can have a significant effect on the availability of capital for economic development depending on how it regulates the financial capital markets. In acting as a manager, the state acts as an overseer of

private sector activity. Though the state does not directly participate in the activity, it does manage the overall operation by determining what can and cannot be done. States regulate the private financial market primarily through their ability to grant charters for new financial institutions or to authorize expansion of existing ones. They can also influence liabilities or sources of funds by various regulations, including the maximum legal interest paid on deposits. Finally, states can regulate the assets of life insurance companies and public fiduciaries in order to protect the public from imprudent uses. A growing number of states, for example, have developed programs for targeting public employee pension funds for beneficial in-state investments.

4. Role as broker. When the state (or province) acts as a broker, it provides both financial and nonfinancial services, with the goal of influencing the private capital allocation process toward publicly desirable investments. Again, the state does not directly involve itself in the capital allocation process, but rather offers services which facilitate the flow of funds. The state can provide subsidies to decrease the high cost of economic development investments. Subsidies, however, have often proved to be an inefficient and ineffective financial development tool. They are typically too small to affect the firm's profitability, distort the market's decision-making process, and cost the state in tax revenues far more than the benefits received (Daniels et al. 1981). A more effective method is reducing the high risks of economic development investments through the use of loan guarantees and credit insurance mechanisms. The state can also increase the liquidity of financial institutions that make economic development investments through the use of secondary marketing and linked-deposit schemes. Secondary marketing mechanisms can substantially increase the availability of capital to potential borrowers and increase the lender's profitability. Under a linked-deposit system, the state agrees to place its current account funds on deposit with a private financial institution on condition that the financial institution make loans which fulfill publicly desired economic goals.

5. Role as investor. The most aggressive strategy for state involvement in the capital allocation process is by direct intervention through the creation of state development finance institutions which are publicly chartered, capitalized, and managed. Although these institutions often implement indirect forms of financial market intervention, they also can operate as direct financial intermediaries, lending or investing in projects/businesses that have inadequate access to private financial institutions.

States have intervened to create both equity- and debt-providing public intermediaries. Although there are few publicly chartered and capitalized equity institutions in operation, these institutions are charged with the mandate of diversifying the economy of their respective states (or provinces). The dearth of these equity-providing development institutions in North America is in sharp contrast to the European and Lesser-Developed Country experience, where public equity institutions play an integral role in the development process (MacDonnell et al. 1982; Habitat North, Inc. 1979). This situation, however, is changing in some of the resource-based states and provinces (particularly Alaska, Montana, and Alberta) where increasing attention is being directed toward utilizing resource tax and royalty payment monies for diversifying economic activity, enhancing resilience to short-term economic shocks, and sustaining production and associated employment over time.

In contrast to equity-providing institutions, there are public debt institutions in nearly every state and province. Public debt intermediaries generally finance projects in one of two ways. The first is tax financing, where the intermediary receives tax funds directly from the state (or province). The funds, in turn, may be used to leverage other state and federal funds. The more prevalent source of funds for public debt intermediaries is the sale of federal tax-exempt bonds to finance enterprise development. Most states have established industrial development agencies with the authority to issue revenue bonds.

Many states (or provinces) have, in recent years, taken some bold new steps toward developing innovative programs that recover, through resource taxes and royalty payments, a portion of the wealth generated by oil, coal, and other nonrenewable resource development. These monies are utilized to strengthen and diversify their local economies and to invest in profitable enterprises outside their region. Illustrations of such innovative programs can be found in Alberta and Alaska.

Alberta Heritage Savings Trust Fund. The Heritage Fund was established in 1976 for the purposes of prudently saving for the future, strengthening and diversifying the Albertan economy, and meeting current needs for its populace. Its funds are derived from two sources: (1) an annual transfer of the Province's nonrenewable resource revenues, primarily from oil and natural gas extraction; and (2) the retention of its investment earnings. Each year, over three-fourths of its new funds available from nonrenewable resource revenue and investment income are invested directly in Alberta. Since 1976, its asset base has steadily increased from $708 million to over $2.8 billion in 1983 (Alberta Treasury 1983).

The investment portfolio is divided into five investment categories: capital projects, Alberta investment, commercial investment, Canada-wide investment, and deposits and marketable securities. A number of the Heritage Fund's investments do not earn income but do provide long-term social and economic benefits for Albertans. Capital projects vary from research and development (e.g., agriculture, food processing, forestry, energy technology), to parks and recreation, hospital and health care clinic construction, and endowment funds for medical research and scholarship programs. Investments are also made in provincial crown corporations, enabling them to deliver programs and initiatives in diverse areas of activity.

In support of Alberta's overall social and economic development objectives, these corporations provide programs to home purchasers and renters, local governmental authorities, farmers, and small businesses. The single largest investment of the Heritage Fund is in the area of housing--providing subsidies to contractors, house purchasers and tenants, and senior citizens. The Alberta Opportunity Company and the Alberta Agriculture Corporation act as debt-providing financial intermediaries, providing loans (and loan guarantees) on favorable terms to Alberta small businesses and farmers. Priority is given to businesses unable to obtain financing from conventional sources and located outside the metropolitan centers of Edmonton and Calgary. Agricultural-related funding is made to foster the establishment and maintenance of family farms and encourage the in-province processing of agricultural products. Equity participation positions have also been made in energy resource projects (e.g., Syncrude) and a grain terminal project.

Previous years have also seen investments made in various projects across Canada. Lending in this division has been suspended indefinitely, however, to help ensure that funds are available to meet priority needs within Alberta for housing, businesses, farms, parks, and other projects.

The remainder of the Heritage Fund is invested in Canadian equities, convertible bonds, and money market securities. The investment strategy for equity instruments involves a diversified portfolio representing a broad range of Canadian industrial sectors and public companies. The major components of the bond portfolio are marketable federal and provincial government securities.

The Heritage Trust Fund is an extremely effective and innovative element in the province's overall economic development strategy. Its diversified portfolio has provided market rate financial returns, spurred business expansion and formation, created more jobs, and ensures a trust account for future generations in Alberta (Alberta Treasury 1983).

<u>Alaska Resource Corporation</u>. As in Alberta, the Alaskan state government is taking a more active role in directing the development of the state's economy, linking revenues from nonrenewable resources to a diversified investment portfolio. Through the Alaska Resource Corporation (ARC), the state supports venture capital investment in private businesses owned by its residents. This financial development institution was created in 1982 as a result of the reorganization of the Alaska Renewable Resources Corporation (ARRC), established by the state legislature in 1978. Initially capitalized with a two-year appropriation representing 2.5 percent of the state's receipts from numerous leases, rentals, bonuses, and royalties (about $42 million), the ARRC suffered from implementation problems and conflicting views regarding its overall purpose. As a consequence, the ARRC received no new appropriations in 1981, and, after extensive evaluation, was restructured as the ARC.

The original goals of the ARRC were to enhance the state's plentiful natural resource base while expanding economic activity and creating jobs in Alaskan-owned businesses that were in the renewable resources of agriculture, forestry, and fishing. The ARRC's project selection criteria were more comprehensive than the private venture capitalist's singular requirement of financial return. Certainly, the Corporation included the standard financial analysis (i.e., the risk and return factors) of proposed business projects. But ARRC criteria also included attention to which new and expanded businesses will add to Alaskan production through value-added and backward linkages that create upstream opportunities for further business development (Olson 1981).

The new ARC inherited the financial assets and investment portfolio of its predecessor organization, but it now has a more limited capital base, a more clearly defined purpose, a more conventional board structure, and specific guidelines concerning the size and terms of its investments. Although the ARC is not authorized to invest in service, retail, or real estate firms, its investment scope has been broadened to include mining, manufacturing, and tourism, as well as the renewable resource industries (Berger 1983).

Investments made by the ARC are limited to under $500,000 and may not be made to enterprises with gross sales above $10 million. The former ARRC was permitted to make equity investments of up to 49 percent, and in the few years of its existence such investments accounted for nearly a quarter of the approximately $38 million in total investments made. Though the new ARC is still permitted to make equity investments, it must provide for divestiture of its equity position beginning at a specified time. Unlike its predecessor, the ARC cannot make outright grants. The ARC is also prohibited from getting involved in the management of the businesses in which it invests.

As in the case with Alberta's Heritage Fund, the ARC is allowed full use of both principal and interest generated by its investments. The latest available annual report (fiscal year 1982) cautions that companies in which the ARC invested may be particularly vulnerable to business cycle troughs because of business size and age. Even with some erosion, ARC's asset base is expected to remain well above $30 million, providing substantial funds for future investments in the state's economy.

The use of public funds to stimulate and broaden private investment in North America is not a new phenomenon. Public involvement in economic development has occurred to guide, direct, and stabilize activity. More recently, specialized public development corporations designed to encourage and assist private investment have become commonplace. Efforts to change the shape of the economic landscape through public investment capital, as opposed to public spending, are altering the incentives for private economic decisions. Resource management and economic policymaking responsibilities are being combined in many resource-based states and provinces to avoid what is known as "Dutch Disease." The Netherlands government consumed revenues generated from the depletion of a nonrenewable natural resource, namely natural gas. Government expenditures rose to meet increased tax revenues. When the resource ran out, as did the gas in Holland, the country was faced with extraordinarily high social service costs, stagnated manufacturing industry, and mass unemployment (Kaldor 1981). The more innovative states (or provinces) are restructuring their tax, regulatory, and expenditure policies to provide the right incentives for private participation in resource investment programs by developing structural growth policies in collaboration with private sources of investment capital and establishing innovative public-private development finance mechanisms to convert resource assets into newly derived and diverse economic activity (Nothdurft 1983). Natural resource severance tax trust funds, such as those in Alaska, Alberta, and Montana, provide capital for further in-state investment to foster economic diversification and thereby lessen their dependence on fluctuating world markets for economic stability.

CONCLUSIONS

The availability of financial capital has direct bearing upon the quality of life in rapid-growth communities. Without the required level of financial capital, these communities will undoubtedly experience some level of fiscal stress, i.e., inability to cope with new demands for public facilities and services. The dilemma faced by many local governments is either to raise local taxes to provide for the needed services and infrastructure and/or to limit government expenditures. Financial capital gaps may also exist within the local private sector with requirements outstripping the availability of capital. Potential indirect and induced economic activity in the region will be impeded without an adequate supply of financial capital.

Numerous fiscal responses and financial mechanisms have been developed and adapted for addressing the fiscal realities that face rapid-growth communities. Though many of these policy responses are internal to the local government, it is widely recognized that some form of outside assistance is necessary. A potpourri of assistance programs is available from federal and state (or provincial) governments, industry, or some level of public/private partnership. These aid programs are designed either to correct supply-side deficiencies or to remove demand-side barriers within impacted communities. Most aid programs, however, deal with those communities experiencing rapid growth; few programs offer counter-cyclical aid to localities undergoing the "bust" phase of boom-to-bust resource development.

Private capital markets are among the most highly developed and competitive markets in the economy. When appropriate mechanisms are in place, money flows to opportunity. Although the private capital market will eventually adjust to the demands of rapid-growth situations, problems may exist in the short term. The level of difficulty experienced by rapidly growing areas depends largely on the rate of growth, their existing financial base, and the efforts made by parties such as the local financial community, resource development company(s), and affected local and state (or provincial) governments. Awareness of financial needs and unmet opportunities in adjustment is an important first step. Further approaches to facilitate private capital availability are required to improve the financing for needed housing and a viable commercial business sector. Critical for these communities will be the effective access to outside capital funds, the establishment of government investment programs, and the development of innovative public-private partnerships.

Public and private sector financing is thus among the most important of all components of impact management. Obtaining knowledge of the likely nature of financing problems in impacted areas and of the alternatives necessary for resolving these problems is an essential prerequisite for those who wish to effectively manage the impacts of any large-scale development.

NOTES

1. Although our focus is on pre-existing communities, there are often no communities in the vicinity of the proposed development site in various regions of Australia and Canada (Robinson 1982; Brealey and Newton 1978).

2. For instance, the popular average per capita expenditure technique is an easy expedient which contains serious limitations, notably that the unique characteristics of the community are overlooked (Stinson 1981). The argument, however, is somewhat flawed. To address the "uniqueness" problem requires an inordinate amount of time and expense. An alternative is for local officials to base their estimates on the experiences of similar communities.

3. The notion of "quality of life," however difficult to define, is strongly associated with the local provision of services (Morse and McDowell 1982).

4. In contrast to the underassessment scenario are situations which encourage assessors to overvalue properties. Although state laws establish property tax rate ceilings, the local jurisdiction can collect more revenue from a given tax rate by merely increasing the assessment ratio. Similarly, state statutes may relate the amount of allowable borrowing by the locality to the value of taxable property in that locality. Thus, increasing the assessment ratio can alter the impact of these arrangements.

5. The debate is centered around whether rates in some states are excessive. Recent challenges on the constitutionality of some of these severance taxes (e.g., Montana, Louisiana) have reached the U.S. Supreme Court. The Court ruled in 1981 that such taxes are within the domain of the state's taxing authority, so long as the taxes are not overly discriminatory. The Court also refused to limit tax rates to those necessary to raise the funds to provide the additional government services required by the development project and its employees (Stinson and Temple 1983).

6. For discussions pro and con, see Krutilla and Fisher (1978); Gilmore (1976); Leistritz et al. (1981); Moore et al. (1979); Stinson (1978); Lamont et al. (1974); Gulley (1982); and Conrad and Hool (1980). The theoretical issue of resource exhaustion has yet to be demonstrated as an important mitigative

reason for severance taxes. Site-specific closings, however, are another matter.

7. There are essentially two basic types of intergovernmental aid programs: (1) formula and (2) discretionary. Formula programs are more important to local governments for their projection of revenues. The amount of funds received under formula aid is based upon verifiable information of some specified characteristic of the locality (e.g., population census, number of school children, amount of locally assessed value). Familiar programs of school aids and revenue-sharing are examples of formula aid. Discretionary programs, in constrast, allow limited basis for predicting future local government revenues. The disbursal of funds is merely at the discretion of those public officials in charge of the particular program. Examples of discretionary programs are grants from such federal or state agencies as the Economic Development Administration, Housing and Urban Development, Environmental Protection Agency, and state economic development departments. Although these grants are used to absorb some of the costs associated with rapid growth (particularly infrastructure construction), the aid level is dependent upon several factors including the "grantsmanship" ability of local governments, perception of need by the granting agency, and level of available funds.

8. The impacted community's access to capital includes such features as the community's bond rating, the interest rate at which it can market its debt, feasible amortization schedules, and marketable debt amount.

9. The major disadvantage these bonds carry in relation to other municipals is the weak character of their obligation. The highest quality bonds tend to be of the general obligation type, bonds which are backed by the full faith and credit of the issuer. Most "impact" bonds, however, cannot be considered true general obligation bonds because the tax base needed to repay them is not yet present. Thus, the most common impact bond is the revenue bond--a limited obligation bond in which the revenues from a government enterprise are pledged to repay a bond issued to improve or build such an enterprise.

10. Economic sectors may be directly or indirectly linked to the resource development project. Directly linked firms may either be input-supplying businesses (i.e., backward linked firms) or output-utilizing businesses (forward linked firms). Indirectly linked businesses generally include retail and service establishments.

11. An important matter to remember with regards to business formation is that financial capital is a necessary, but not sufficient, aspect in the economic development process. Without financial capital, business formation cannot occur, but often capital is only part of the problem. The presence of capital, for instance, cannot make up for deficiency in markets or management, or overcome the high costs of labor or land (Daniels 1982).

12. Capital market failure occurs for a number of reasons, necessitating some form of intervention (Shaffer 1983; Daniels and Kieschink 1979). When intervention is required, our bias is

towards having it as unobtrusive and of as short of duration as possible. There is also a bias towards interventionist schemes that provide the greatest level of return for the smallest investment made by government or industry.

13. Some banking critics, however, contend that small rural banks frequently are not successful in tapping these outside funds--an obvious restraint on their ability to meet local economic development needs (Staniforth and Haggard 1982).

14. Although financial resources are a major factor, other factors may lead to the dissolution of the business, such as lacking the needed management capacity to adapt and compete in the new market environment.

15. For a review of these common housing issues, including short-term shortages and supply lags, lack of choice, existence of a segmented housing market, and inappropriate unit and residential environment design, see Detomasi (1982).

16. Resource development companies have also utilized approaches to encourage the development of housing. Companies reduce the risk of construction financing by either assuming a contingent liability (e.g., co-signing construction loans, minimum price contract) or directly assuming up-front development costs (MacDonnell et al. 1982).

9 Planning for the Inevitable? Closure Issues in Resource Development

In the early 1980s, the small community of Parachute, Colorado underwent enormous growth when Exxon Corporation initiated development on a nearby $8 billion oil shale project. Later in May 1982, after the energy conglomerate had already invested over $2 billion in the Colony project including numerous community infrastructure items (e.g., schools, roads, street lights, recreation center, fire and police stations, shopping center), the oil shale development was abruptly cancelled. Many of Parachute's remaining 900 residents--down from a 1981 peak population of 4,000 people--still wait for that large-scale resource development project that may never arrive.

By contrast, the recent closure of Anaconda Company's copper mining-smelting operations in Butte and Anaconda, Montana, terminated an enterprise which had been the area's predominate employer for nearly a century. The closure resulted in a depressing impact on the communities' employment and income as well as on their ability to finance public services and maintain a viable fiscal position. Despite the numerous mitigation efforts and economic development activities initiated by both the company and communities, economic readjustment continues to be difficult (Halstead, Chase, and Leistritz 1983).

The above examples are illustrative of a recent type of impact phenomenon plaguing many resource communities--the closure of large-scale resource development projects. Recent attention has focused on the increasing number of large-scale manufacturing closures (Harrison and Bluestone 1982; Shapira 1983; Aronson and McKersie 1980). This recent spate of manufacturing closures has resulted in national attention being directed toward various mitigative issues ranging from macroindustrial policy and legislative restrictions to microeconomic recovery measures and manpower strategy responses.

Plant closures, however, have not been confined solely to the U.S. manufacturing sector. Recent years have seen extensive restructuring of certain economic sectors in many of the advanced industrialized countries (McKersie and Sengenberger 1983; Sweet 1981). A plethora of closures has occurred as a result of the economic restructuring in such sectors as textiles, steel, automobiles, and shipbuilding. The most widely publicized changes have occurred in the United States' steel industry (Buss and Redburn 1983; Bluestone and Harrison 1982), where 45 percent of the work force have been idled and 20 plants closed since 1977 (Miller 1984).

Public attention has also been drawn to recent closures and cancellations in natural-resource-based economies. Closures have occurred in both renewable resource systems (e.g., forestry, agriculture) and nonrenewable ones (e.g., mining, energy conversion). Five years ago, no one conceived that large-scale projects would be terminated at or near their completed construction stage. The sheer magnitude of investment in sunk costs alone in cancelling a resource development project is staggering. And yet, the heretofore incredible has become a reality. Since 1981, for example, Colony oil shale (Colorado), Washington Public Power Supply System (Washington), and Alsands heavy oil (Alberta) facilities were either substantially scaled down (i.e., "downsizing") or cancelled, leaving behind in each case an investment loss in excess of $1 billion.

Such events invariably raise questions about the extent of large-scale project closures and cancellations, the reasons behind and consequences of facility closures, and the strategies available for local economic recovery. However, only a modicum of research has been conducted on resource development closures in rural areas (McGinnis and Schua 1983; Keyes et al. 1982; Root 1982). In this chapter, we will survey the various issues involved with facility closures in resource development. In this overview, we will briefly review the incidence of facility closure, discuss the reasons why resource development projects terminate their operations, assess the various impacts of facility closure and associated job loss on communities and individuals, and finally, discuss the available mitigative strategies for economic recovery.

First, it is important to define terms. As used here, a facility *closing* refers to the cessation or disinvestment of operations where at least 50 persons will be (or were) permanently unemployed.[1] *Cancellations* occur when the owners, after deciding to construct a facility and making a significant commitment of resources to building the plant, subsequently reverse their decision to complete construction or place the facility in operation after construction. In contrast to abrupt terminations, *decommissioning* refers to that process by which facility closure is phased over a period of several months or even years. *Decommissioning* is often used in the context of military installations (Lynch 1970; Daicoff 1973; Shen 1980). These terms are graphically illustrated along a hypothetical time line (Figure 9.1). Since our principal concern is with large-scale resource developments, the focus lies with those closures and cancellations which have occurred in such economic sectors as forestry (Quinn 1979; Clawson 1980), agriculture (Bowen and Foster 1983), mining (DiNoto and Merk 1982; Hansen et al. 1981; Keyes et al. 1982), and energy conversion (Root 1982; Energy Information Administration 1983; McGinnis and Schua 1983).

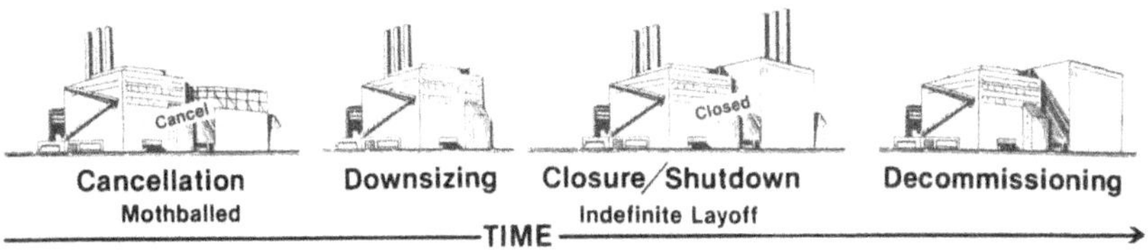

Figure 9.1. A graphical depiction of closure terminology

THE EXTENT OF FACILITY CLOSURE
IN RESOURCE COMMUNITIES

Although plant closings are becoming increasingly common, closures are not a new phenomenon. Economic history is replete with businesses which open and close. Indeed, businesses are constantly going through the life cycle of birth and death. For the most part, these changes occur gradually and affect small-scale enterprises. The inevitability of this economic process of "sifting and winnowing" is generally perceived as indicative of a dynamic, vibrant economy.

Industrialized societies are continually facing structural change. Within their economies are movements of industrial contraction and expansion, incidences of capital disinvestment and reinvestment, and the elimination and creation of jobs. These occurrences happen in various enterprises and sectors with varying scope and pace. The extent of structural change has been enormous with such visible economic dislocations as plant shutdowns, mass layoffs, and project cancellations. This concept of structural change was labeled by the eminent economist, Joseph Schumpeter, as the "process of creative destruction [and reinvestment] of capital" (Schumpeter 1942). In order for an economy to remain prosperous, it must undergo constant transformation, where capital is disinvested from less efficient enterprises for reinvestment in more productive ones. Such a process, however, does not occur smoothly, nor does structural change proceed evenly. Imbalances invariably develop, especially to the extent that expansion in growing industries, sectors, and regions may not be adequate compensation in the short or middle run for losses in contracting sectors and locations. Thus, this "process of creative destruction" has temporal and spatial dimensions (McKersie and Sengenberger 1983). In a temporal sense, this reinvestment of capital may not keep pace with capital disinvestment. Such dissynchronous developments are likely to occur when displacements emerge precipitously or abruptly. In addition, this destruction-creation process may not happen in the same location but may leave spatial imbalances across areas and regions. Consider, for example, the highly publicized business movement between the Frostbelt and Sunbelt in the United States. Although the older manufacturing states within the Northeast and Midwest have been afflicted by a vast number of plant closures, recent evidence indicates that no one region in the country is immune from such changes (Bluestone and Harrison 1982; Hekman and Strong 1980). David Birch, for example, states that the rate of job loss due to plant closings or contractions between 1969 and 1976 was about the same across regions (Birch 1979).[2]

In the United States, the information needed to understand the extent of the problem is lacking. No comprehensive data base exists at the federal or state level that tracks plant closings and the reasons for closure. Without hard data, it is rather difficult to support or deny the impression that economic dislocation is a widespread and spreading phenomenon (Schweke and Jones 1982). Faced with a growing problem, many states have begun to collect data on local business closures (e.g., California Employment Development Department 1983a; Shapira 1983). However, much key information is proprietary; employers are not obliged to inform the state or federal government of imminent closure. In this regard, the United States appears to be an exception compared with other industrialized nations, such as the United Kingdom, Sweden, Canada, and West Germany (Sweet 1981; Labor Union Study Tour Participants 1979). These countries require, as part of their business closure regulations, that corporate employers inform the government of impending closures, including economic reasons and the number of affected workers.

The dearth of closure data is also evident when one attempts to delineate the extent of closings for large-scale resource developments. As in the case of plant closing in urban areas, much of the resource development closure research is presented in case study format. There are, however, a couple of available exceptions--mining communities in Canada and nuclear power plants in the United States--that suggest that closures are both common and costly.

<u>Canadian Mining Communities</u>. The single-industry community is a prominent feature in many resource development regions in the advanced industrialized countries (Vatne 1981; Robinson 1982). In the resource-oriented economy of Canada, scores of communities exist to serve nearby forest, mining, power, and oil and gas developments. Researchers have identified about 160 of these resource-based communities, located beyond the continously settled parts of Canada (Robinson 1962; Bradbury 1979). A related study identified 142 communities as primarily dependent on metal and nonmetal mining, smelting, and refining (Department of Regional and Economic Expansion 1979). In 1982, a task force was established by Canadian federal, provincial, and territorial ministers to examine the special problems of communities dependent solely on the mining industry. While the task force's final report focuses on the effects of mine closure on these single-industry communities and possible mitigative strategies, it does include a comprehensive, albeit one-year, record of layoffs,

closures, and extended shutdowns in the Canadian mining industry (Keyes et al. 1982).[3] During the recessionary period of 1981-82, the closure of nearly 90 mines in Canada affected 59,000 direct workers. Approximately 20 percent of these workers were affected by permanent shutdowns.

Nuclear Power Plant Cancellations. In the United States, the first commercial order for a nuclear steam supply system (NSSS) was placed in 1953. By 1974, the electric utility industry had nearly 30,000 megawatts (Mw) of nuclear plant capacity licensed for commercial operation (Energy Information Administration 1983). That year also represented the high-water mark in terms of the industry's commitment to future additions of nuclear plant capacity, with orders placed for over 217,000 Mw exclusive of about 13,000 Mw which had been previously cancelled (Table 9.1).

TABLE 9.1.
U.S. commercial nuclear units ordered and cancelled, 1972-1982

Year	Orders Placed		Cancellations		Cumulative Orders	
	Number	Mw	Number	Mw	Number	Mw
Pre-1972	131	109,392	0	—	131	109,392
1972	38	41,315	7	6,117	162	144,590
1973	41	46,791	0	—	203	191,381
1974	28	33,263	7	7,216	224	217,428
1975	4	4,148	13	14,699	215	206,877
1976	3	3,804	1	1,150	217	209,531
1977	4	5,040	10	10,814	211	203,757
1978	2	2,240	14	14,487	199	191,510
1979	0	—	8	9,552	191	181,958
1980	0	—	16	18,001	175	163,957
1981	0	—	6	5,781	169	158,176
1982	0	—	18	21,937	151	136,239
Total	251	245,993	100	109,754	151	136,239

SOURCE: Energy Information Administration 1983.

The first cancellations of nuclear power units occurred in 1972. This marked the beginning of a trend which has continued up to the present. By the end of 1982, the industry had cancelled 100 plants at 56 sites, totaling nearly 110,000 Mw in lost electrical capacity and representing 45 percent of the total commercial NSSS capacity previously ordered. In contrast, only 39 fossil-fuel-fired units, totaling about 23,000 Mw, were cancelled during the same time period (Energy Information Administration 1983).

Initially, the utilities terminated only units that were in the early stages of planning, i.e., the "paper" plants. In recent years, nuclear units in the more advanced stages of development have been cancelled. By 1980, none of the plants underway were in the "paper" stage. Utilities were cancelling units where construction permits had been applied for and, in some cases, already granted by the Nuclear Regulatory Commission. The latest round of terminations have seen a number of plants well into construction being abandoned (McGinnis and Schua 1983; TVA 1982; *Time* 1984).

The costs associated with these nuclear power plant cancellations have been substantial. The Energy Information Administration (1983) has estimated that about $10 billion was expended on these 100 nuclear unit cancellations since 1972; this amount represents approximately 7 percent of all utility expenditures for power plant construction during that time. Most of these cancellation costs have been incurred since 1977, during which time 72 nuclear reactors were cancelled. Of these cancellations, over 40 units experienced abandonment costs of at least $50 million.

REASONS UNDERLYING FACILITY CLOSURE AND CANCELLATION

Resource development facilities close for a variety of reasons. With the number of factors that influence a business operation come myriad possible reasons why a facility closes. Usually, no single factor can be pointed to as the precipitating reason; rather facility closures occur because of a culmination of problems, many of which are economic in nature. In a study by the Congressional Budget Office (1982), a number of macroreasons for facility closures were cited, including restructuring of basic industries, continued lagging (or actual declining) in some industries, modernization of production through labor-saving technologies, and shifts in growth away from basic industries to energy, high-technology, and service sectors. Poor business climate in subnational entities is another major factor contributing to plant closings. This factor of poor business climate (or the "high cost of conducting business") is actually a euphemism that covers any number of business complaints and criticism that is illustrated by such restrictive state and local policies as environmental and work-related regulations, high taxes, and zoning regulations. Other factors cited as contributors in facility closures fall under the heading of corporate business strategy. Businesses, for example, may decide to disinvest in older facilities rather than upgrade them, to shift production machinery from old to new locations, or to reallocate financial resources away from less profitable enterprises into other more profitable uses.

Yet there exist other factors that are not so easily explained by economic forces. Although no all-inclusive list has been assembled, research has found a number of frequently cited reasons for facility closings (Mazza et al. 1982; Gordus et al. 1981; Hansen and Bentley 1981):

- •resource depletion
- •plant and equipment obsolescence
- •volatile commodity prices (e.g., long-term depressed)
- •inadequate capital investment
- •rising costs (e.g., labor, energy, taxes, transportation)
- •declining market demand
- •increased competition, both foreign and domestic
- •unmet profit expectations
- •discontinuance of product line
- •decline in productivity
- •mismanagement
- •poor long-term planning
- •government regulations
- •relocation of facilities
- •labor-management conflict

For some facilities, the reason for closure has been axiomatic--exhaustion of the economically extractable resource. This is a common malady that plagues substantial numbers of fossil fuel and metal-mining facilities. Mining companies realize that their prosperity rests on a declining and ultimately vanishing natural resource. In some cases, all available ore or fossil fuel has been extracted. There have been numerous examples throughout history of such mining facilities (Clawson 1980). In other cases, there still may be significant quantities of mineral-bearing rock in place, but due to mineral prices, mining costs, environmental regulations, taxes, technology, economic circumstances, the mining plan, and so forth, it may no longer be profitable to mine. In other words, the remaining reserves have become resources that are economically infeasible to extract, and the long-term prognosis may indicate no real improvement (Keyes et al. 1982).[4]

For other facilities, such as smelting operations, lumber mills, and electric power plants, the reasons have been less conspicuous. Consider, for example, the 1980 closure of copper smelting operations in Anaconda, Montana. Several reasons were postulated for the abrupt termination, including noncompliance with environmental regulations, increased cost of production, depressed mineral prices, technological obsolescence, and corporate policies (Halstead, Chase, and Leistritz 1983; Gold 1981; Bluestone and Harrison 1982).

Reasons Behind Nuclear Power Plant Cancellations. In their recent survey of nuclear reactor cancellations in the United States, the Energy Information Administration (1983) has attributed the dramatic reversal in nuclear generating capacity to five major underlying reasons. First, significant downward revision in forecasted load growth was the reason cited most frequently in the survey, being involved in about half of the units cancelled. Although this reason alone may not be sufficient for cancellation, a reduction in forecasted peak load growth in conjunction with other reasons (say, difficulty in financing new capacity) will make nuclear plant cancellation all the more attractive an option. Second, severe financial constraints have plagued many investor-owned utilities. During the last decade, most utilities were unable to earn acceptable rates of return, resulting in access to external capital being substantially limited. In light of such difficulties, many utilities adopted a strategy of restricting new investment to only those projects absolutely necessary to service near-term obligations. Nuclear plants, as such, became particularly vulnerable to cancellation due to their long lead times, high capital intensity, and the uncertainties shrouding their ultimate costs and completion dates. Third, nuclear power no longer offers a clear cost advantage in electrical generation. Unanticipated construction delays and substantial cost overruns, as typified by the Washington Public Power Supply System (WPPSS) nuclear reactor units have led some to question the competitiveness of the nuclear option. This relative decline in economic advantage, along with the perceived riskier investment, is behind the cancellation of several recent nuclear plants. Fourth, the regulatory environment, with its continuously changing regulations, licensing delays, and uncertainty regarding future standards, has substantially contributed to the cancellation of nearly 40 units. This reason can also create sufficient conditions for cancellations by increasing planning lead times and construction costs. Finally, state siting authorities forced the cancellation of six nuclear units by denying certification.

In summary, the reasons behind closure or cancellation, though numerous and complex, can be categorized into (1) macroeconomic forces, (2) subnational economic climate, and (3) corporate business strategy. Facility closures are symptomatic of profound changes occurring in the economies of industrial nations. The location of economic activity and methods of production have taken on global dimensions, and consumer preferences are changing.

All of these reasons combined produce an employment problem of significant proportions. Ultimately, the decision to close, relocate, or remain open *in situ* rests with management. This decision affecting the future of the business enterprise is essentially a private decision based on economic efficiency. However, such decisions are not made within a vacuum. Both the community and the individuals involved experience serious impacts from the decision to shut down a facility. These "rippling" effects will be elaborated next.

THE COSTS OF FACILITY CLOSURE

Economic dislocation differs significantly from other types of job and income loss in terms of both permanency and scale. Resources other than human labor (e.g., plant, machinery, raw material stocks) are either permanently removed or no longer available for production at a specific location. Dislocation has social and economic consequences because those who bear the costs and those who gain from the decision to shut down the facility are typically two distinctly different groups. Such decisions create distributional externalities, whereby various costs are borne by the dislocated workers and communities in which they live, while others may not only escape the costs entirely but actually experience an improvement in their economic well-being.[5]

Changes of the magnitude inherent in large-scale facility closures exert substantial impacts on the individuals and regions involved. In this section, the ramifications of closure will be analyzed from the perspective of the community and the individual, and in terms of both the economic and noneconomic effects.

Area and Community Consequences

The closure of a community's major industry will have a cluster of economic effects that emerges over time. The immediate, direct effects are quite visible with mass layoff of workers, a curtailment of discretionary spending income, and loss of tax revenues. The multiplier effect on employment may initiate a slow but steady process of decline in the community's economic base. In addition, there may be a short-run exodus of the skilled craftsmen which could impede the long-run re-establishment of local industries (McKersie and Sengenberger 1983). Finally, in small and single-sector (or single-company) communities with little economic diversity, the process of decline following closure may be practically irreversible (Vatne 1981; Clawson 1980).

Decline: A Community Impact Statement. When there is a facility closedown, the immediate and obvious effect is a loss of payroll. A related effect is loss of retail sales due to dimensioned spending, altered spending patterns, or even worse, exodus of workers and their families. This curtailment of spending by former wage earners is further aggravated by the discontinuance of local purchasing of goods and services by the closed facility. The combined effect is the loss of secondary jobs in the community, including trade, service, construction, transportation, and public services. When the local community reaches its new equilibrium, the multiplier effect will probably be seen to have taken its toll of one and one-half to two times the initial employment and income loss due to the facility closure (see Table 9.2).

Local governments may experience a revenue-expenditure squeeze resulting from a loss in property tax revenue because of the facility closure, tax delinquencies, population outmigration, and general decline in property values. Further losses to local governments may be incurred with declining sales tax revenues. At the same time, there is pressure to increase local government spending due to increased demand for certain services (e.g., welfare and social services) resulting from the facility closure, and increased expenditures for recruiting replacement industry.

In addition to the economic effects, a facility closure may seriously impair the quality of life within the community. There

TABLE 9.2.
Effects of closure on the community

Effects			
Direct	Indirect	Induced	Mitigating Influences
-Reduced salaries and wages of displaced workers	-Decreased retail purchases in community	-Increased demand for social services	-Level of transfer payments (pensions, unemployment compensation, severance pay, etc.)
-Loss of local supplier purchases	-Reduction of salaries in supplier firms	-Decreased employment in producer services	-Company grants
-Loss of property tax revenues	-Increased unemployment in community	-Decline in public sector expenditures	-Deferred or staggered layoffs
	-Loss of population		-Government forms of impact assistance
	-Increased tax burden for residents		

SOURCES: Bowen 1983; Morse 1983; Aronson and McKersie 1980.

is evidence that individuals experiencing job loss withdraw from community life (Gordus et al. 1981; Hansen and Bentley 1981). Thus, stricken communities experience reduced participation in such social organizations as churches and volunteer groups. This withdrawal dampens community vitality, weakens the social fabric, creates a dreary climate that encourages outmigration, and thus exacerbates community morbidity (McKersie and Sengenberger 1983).

The manifestations of social withdrawal listed above are merely the milder symptoms. Economic decline is also associated with social deviancy. In other words, one possible reaction to job loss is anomie. For example, a study by Harvey Brenner (1976) found that there was a direct correlation of increased unemployment rate with increased rates of homocide, mental illness, prison admissions, and suicide.

Estimating Magnitude of Economic Decline. While there has been a considerable surge of interest in the use of various types of socioeconomic impact assessment models to analyze the local and regional impact of large-scale resource developments (Hushak and Morse 1979; Leistritz and Murdock 1981), the current economic circumstances of closures and contractions should not diminish the need for sound and systematic analysis of local repercussions. In fact, it could be argued that there is an even more acute need for a sound analytical methodology which might provide some guidance to those public decision-makers faced with a major closure.

The all-important issue facing many public decision-makers and analysts is whether these growth-oriented models can simply be put into reverse to address economic decline and facility closure. In other words, if a facility closes, are the local economic and fiscal impacts simply the negative mirror image of the same facility opening? Or, to what extent does the economic multiplier hold true in declining situations?

Many case studies analyzing the economic impacts of closure have simply ignored the issue, assuming that the multiplier is equivalent in the bipolar situations of growth and decline (Ayer and Layton 1972; Bartholomew et al. 1977; Shen 1980; Bagshaw and Schnorbus 1980; Shapira 1983; DiNoto and Merk 1982). Other recent studies (Morse 1983; Bowen 1983; Brownrigg 1980; Batey and Maden 1983), however, contend that without appropriate modifications the mechanical and unthinking application of the growth-oriented multiplier will most likely overstate the implied economic effects of facility closure. The necessary adjustments include (1) public and private income maintenance programs (e.g., unemployment compensation, severance pay, early retirement, food stamps); (2) demand change for various public sector services from unemployed workers; (3) migration reaction of workers; and (4) reaction toward redundancy by indirect workers. The combined effect of these modifications is to reduce substantially the overall economic effect of the facility closure. Thus, the urgent necessity of addressing the real and hurtful problems of facility closure should not be taken as an excuse to avoid carrying out an objective and systematic evaluation of the situation.

Consequences of Job Loss on Individuals

Aside from the aggregate impacts of facility closure, individuals experience very personal effects of job loss. The vast majority of plant closure research has centered on the dislocated worker (e.g., Root 1979; Hansen et al. 1981; Berth and Reisner 1983; Congressional Budget Office 1982; Gordus et al. 1981), with the focus either on program impacts or the job search methods and re-employment experiences of workers. Many researchers concur--dislocated workers experience significant difficulties that not only are economic but cover the gamut of personal and social relationships. Even when overall statistics might suggest no real difficulties, it is more than likely that individuals will face severe transitional problems. In this section, we will address the impacts of job loss on individuals, both with respect to economic and noneconomic dimensions.

Economic Impacts on Individuals. The most concrete and visible impact of job loss is in the economic arena (McKersie and Sengenberger 1983). Workers are faced with the sudden and unexpected loss of their jobs; many experience substantial income loss. The severity of income loss varies depending on such factors as labor market characteristics (number of available jobs, occupational mix), personal characteristics (age, sex, skill level, work experience), and extent of mobility. The continuum of economic experience can be quite wide, ranging from a small number of workers who ultimately do better as a result of the change to a group that suffers from long-term unemployment. For this latter group, job loss could be catastrophic by leading to the loss of all savings and the forced sale of such capital items as automobiles and houses.

The loss in earnings experienced by the dislocated worker results not only from the initial layoff but also from lower earnings in subsequent jobs. Thus, the worker takes a capital loss in that the human capital developed for a particular situation cannot be marketed in like manner for the same value. Beyond human capital losses are other losses such as out-of-pocket expenses in employment search, moving expenses, and decline in value of housing (Hodge 1984).

Quality of Life Impacts on Individuals. Traditionally, job loss has been viewed as solely an economic phenomenon. An increasing body of information, however, leaves no doubt that the costs to the dislocated workers are more than economic. A number of researchers have investigated the problems experienced by individual workers and their families when faced with facility closings (Root 1979; Buss and Redburn 1983; Hansen et al. 1980; Grayson 1983), specifically how dislocated workers react behaviorally, psychologically, and physiologically to job loss. The individual response to job loss ranges over a wide spectrum, depending upon his or her adaptative capacity, i.e., the extent of economic resources available, existence of transferable skills, and access to a familial support system (Hansen and Bentley 1981). Job loss is one of the most stressful and disorienting of life changes and, consequently, can have devestating and long-term effects on the worker and his family. Common emotional reactions to termination notices are confusion, acute anxiety, anger, resentment, and a sense of worthlessness. The psychological reaction tends to follow a common pattern of sequential states: (1) initial shock with panic and anxiety; (2) defensive retreat, including denial, reality avoidance, and indifference; (3) acknowledgement; and (4) adaptation (Hansen and Bentley 1981).

It must be emphasized that the type, scale, timing, and context of facility closure are critical factors in explaining the magnitude and extent of consequences on the area and its workers, as well as determining the range of appropriate mitigative responses to address closure. The type of firm refers to (1) the enterprise's orientation, e.g., resource-dependent; and (2) industrial structure, e.g., unaffiliated independent, branch facility of multinational corporation. Closure scale refers to the percentage of the area's labor employed in the facility. There are at least two aspects of the timing of closure: one is the amount of lead time provided by the company to the community and the workers, and the other aspect involves the displacement pattern of the shutdown (e.g., whether everyone is displaced at once or there is a gradual reduction in force over time) (Root 1982). A final factor that influences both consequences and mitigative responses is the closure context. Such contextual aspects include local economic structure (e.g., single-company town, diversified economic base), community organization, and government intervention. In sum, the closure of a large-scale facility may have significant impacts on the area's communities and on their residents.

MITIGATIVE RESPONSES TO FACILITY CLOSURE

In this final section, we examine a broad spectrum of mitigative responses to closure ranging from purely remedial efforts that only deal with the consequences of economic dislocation to programs that are essentially preventive; that is, they deal with the potential of closure by preventing its occurrence. Underlying these various mitigative strategies are two competing philosophical approaches to economic policy.

On the one hand, there is the laissez-faire approach that embodies the belief that the free enterprise system along with reliance on market forces will produce the most efficient outcome in the process of economic adjustment. Any interference with the free mobility of capital and labor in response to market forces will inevitably impair an optimal resource allocation and prevent the best solution from occurring. Facilitating capital mobility is based on the premise that the gains from the economic change (e.g., facility closure) will more than compensate for the losses. Even though losers may not be compensated, society overall will be better off due to the economic change. In such an approach, jobs are not protected and the affected workers may not even be cushioned from the impact of closure. The United States most typifies the laissez-faire approach, though there has been growing concern about the consequences of closure even in the United States. Thus, a number of remedial programs have been recently instituted in the United States to help ameliorate the effects of closure on workers, firms, and communities.

In contrast, there is the government interventionist approach whereby jobs are protected and employment is stabilized. Such an equity strategy is justified on the grounds of trauma caused by job loss, i.e., workers affected by closure are adversely impacted through no fault of their own. Thus, policy programs utilized under the rubric of government intervention attempt to avert economic dislocation. Using an accounting stance (with different assumptions and explicit tradeoffs), such an approach concludes that if a facility closes down, the costs for those potentially involved would be higher than the overall gains benefiting the economy.[6]

In between these two bipolar approaches is one that seeks to emphasize the gains realized both from capital mobility and from protecting the workers (McKersie and Sengenberger 1983; Batt and Spring 1982). Underlying this approach is the belief that while economic change is inevitable and desirable, a pure market solution to change tends to produce social injury too high to be acceptable, or lead to a solution which places the burden of adjustment unilaterally on a particular group, thus creating socially inequitable results. For a more socially equitable distribution of costs and benefits of economic change, some intervention in the market place or some cooperative program is required that assists to ameliorate the consequences of facility closure for workers and communities (McKersie and Sengenberger 1983). This blending of the bipolar perspectives, called the integrative or synthesis approach, is implicit in the remaining discussion of various mitigative programs and responses to facility closure.

While the decision to close, remain open, or relocate the business establishment is a unilateral one, it does create a situation to which several groups must respond. Management, labor, local community leaders, and government agencies all have available to them a multiplicity of options for dealing with facility closures, some of which ameliorate the effects of economic dislocation, while other programs attempt to prevent the potential job loss. While management has a key role to play in mitigation, these other groups (i.e., labor, community, government) are in a position to make a significant contribution. In fact, no program for dealing with economic dislocation and readjustment can be successful without the participation of a variety of institutions representing this quadpartite. Each of these groups responds to facility closings based upon a set of assumptions concerning its rights and obligations, and perceptions as to the appropriate, permissible, or feasible point of action (Gordus et al. 1981).

Private Sector Initiatives

Management maintains that capital mobility is a fundamental tenet and efforts to restrict mobility are deemed both inappropriate and costly for business. Management has the right to make its own decision and publicize it at its own discretion. Once the decision has been made to relocate or close the facility, the policies selected by management can either facilitate or hinder the successful adaptation of workers and communities.

Efforts to Avoid Job Loss. Providing it can be done on some sensible basis, the best method to deal with potential job loss is to prevent its occurrence. Perhaps, the most suitable response for resource development firms is the phasing out of operations on a gradual basis so few, if any, individuals are actually terminated. Under this attrition strategy, jobs are eliminated only as people depart, either through natural attrition (e.g., employee turnover) or accelerated attrition (e.g., early retirement). Such an emphasis is at the heart of the approach taken in many European countries and Japan where economic change is implemented on a gradual basis and few if any workers lose their jobs (Sweet 1981; Batt and Spring 1982).

Another effort available to make the operations of the business more competitive is making appropriate changes to the enterprise's cost structure. Several variations on this theme exist including "rollbacks" in established wages and fringe benefits, and productivity improvements. Many of these measures stem from labor-management bargaining agreements. Both rollbacks and productivity improvements have the potential for lowering costs to the point that jobs that were in jeopardy can be saved at least in the short term, and perhaps even for a longer period of time.

Ameliorative Programs. Efforts directed to avoid job loss are generally taken early on, while programs to cushion the impending closure are essentially remedial. In many situations, the prospect of a facility shutdown must be confronted directly, and steps must be taken to ameliorate the impact of the change.

Prior research has indicated that plant closings can be exceedingly costly to corporations as well as to workers and communities. Buss and Redburn (1981, 1983), for example, contend that management has a vested interest in following a different strategy than the "cut-and-run" tactics typically employed. Plant closings have elicited public resentment which may lead to restrictive legislation. Assuming that management wishes to avoid further legal restrictions on their future decisions regarding capital mobility as well as minimizing their costs of closings, how should a firm go about shutting down a facility?

1. Preparing for a Closing. For many companies, there are no agreements in force with workers concerning company obligations for prenotification of a closing, re-employment assistance, retraining provision, severance pay, and health and social services provision. In order to meet the needs of management and workers, both parties may wish to negotiate in advance the rights and obligations of each prior, during, and after a facility closing (Buss and Redburn 1983). A related issue is the "decision bargaining" consultation between management and labor concerning a facility closing (Batt and Spring 1982). In spite of its controversial nature and recent court decisions,[7] some companies have felt that it was imperative to provide reasons to labor for closure and to negotiate steps to facilitate readjustment.

2. Advance Notice. Most observers (Gold 1981) advocate that management inform workers well in advance of a facility closing. Many recommend anywhere between six months to a full year's lead time for labor, so that workers have the opportunity to either search for new employment or to retrain. Employers can play an active role in the process. The notification periods are often short, however. Statistics show that only about 10 percent of collective bargaining agreements in the United States required any provision of prenotification, and the time requirement usually was only one week's notice or less. (Harrison and Bluestone 1982). Prior research has indicated that most resource development companies have provided little, if any, advance notification (Gold 1981; Keyes et al. 1982; DiNoto and Merk 1982; Hansen et al. 1980). These studies indicate that the advance notice requirement is a contentious issue with many companies, due to such concerns as deteriorating worker morale, loss in worker productivity, increased worker absenteeism, and loss of potential customers and investors to competitors. It would appear that three months would be ideal by providing an adequate period of time for concrete steps to be planned but not too long to provide a period of unproductiveness and idleness. If an early warning requirement may harm the company, management must seek other ways to offset the problems of closure.

3. Re-employment Responsibilities. Management closing facilities may assist workers in a variety of ways including job

counseling and motivation sessions, inter-company transfers, and reorientation programs. Several case studies have emphasized the need for dislocated workers to become active in the readjustment process (Berth and Reisner 1983; Buss and Redburn 1981; Hansen and Bentley 1981). Employees who have spent their entire working lives at one facility need assistance in developing skills for finding employment such as filling out job applications, preparing resumes, interviewing, and so forth.

Management may also assist workers in offering intercompany transfer opportunities. Previous findings, however, suggest that transfering to another geographical area is not a viable option for many dislocated workers (Batt and Spring 1982).

Another method companies can use to help workers is to act as an advocate in their contacts with other potential employers. The discharging company knows considerably more about the experience, skills, and other characteristics of their long-time employees than any other institution in the labor market. This is why employers in many European countries are charged with the responsibility of returning workers to the labor market in a state of readiness (Berth and Reisner 1983). Companies have, at their disposal, a wide range of employment-rostering devices that can be utilized to help identify opportunities and to direct dislocated workers along the right channels. Readjustment efforts may include such activities as acting as a job broker, sponsoring a job fair, or supporting a community organization which serves as a convening center for re-employment activities in the local labor market.

4. Retraining Responsibilities. Research has indicated that most retraining programs for dislocated workers in the United States have been either ineffective or otherwise undesirable (Buss and Redburn 1983). Training programs are often operated without knowledge of the skill requirements for local business or for firms which might locate in the community in the future. From the workers' perspective, training programs are also undesirable because many workers are reluctant to change occupations, especially when potential local opportunities are for lower-salaried jobs. Even so, management can supply private and public agencies with detailed information on the skills and occupational background of workers. This will help agencies to identify the groups of workers most amenable to retraining as well as the retraining programs most likely to lead to re-employment. Providing there is enough lead time, the "last employer" may implement their own in-house training programs to assist workers to take advantage of the local labor market. Such programs might provide retraining in jobs similar to those lost, or in different jobs altogether.

5. Compensation and Income Protection. The purpose of compensation is to provide financial support during the transition period. Designing an adequate, fair package of compensation benefits, however, is not easy. One essential requirement is to assure continuation of health insurance benefits for dislocated workers. Although companies can ill afford expensive fringe benefit packages once the facility closes, they could press

communities for the development of deferred payment plans for workers funded through a risk pool.

Another way management can reduce the impact of job loss on individual workers is to offer severance pay extending unemployment compensation benefits beyond the customary 26 weeks. Companies could place such payments in a fund to be paid to workers only after other benefits, including unemployment compensation, SUB pay (supplemental unemployment benefits), and TRA (Trade Readjustment Allowance, i.e., workers who lost their jobs because of foreign competition), are exhausted. The rationale behind severance pay is that it represents partial compensation for the loss of human capital that the worker has invested in his or her job. However, there are some difficulties with severance pay, namely it provides little incentive for workers to find another job, and some companies simply do not have the requisite funds.

In sum, management has at their disposal numerous methods to either avoid job losses or ameliorate the effects of facility closure. Prior research indicates that companies do have an incentive to behave in a socially responsible fashion out of profit and loss considerations (Buss and Redburn 1981, 1983; McKersie and Sengenberger 1983; Batt and Spring 1982). If firms take a proactive approach, the need for costly regulation may be minimized, the economy may retain its capacity to renew itself, and the costs to the company, workers, and the community may be substantially reduced.

Labor-Initiated Programs

Theoretically, unions have the option of negotiating during each contract round for shutdown provision. Unions have attempted, although often unsuccessfully, to secure access to the decision-making process of companies. By and large, unions assume that management has the right to close a facility, and thus, have directed most of their efforts toward obtaining a favorable closing process including early notification, employment continuity, income maintenance, adjustment assistance, and pension protection. Perhaps the greatest problem unions face in the advent of a closing is a contract that does not address the issue at all. Hence, unions must resort to *ad hoc* bargaining at the time of closing to forge a favorable agreement (AFL-CIO 1982; Gordus et al. 1981; Langerman et al. 1982).

Although there is a dearth of evidence about *ad hoc* bargaining at the time of closing, researchers have indicated, in a recent case study of mine closures, that the union was essentially rendered powerless in the wake of the decision (Hansen et al. 1980). Beyond ensuring that the terms of the contract were carried out (e.g., severance pay), the union demonstrated little leadership in encouraging or assisting in a community response or in launching other initiatives to aid the dislocated workers. The lack of positive union involvement in mine closures reflects the problems faced by unions and their general unpreparedness for coping with this phenomenon. Unions are obviously dependent on employed workers for their income; i.e., through payment of dues. When the source of jobs is eliminated, their membership effectively dries up, making it difficult for unions to maintain contact and deliver supportive services. Nevertheless, the group identity fostered by the union appears to be the most useful in various supportive services such as providing accurate information obtained from the company management, facilitating assistance in securing company benefits, and job search and training programs (Hansen et al. 1981).

Labor-Management Cooperation. Although the union's role has been relegated largely to negotiating transition arrangements for displaced workers, the union can become an important party in the readjustment process. Perhaps the best example of this active role comes from Canada where under the Manpower Consultative Service (MCS) the union becomes a formal party with management in the establishment of a local employment committee (Berth and Reisner 1983; Batt and Spring 1982). Participation by management and labor in forming a committee is voluntary, but these cooperative committees appear to have had considerable success. Of those dislocated workers who request committee assistance, some 65 percent are placed in new jobs with a cost per placement of under $100 (Berth and Reisner 1983). Although there are recognizable institutional and labor market differences between the United States and Canada, the key aspects of MCS could be profitably joined with other locally based labor-management cooperative arrangements.

Although some labor-management committees have helped to plan and implement readjustment programs for dislocated workers, it appears that this arrangement has not been sufficiently utilized. The union, for instance, knows as much or more about the needs and capabilities of the workers as any other agency. If the union is involved, the program will have more acceptability and credibility with the workers being served. In spite of their desire to become more involved in the readjustment process, unions often do not have the resources to assist dislocated workers, especially where dues income has been terminated and where there are no long-term collective bargaining opportunities. This is why the Canadian Manpower Consultative Service has been hailed as an idea whose time has come.

Worker Ownership. An increasingly popular alternative to stave off facility closure and worker dislocation is the labor-initiated employee-ownership strategy (Bluestone and Harrison 1982). Certain declining companies convert, with federal assistance, into wholly or partially employee-owned enterprises or possibly to enterprises owned jointly by their work forces and local communities. Such a strategy is seen as a potentially superior alternative, in certain cases, to the more usual subsidization or protective measures, and as a useful component of a national program of reindustrialization (Bradley and Gleb 1983). Complete or partial takeovers of certain firms is not an unnatural response to threatened closure; rather such responses, if appropriately aided by government, may provide a useful supplement to the current arsenal of industrial support policies.[8]

Worker ownership is defined as a form of industrial organization where at least part of the equity is owned by members of its work force who also assume a large degree of responsibility for the economic survival of their enterprise. This terminology might tend to obscure the large differences in ownership and control structures that vary between producer cooperatives, self-managed enterprises, and employee-owned businesses (Jones and Svejnar 1982; Bradley and Gleb 1983). The most common form of worker ownership in the United States is the Employee Stock Ownership Plan (ESOP), whereby a company deposits part of its profits in an employee trust fund. Eventually, these profits are vested in the workers who purchase shares of the trust either out of their current wages or from the company-paid, union pension fund (Bluestone and Harrison 1982). Recent federal legislation has provided technical and financial assistance to workers seeking to purchase existing enterprises (U.S. Senate 1980). From a narrow economic view, public policies to assist adjustment are preferred over those designed to preserve outmoded, archaic enterprises indefinitely.

There are several factors necessary for the success of a worker-owned enterprise, especially those firms that were purchased to prevent a threatened closure. These factors include (1) an adequate lead time of several months; (2) access to company information; (3) sources of financial capital; (4) a defendable feasibility study and operational plan; (5) worker education regarding rights, obligations, and expectations; (6) cooperation and support of the existing owners, union officials,[9] and local community; and (7) existing management expertise (Blasi and Whyte 1982). Few models of these worker-owned firms exist in the United States; most firms are urban-based manufacturing enterprises. Although only a small number of these employee-owned enterprises are resource-based (e.g., plywood companies), worker-ownership is a potential alternative to closures in resource developments.

The role of organized labor, constrained by the relative failure of collective bargaining to provide job security, has recently shifted its emphasis toward a closing-specific posture. Unions have engaged in aggressive *ad hoc* bargaining to extract as much adjustment assistance as possible. Organized labor has also vigorously supported the legislative enactment of those provisions that have not been achieved through collective bargaining. Although these reactions correspond to the normal range of union activities, the most positive assistance organized labor can make is in the area of building coalitions and achieving cooperative arrangements with management.

Community Responses

Rarely is a community prepared to manage the problems of an unexpected shutdown. In most cases, notification of the possible closure comes from a rumor circulating in the plant or from a local newspaper article. In the past, most communities responded passively when faced with a facility closure. Communities are now, however, taking a more active role in perceiving the problem, mobilizing and coordinating resources, formulating a plan of action, and implementing that plan.

Communities have a wide spectrum of available response strategies, ranging from anticipation of the facility closure and attempts to retain the firm to long-range economic development planning and economic recovery prospects. Thus, the components of a management framework for communities facing potential or actual closures are (1) anticipatory actions including early warning information systems and contingency plans; (2) short-term reactive response mechanisms such as strategies to avert the closure and mitigation of immediate effects; (3) economic recovery strategies including employment preservation and creation measures and financial assistance programs; and (4) long-term economic diversification plans, both vertical and horizontal diversification.

Anticipatory Actions. In an uncertain environment, communities must develop mechanisms which anticipate major facility closings. Such anticipatory actions include the development of early warning information systems as well as contingency plans should a closure occur. The utility of an early warning system lies in its ability to provide the community with the capacity to detect or intercept signals from the local economic environment in sufficient time to apply appropriate interventions (Buss and Redburn 1983). According to Mazza and associates (1982), there are three categories of early warning indicators communities can watch for: (1) changes in the company's market or marketing strategy; (2) changes in management behavior, investment patterns, and production programs; and (3) changes in the work force, reduction in personnel, and protracted labor-management disputes. Federal initiatives to assist communities in providing this capability have been designed (Nathanson 1980), but formal mechanisms have yet to be implemented and tested.

Communities should also have well-developed contingency plans for dealing with the potential impacts of a major facility closure. A coalition of labor, management, and community leaders can predetermine the steps to be taken should a closing be announced. The outcome of such a process is a set of formal agreements among the community's major institutions on how they will respond in a major closure situation.

Short-Term Reactive Measures. Perhaps the most difficult aspect of any community's mitigation efforts is acting promptly and decisively at the first signs of an imminent closure. Although ideally, the community ought to have contingency plans in place for dealing with closure impacts, more than likely these "best laid" plans will be left undone until the community is faced with a potential closure crisis. The principal requirement for crisis management in this setting is a rapidly deployed and well-coordinated response program consisting of an economic action coalition. This coalition usually serves in the capacity of either advisory and support or guidance and planning. Whether the economic action coalition acts in an advisory or directive manner, committee membership should be composed of a broad spectrum of parties that have a vested interest in the program's success, including the company, the union, the local government, the state government, the social service agencies, the banking community, the local educational system, the private industry council, the chamber of commerce, the religious community, and the local media (California Employment Development Department 1983b). Each of these parties offers a unique and essential area of expertise. This assemblage becomes the planning and implementing agent for the community's economic recovery.[10]

After the coalition is created, two sets of strategies can be pursued: strategies to avert a facility closing or, if this is not possible, mitigation strategies to ameliorate the most immediate effects of closure on the community. Although prevention should be the first avenue explored by the action coalition upon notification of an impending facility closure, in the majority of cases the announced closure is inevitable. In general, prevention is a viable strategy only if the facility is still turning a profit, if there is a stable demand for the product, if the firm is shutting down to relocate, or if there are feasible alternatives to the facility's present use. If any of these conditions exist, options available to retain the facility might include initiatives in local development finance, tax incentives, seeking new corporate ownership, and exploring employee ownership (Mazza et al. 1982; Vaughan 1980).

If prevention proves not to be a realistic option, the community's economic action coalition will need to institute various mitigation strategies to cushion the immediate effects of the closure. Crucial to impact mitigation is negotiating a beneficial closure agreement with management. As indicated above, the more gradual the closure (e.g., phased layoff, early retirement), the better the local economy and social services will readjust, and the better equipped the work force will be in handling the problem. Other immediate responses might include creating both an *ad hoc* community services program along with an employee services program. The community services program acts as a conduit in collating information on employee needs and problems and directing them to existing social service resources. Ideally, the employee services program ought to be comprehensive, offering such services as job counseling, retraining, and job search assistance. These programs, however valuable as crisis-response measures, do not serve as long-term solutions. The community must turn its energies and efforts to the development of various economic recovery strategies.

Economic Recovery Actions. Once it becomes certain that a facility will close, the aggravation of mounting problems can be prevented through an active policy of countering the losses that have occurred and strengthening the productive resources available locally. In order to accomplish the goal of creating new jobs, the community must take the initiative and devise a well-planned economic recovery program. Although the goals of job creation and long-term economic stability are axiomatic, there are a variety of available approaches from which to choose in attempting to achieve the desired goal.

In general, prior to selecting a strategy set, the community will need to carefully analyze their available resources--human, natural, capital, and so forth. Undoubtedly, such an examination will uncover the community's strengths and weaknesses, thereby influencing the design of the local economic recovery program.

There are two important dimensions by which to analyze the policy topic of economic recovery programs. The first relates to the target of the program, i.e., whether the emphasis is placed on creating jobs for those who have been recently dislocated from closed enterprises, or on creating jobs for those who have been unemployed for a substantial period of time. The second dimension relates to the stimulus and the source of financial support for the job creation. Ultimately, the auspices for the creation of jobs will be the private sector employer. Although government agencies by themselves do not create jobs, government can provide financial assistance (McKersie and Sengenberger 1983).

In light of these distinctions, an economic recovery program should be comprehensive, consisting of three strategic approaches: (1) improving the efficiency of existing businesses, (2) attracting new basic employers, and (3) encouraging business formation (Pulver 1983). Each of these approaches has its strengths and limitations, and for this reason most recovery plans should incorporate elements from all three approaches. Job creation efforts in the past have effectively utilized these approaches.

In order to improve the efficiency of existing firms, communities can assist businesses by offering educational programs on new technology, management capacity, and nonlocal marketing; by identifying new capital sources; improving work force quality; and developing community and regional facilities. The more efficient existing businesses are (hence, the more competitive they can be in their respective markets), the more net income and jobs they are able to return to the community.

Attracting new basic employers (i.e., manufacturing, nonmanufacturing, and nonlocal government) can be a risky undertaking, because it often requires substantial investment by the community. Communities frequently invest large sums of money in buildings, infrastructure improvements, or tax incentives, only to compete with each other for a limited number of branch or relocating businesses. Efforts to lure new businesses should proceed cautiously, weighing both the costs and benefits. If successful, attraction strategies have the overwhelming advantage of replacing substantial numbers of lost jobs. In addition, the attracted businesses are generally smaller than the closed plants, permitting the community to diversify its economic base while gaining new jobs. Attraction strategies include various support efforts such as site preparation, provision of requisite infrastructure, financial assistance, and directed marketing.

Research has indicated that small, young businesses can play a crucial role in generating replacement jobs (Birch 1979).

Encouraging business formation in the community can occur through organizing community capital resources, identifying and training entrepreneurs, providing programs of continuing advice and support (e.g., incubator centers), organizing product and market technical assistance, and providing a "one-stop" service center for licensing requirements.

The above three strategies form the basis for the community's comprehensive economic recovery program in job creation and income growth. Crucial to the success of the local economic recovery program is the provision of necessary financial resources. Adequate financing for development purposes is obtained from a variety of sources including local and nonlocal financial institutions, public sector resources (e.g., bonds, loans, grants), and public-private partnerships (see Chapter 8).

In attempting to assess whether these strategies are effective, one would need to take account of gross and net employment effects, dislocation effects, and other economic relationships. Nevertheless, a few comments are in order about the three above strategies. First, empirical research has indicated that some targeted job creation policies have been largely ineffective in directly assisting those workers being dislocated from their places of employment. Typically, what happens when new jobs are created in an area is that they go to younger workers in the labor market or to others who migrate into the area to take advantage of the new opportunities. The middle-aged and older workers, who represent the bulk of the dislocated workers, remain either unemployed or fill lower-paying positions in the labor market (McKersie and Sengenberger 1983).

Secondly, the jobs created in an economic recovery program may not represent long-term jobs. Firms may view the inducements to locate in a community and to create jobs as a type of asset that they deplete over a five- to ten-year period. At the end of this time, these "footloose" firms simply move to another community to capture another set of inducements.

Thirdly, the number of jobs created in small businesses represents a small fraction of the workers being dislocated. Despite the assertion that "small is beautiful," it is a fact of economic life that individually these small businesses do not generate many jobs (McKersie and Sengenberger 1983). Finally, the types of jobs (e.g., skill requirements, occupational mix) being created will help determine how many dislocated workers benefit. Essentially, the closer the linkage between the dislocated worker and the new job, the better the match. If, for instance, the newly created job is by a similar employer type, then the gap is not vast and the dislocated workers stand a good chance of being rehired. On the other hand, introduce a new employer type where the work is different and requires retraining, and chances of these new jobs benefitting the dislocated workers become meager (McKersie and Sengenberger 1983).

Long-Term Economic Diversification. Although most of the preceding job creation approaches are designed to stabilize the local economy in the short run, communities are faced in the long run with the prospect of restructuring their economies. In order for their economic future to be secure, communities must pass through a painful transition period to obtain eventual economic health. A program for restructuring the community's economy will help to counteract community vulnerability to economic downturns and facility closure by creating a new economic base which in the long run will be more diversified, stable, and self-renewable.

Economic diversification can be subdivided into two categories of activities, vertical and horizontal diversification (Keyes et al. 1982). Vertical diversification consists of those activities that are directly linked to the locally based facility. These economic linkages are vitally important for it is through this network of interdependent firms that growth is transmitted in the local economy. The supply of goods and services (i.e., *backward linkages*) to the facility and further processing of the facility's product (i.e., *forward linkages*) are examples of activities that fall into this category. Many small resource-based communities have poorly developed linkage networks (Vatne 1980). In addition, vertical activities may accentuate community dependence on its existing economic base. For this reason, they are usually not very effective in offsetting community problems associated with economic downturn or facility closure (Keyes et al. 1982). This is especially applicable to backward linkages. In contrast, forward-linked firms may not be as vulnerable to facility closure. A smelting operation, for instance, may continue to operate by utilizing concentrate from other mines, in spite of the local mine closure.

Horizontal diversification consists of activities that are independent of the local facility. These activities can continue largely unaffected by what happens to the local facility. Among the activities in this category is the development of other local resources for regional or export markets or the extension of locally provided goods and services to customers outside the community. Horizontal activities operate in parallel with facility-related activities, and thus reduce the vulnerability of communities to facility closures. A community that has survived through horizontal diversification is Bisbee, Arizona. Formerly dependent on mining, Bisbee is now a tourism, service, and retirement-oriented community (Francaviglia 1983).

There are a number of important factors for communities to consider in implementing diversification planning including careful analysis of the community's opportunity potential (resource endowment, accessibility, location); amount of advance notice of impending closure; designation of a local agency or group with overall responsibility for diversification; involvement of senior government in terms of attitudes, programs, and financial resources; and access to financial and other resources (Keyes et al. 1982). Prudent consideration of these factors will assist the community in not excessively relying on diversification to alleviate the problems associated with closure. The usefulness of diversification is limited by (1) local job replacement, (2) local skill requirements, and (3) timing uncertainty. While diversification may reduce the community's dependency on the facility, rarely will it counterbalance the dominant role played by the facility in the local economy. In addition, without extensive retraining and alternative skill development, diversification activities are not likely to be an effective sponge for absorbing the dislocated workers. Finally, there is little confidence that diversification opportunities will coincide with the facility closure.

Despite such limitations, economic diversification is still an important tool for dealing with the problems of communities facing facility closure. In addition to reducing community vulnerability, it can assist in strengthening the social fabric. A diversified economic and social structure provides residents with a wider set of employment and lifestyle choices. Although the immediate consequence of a closure is a glut of unemployed workers, a more diversified economy provides individuals with the prospect of employment alternatives, and hence, reasons for staying in the community to pursue those alternatives (Keyes et al. 1982).

In summary, the community has a wide range of available mitigative responses, both reactive and proactive, for use in facing a facility closure. An additional perspective on mitigative measures stems from the particular circumstances of any given community. Local economic features, in fact, play a significant role in the design and success of community response strategies. Such features include the degree of community dependency on the facility, the level of diversity in the local economy, current economic conditions (i.e., economic stability or crisis), and single closure or multiple closures in unrelated industries. These conditions are important to consider during the initial planning stages of a local economic development effort.

Government Responses

Government initiatives consist of activities that aim to facilitate community and worker adjustment through early notification legislation, provisions for continuity of employment, maintenance of income, and the offering of various services that will make for a smooth economic transition and rapid re-employment.

Mitigative Legislation. Legislative initiatives concerning plant closures stem in part from a rejection of the argument regarding unrestricted capital mobility. While most legislators, community officials, and (even) labor leaders would continue to accord management the prerogative of closure decision, there is a growing movement to restrain management's unilateral investment and disinvestment decisions and the timing of disclosure. Over the past ten years, a great deal of political activity in the United States has centered on the issue of plant closings. Although this activity has not been successful in passing legislation on the national level, workers have been enabled to buy facilities threatened with closure through broader legislation (i.e., U.S. Small Business and Employee Ownership Act of 1980). Efforts at the state level have been more successful, but existing state statutes (Maine, Michigan, Wisconsin) are considered relatively weak. Other states are reluctant to pass legislation due to the potential negative effect on business climate.

Key features of the proposed remedies include advance notice of 6 to 12 months, depending upon the number of employees; severance and other payments for income and benefit protection; community impact statements; assistance funds for community adjustment; government assistance to business concerns (e.g., economic and technical assistance to keep a facility from closing); and assistance to dislocated workers for retraining. These proposed legislative provisions for economic adjustment for communities, businesses, and workers have evoked considerable debate over such issues as cost effectiveness, corporate social responsibility, government control, and economic liberty (Bluestone and Harrison 1982; Foltman 1982; McKenzie 1982).

The successful management of facility closings in some European countries has served as a leading source of program and policy models for many political officials, labor leaders, and community activists in the United States. Most European countries, in contrast to the United States, have some form of legislation intended to mitigate the hardships following a facility closing. The European legislation has generally provided an active and helpful approach for dislocated workers, with the keystone being early notification, which enables workers to make the necessary adjustment more easily. The government also plays a major role by expeditiously providing compensation, services, and transitional assistance (Gordus et al. 1981).

Readjustment Programs and Agencies. A large variety of programs involving training, placement, or job search assistance have been undertaken by the United States during the last 20 years. In the recent past, the basic program for targeting federal monies to the economically disadvantaged was the Comprehensive Employment and Training Act (CETA). This program, however, offered very few services to dislocated workers and provided little flexibility for localities to initiate new programs according to preferences or needs.

In 1983, the Job Training Partnership Act (JTPA) replaced CETA as the nation's basic employment and training program. Among the most important provisions of JTPA is Title III, which for the first time puts into place a national employment and training program focused on dislocated workers. Through this Title III, state governments receive substantial resources and responsibilities for carrying out programs for the re-employment of dislocated workers.

One innovative state program is the California Economic Adjustment Team (CEAT), an interagency group that organizes dislocation responses. CEAT provides rapid state response to facility closures and is capable of assisting local communities in marshalling responses to assist workers, communities, and affected firms. The responsibilities of CEAT include providing technical assistance to help communities develop coordinated economic adjustment plans and identify available state and federal resources for worker adjustment (California Employment Development

Department 1983b; Berth and Reisner 1983). The basic vehicle for the provision of services to workers is the re-employment center, with such services as skills transference, intensive job development and placement, retraining, and job search workshops. In general, CEAT discovered it is most effective as a catalyst, bringing together the affected company, labor, and community representatives who in turn organize and administer a worker adjustment program. This enables the state to concentrate on providing technical and financial assistance to the local coalition (Fedrau 1982).

Most existing institutionalized placement programs have not been successful in assisting dislocated workers (Batt and Spring 1982; Aronson and McKersie 1980). Most state employment agencies do not have the necessary funds or expertise to handle the special demands imposed by dislocated workers. Often, these workers find themselves combined with other groups regularly served by employment services. Clearly, these employment agencies need to develop responses tailored to large-scale work force dislocations.

Finally, income replacement programs have been found to be double-edged. Undoubtedly, dislocated workers' lost incomes must be replaced to some extent. And yet, previous research has indicated that income maintenance impedes worker adjustment, although some workers clearly use the cushion of income replacement to search for, and find, better jobs (Berth and Reisner 1983).

Unless some explicit steps are taken, labor market services for dislocated workers in the United States will, by and large, continue to remain inadequate. An effective program for dislocated workers should consist of several essential features including (1) public-private coalition of employer, labor, and community; (2) early and locally led involvement; (3) flexible reallocation of resources to emerging situations; (4) coordination of resources, services, and activities (e.g., a clearinghouse or "one-stop" center); (5) a catalytic and supportive role for local efforts; and (6) a comprehensive and long-term perspective. A program with these characteristics must deliver specific services in specific contexts. Service delivery should not only be dictated by the particular situation, but also by those who know the workers, their potential, and the job opportunities in the local area.

CONCLUSION

It is essential to recognize that facility closures are an economic fact of life. As one reviews prior economic history, impermanence is more striking than permanence. In our preoccupation with the growth-oriented present, we casually assume that what we know will continue, even indefinitely. Perhaps, but statistical experience is against any such easy assumption (Clawson 1980). Such impermanence is amply evident in resource-based developments where ephemeral mining towns and lumber camps are common. Even though the ultimate exhaustion of economically extractable resource is inevitable, the timing is often uncertain.

The starting point of any management program is to develop and maintain a capacity to anticipate and respond to a potential facility closing. It is essential to recognize that an adjustment program should treat facility closures as emergencies that are both predictable and natural in a changing economy. By preparing for the inevitable, it is possible to soften the adverse effects for individuals and communities. Proactive planning has been shown to be the key to effective and equitable management of facility closures. Unfortunately, we often give attention to this only when the next crisis emerges and then we tend to scramble only to muddle through.

NOTES

1. The closure literature has certainly spawned its own share of jargon. Facility closings are described with such assorted terms as *shutdowns* (Buss and Redburn 1983), *rundowns* (Habitat North, Inc. 1979), *rampdowns* (McGinnis and Schua 1983), *slowdowns* (Planning Center 1982), and *mass layoffs* (Fedrau 1982). In this chapter, we use the terms *closures*, *shutdowns*, and *closings* interchangeably.

2. Although business closings and contractions are equivalent, regions vary markedly in their ability to replace these lost jobs. Net job creation has, by and large, been greater in the Sunbelt than in the Frostbelt. For further information, see Birch 1979; Bluestone and Harrison 1980; Armington and Odle 1982; Armington 1983; and Schweke and Friedman 1983.

3. The task force distinguishes between layoffs, extended shutdowns, and closures. Basically, layoffs and extended (or indefinite) shutdowns are temporary in nature caused by cyclical swings in the mineral markets, whereas closures are permanent due to structural problems.

4. Mining, perhaps more than any other industry, is subject to regular fluctuations of activity. Given its susceptibility to cyclical swings in mineral markets, mining has been characterized as a classic "boom-bust" industry (Clawson 1980). Recent case studies of mining closures aptly illustrate the volatility of the industry (Michels 1980; Gulliford 1983; Keyes et al. 1982; DiNoto and Merk 1982; Ayer and Layton 1972; Hansen et al. 1980).

5. Under the prevailing rules, there is no obligation of the "gainers" to compensate the "losers." If, however, there are rule changes (i.e., changes in public policies or programs), such changes need to be based on knowledge of the extent and nature of problems associated with facility closure.

6. In the debate over facility closings, the cases made for and against government intervention have been increasingly heard. Principal spokesmen for these two ideologies of laissez-faire and prevention are respectively McKenzie (1982) and Bluestone and Harrison (1982).

7. The U.S. Supreme Court, in the 1981 Broadway Maintenance Corporation case, struck down a lower court decision that the company was required to bring entrepreneurial decisions within the sphere of collective bargaining (Batt and Spring 1982).

8. Worker capitalism arouses emotions over a broad range of the political spectrum. It should be stressed that the rationale behind the inclusion of such a seemingly radical suggestion is not ideological. Neither need it hinge on any assumed long-term superiority of the employee-ownership form over the more conventional ownership-management structures in terms of productive efficiency. On this issue, the adopted stance is mildly positive--at least in intent.

9. Although most of the U.S. firms taken over by workers were unionized, union leaders at the national level have been circumspect, adopting a "wait and see" attitude towards the change of ownership, and generally unwilling, if not openly hostile, towards extending themselves to help. Their greatest concern has been over the dismantling of often hard-won pension provisions as the basic source of capital for financing the buy-out. Additionally, the traditional adversarial relationship between labor and management is muted when workers own the plant. How, they ask, can unionists collectively bargain with themselves? (Bluestone and Harrison 1982).

10. There are two general models of these economic action coalitions: the public-private model, where the tripartite of company, union, and government assist in the design, funding, and implementation of the plan; and the community model, where the community generally plays the principle role, while company participation is minimal or nonexistent.

10
Summary, Conclusions, and Future Directions

In this volume, we have attempted to provide a broad overview of impact management. This has included a discussion of general principles, processes, and approaches to impact management as well as detailed case study examples of such efforts. In this final chapter, we briefly summarize the work, discuss some of the broad conclusions and generalizations that emerge from such an analysis of the impact management process, and outline some of the future policy and research analyses that we believe are essential to the establishment of a useful and empirically based field of impact management.

SUMMARY

Chapter One presents both an overview of the context of impact management and the focus and limitations of the volume. This chapter describes the historical and legislative precedents of impact management, a process essential in rural areas because of the magnitude of resource developments relative to the capacity of affected communities. It indicates the utility of impact management for developers, the residents of communities in impacted areas, and the society at large. The chapter delineates impact management as a broadly based process requiring theoretical guidance and involving a wide range of considerations, such as public participation, service provision, financing, assessment, and monitoring. Finally, it points to the focus of the book as being on the conceptual, methodological, and implementation dimensions of impact management as it relates to large-scale resource developments in rural areas of the United States and Canada.

Chapter Two examines the role of theoretical perspectives of the social sciences in the impact management process. This chapter emphasizes that such perspectives can assist the analyst in better understanding the context of impact management and in designing more effective impact management plans. Although numerous perspectives might have been used, the discussion focuses on the utility of three sets--functional, ecological and systems theories; conflict theories; and exchange theories--for providing alternative explanations for key impact management events. We suggest that the use of such theoretical perspectives can assist in resolving such key issues as how impact areas should be delineated, who should be involved in the management process, the nature of the processes likely to characterize impact management, the probable reactions of local residents to project-related changes, and what mechanisms may be most effective in impact mitigation. The chapter concludes with the premise that additional theoretical development is essential for the advancement of the field of impact management.

Chapter Three describes means to assess what level of management may be necessary for a given impact situation. The chapter reviews some key dimensions that affect the magnitude of impacts and describes factors that must be examined in the preproject and project-development phases. In addition, it presents an overview of findings from analyses of impacted areas that bear on major dimensions of a project's impacts and describes how such knowledge can be used in conjunction with information on a project's characteristics to discern the general magnitude of impacts likely to occur in a siting area. The chapter thus provides an admittedly abbreviated introduction to impact assessment and evaluation--key preliminary steps in the formulation of an impact management plan.

The fourth chapter examines one of the most difficult dimensions of impact management--public participation. The chapter examines the importance of the participation process for both the developer and the public and the difficulties each may encounter in achieving their objectives. Chapter Four also presents several case studies that identify the difficulties encountered in past public participation efforts for large-scale developments, and examines several approaches which have been recommended. Finally, the chapter stresses that the public participation process is one that is likely to be most effective, both for the developer and the citizens of impacted areas, if it is initiated early in the development cycle and takes place in a context of mutual trust and open sharing of information.

Chapter Five examines the alternative roles of legal and formal (institutional) impact management mechanisms. The chapter presents an overview of some existing siting laws and ordinances, discusses several systems to enhance the availability of revenues for impact management (such as severance taxes and trust funds), and describes alternative approaches for impact compensation, monitoring, and arbitration. The chapter provides numerous case study examples of these approaches. The examples clearly point to the reality that institutional mechanisms must be tailored to reflect the unique legislative, jurisdictional, project, and management characteristics affecting each impacted area.

The sixth chapter reviews means of reducing the impacts of a project by reducing the number of project-related inmigrants who are the major source of socioeconomic impacts. This chapter examines factors that affect the number and the characteristics of these inmigrants. It then evaluates the feasibility of several approaches for decreasing the number of inmigrants including such steps as altering the project's construction schedule, increasing local-hiring rates, increasing commuting to the site from distant areas, and providing on-site housing. The chapter highlights the fact that careful attention to such dimensions can alleviate the difficulties entailed in impact management by eliminating the very source of impacts.

Chapter Seven examines means of enhancing communities' capabilities to manage impacts. The chapter analyzes means for organizing community residents to become involved in impact management and examines major management areas likely to require extensive community efforts. The areas examined include the provision of housing, education, law enforcement, medical services, and social services. The chapter emphasizes that among the keys to the effective management of such needs in impacted areas are careful planning and close cooperation between the public and private sectors.

Chapter Eight presents an overview of alternatives for financing impact management. The chapter describes the problems likely to be encountered by public and private concerns attempting to obtain financing during periods of rapid growth. It overviews alternative financing programs and sources, and discusses the advantages and disadvantages of each. The chapter emphasizes that the financing problems encountered during rapid growth often require solutions that involve unique partnerships between local, state (or provincial), and federal government concerns, private financial institutions, and developers.

Chapter Nine discusses the difficulties entailed in the closure of a facility. The chapter describes the factors that affect the nature of the impacts experienced during a project's termination as well as alternatives for alleviating the impacts of project closure. A central premise of this chapter is that the closure phase of a project is one that must be recognized and planned rather than ignored. The chapter stresses that only through careful planning can the impacts of this nearly inevitable stage of a project be successfully managed.

These nine chapters address many of the critical dimensions of impact management. Together, we hope these chapters provide a useful overview of impact management that can be used by practitioners, policymakers, and researchers.

GENERALIZATIONS AND CONCLUSIONS

Any attempt to draw conclusions from an analysis of a process that is as specific to given sites and circumstances as that of impact management must be completed with clear recognition of the limitations of such an attempt. The generalizations presented here are thus only some of the many that might be drawn concerning impact management and admittedly reflect the authors' biases and perspectives. They are ones, however, that we believe merit special consideration.

One generalization that we believe merits emphasis is that managing the impacts of rural resource developments is a unique process reflecting circumstances that may also be unique. Although many general principles of management and planning apply to impact management in rural areas as well as urban areas, many others do not.

This generalization is, of course, central to the premises underlying the development of this volume, but the case studies and analyses presented in the volume clearly reinforce these premises. The level of infrastructure development, the availability of full-time management and planning personnel, and the level of private sector development in rural areas are simply not sufficient to handle the problems likely to be encountered when developing a large-scale project in a rural area. As a result, problems such as inadequate housing and public services, the lack of adequate institutional means for dealing with rapid growth, inadequate financing for both traditional economic sectors and new growth sectors, and a lack of mechanisms for appropriate public participation occur more frequently in rural than in urban development situations.

This fact must be emphasized because the greater likelihood of difficulties in such situations requires more effective anticipation and management of such problems. The fact that such problems are more endemic in situations involving large-scale developments in rural areas will hopefully lead to the recognition that the management of such developments must be a proactive, rather than a reactive, process. The content of this volume clearly suggests that the most negative results have occurred when the impacts of such developments have not been anticipated. In sum, the option of choosing not to manage such processes is often one of limited utility when a large-scale project is to be developed in a rural area.

A second generalization that is evident from the discussion in this volume is that the characteristics of the project, of the siting area and its residents, of the inmigrating work force, and of the legal, governmental, and management context of impact management tend to be site specific. This generalization does not negate the importance of general knowledge of impact management principles, but it clearly asserts the importance of tailoring these principles to the unique characteristics of the area to which they are to be applied. The analysis reported here supports the importance of gaining thorough familiarity with a given project and its siting area and of involving local residents who possess extensive historical knowledge of local social, economic, and cultural conditions in the management process.

The two generalizations noted above are closely related to a third. The characteristics of large-scale projects in rural areas not only involve unique circumstances, they often require unusual levels of cooperation among government, the residents of impacted areas and the larger society, private developers, and labor. Attempts to alleviate the impacts of a development by limiting the inmigration of workers, for example, may require that developers utilize and finance employee training programs, that local governments or similar entities assist in identifying eligible employees, that residents train for such employment, and that labor organizations relax initial hiring restrictions to allow locals to be hired for project-related jobs. The need for the integration of multiple interests toward the solution of common problems must be recognized by all parties involved in impact management.

The fourth generalization is again one that reflects a major premise behind the development of this volume, but it is clearly re-emphasized by the discussion and analysis reported in the effort: the field of impact management requires substantial systematization, conceptual development, and empirical analyses. The area is, in fact, one which can perhaps only optimistically be deemed a field. There are simply few analyses that identify the relative advantages and disadvantages of different types of public participation processes, different forms of financing, or different types of public service provision. In like manner, there has been virtually no conceptual guidance provided for understanding or interpreting the impact management process. Much of the literature in the area has simply involved a chronicling of actions taken to resolve the problems occurring in diverse locations. The skills of academics, policy analysts, and planners must thus be brought to bear to ensure that the critical decisions that must be made during the impact management process are theoretically and methodologically informed.

These generalizations thus reassert that impact management is essential in rural areas undergoing large-scale developments, that the field of impact management is in need of extensive development, and that the area is one in which traditional approaches to resolving problems must be supplemented, and in some cases supplanted, by new approaches that bridge the gaps between traditionally distinct interest groups. These generalizations suggest that the area of impact management is indeed an area meriting the concern and attention of researchers, policy analysts, and decision-makers.

FUTURE DIRECTIONS

Impact management is both a pragmatic process and an area of empirical and conceptual research analyses. In this final section, we discuss some of the research and policy areas requiring additional attention. As with the discussion of generalizations, this discussion delineates only some of the many policy issues and research areas that might be examined.

The research issues related to impact management are both general and specific. Several general topics are discussed first followed by an examination of specific research needs.

One general research need in impact management is also endemic to most areas of social science--that is, the need for additional research that is both longitudinal and inclusive of additional geographic, social, economic, and cultural locales. Although the need for such multisite and longitudinal analyses is noted in nearly every social science study, such efforts are essential in impact management. Only if the effects of different management processes can be assessed in different locales, over extended periods, will it be possible to discern which impact management approaches are most useful. Presently, the evidence concerning impact management has been taken largely from sites that are in the construction or early operational phases of project development or from projects that have experienced premature closure. Findings from projects in multiple areas that have experienced the full cycle of impact events are necessary to identify those factors with major effects on management decisions.

Another area requiring attention is that of the analysis of the basic values underlying alternative approaches to impact management. One of the realities in impact management is that nearly every process enacted reflects a given value emphasis. Thus actions often appear to favor development or preservation of the existing area, to be prodeveloper, proenvironmentalists, or to reflect a procommunity bias and perspective. We are aware, for example, that the discussion in this volume sometimes reflects one or the other of these perspectives. Impact management is in need of substantial research to establish the range of such perspectives and the value structures that foster each. Although recommending such analysis may seem unusual, given our scientific emphasis, the fact that the impact management process is, at present, so imbued with implicit value-oriented actions makes it essential that these values be delineated and made explicit. As in other applications of analysis (see Peters 1983), the purpose is not to discredit any given value position nor to eliminate the roles that value structures play in impact management, because the elimination of these positions is neither desirable nor possible. Rather, the intent should be to make these positions explicit and to identify more effectively the interests that should be involved in the impact management process.

There is an equally critical need for basic conceptual development. Chapter Two attempts to provide an initial example of the need for, and utility of, theory in impact management, but much more extensive development is required. Thus, the utility of additional perspectives, such as those from classical economics and those bearing on political behavior, as well as additional social theories, should be examined. In like manner, the application of such theories must go beyond the stage of demonstrating their likely utility to the formulation and testing of specific hypotheses derived from such theories. This need for conceptual development is clear and extensive.

A final, general research need is for basic evaluation studies of the feasibility and effectiveness of alternative procedures in each of the major dimensions of impact management. It is essential to know which techniques for limiting the number of inmigrating workers, which institutional mechanisms, which methods of housing and service provision, which methods of financing, and which closure policies are most efficient and effective and under what circumstances each can be applied most appropriately. Such basic evaluations are essential to the area of impact management and are necessary to move the field toward an empirical basis and away from speculation and supposition.

The specific research needs of the area are also numerous. It is essential, for example, to more clearly establish the linkages between project, area, and inmigrant characteristics and the levels of project-related impacts. Although these represent basic research dimensions for the entire field of impact analysis (Murdock and Leistritz 1979; Leistritz and Murdock 1981), they are also central to impact management. Better knowledge is needed of how the level of impacts experienced by an area is affected by such factors as project timing, construction work force size, alternative types of employee training programs, worker characteristics, and different forms of community service structures. Research to establish such relationships is critical to impact management as well as to the general field of impact analysis.

Equally pressing needs occur in the area of public participation. Democratic ideals have led social science analysts to *assume* that the more extensive the level of public participation, the better the results of the process for all concerned. There is, however, limited empirical support for this supposition. It is not clear, for example, whether "the public" or specific interest groups are best served by such programs. In like manner, limited information is available on the effects on participation programs of such factors as the timing of their initiation, the nature of participants, and the length of the participation period. Thus, our knowledge base concerning the participation process must be moved from one based on idealism to one based on empirical research.

In like manner, additional information is required on what levels and types of intergovernmental mechanisms should be initiated to resolve impact management problems, what levels of jurisdictions can most effectively manage given types of problems, and the relative advantages and disadvantages of different forms of compensation and mitigation. How such factors are affected by different types of local legal, economic, social, and cultural contexts must also be established. Additional research is thus required on institutional mechanisms in impact management.

There is also a critical need for additional research bearing on the reduction of the size of the inmigrating work force. Additional research is needed on employment and income multipliers and on the timing of secondary employment growth that is likely to occur in impacted areas. In addition, more extensive analyses of the costs of employee training, employee turnover, developer-supported commuting and housing programs, and similar factors are necessary to provide better bases for decision-making.

Similarly, additional research is needed on the provision of housing and services in rural areas. For example, the information base is limited in regard to the long-term effects of different housing policies. What are the types of housing and service programs that can most effectively serve sparsely settled rural populations, and what are the costs and benefits of given programs? In fact, basic data on rural services that are comparable from jurisdiction to jurisdiction across states are difficult to obtain for small rural areas. Additional research is thus critical in order that the bases from which impact management is to be initiated can be known.

In regard to impact management financing, numerous research needs are evident. Additional analysis of the implications of local versus regional financing programs, of the uses of alternative mineral and other taxation systems, and of the different plans for sharing financing responsibilities must be completed. It is particularly critical to conduct research to establish the role that uncertainty plays in financing institutions' decisions concerning investments in rural rapid-growth areas and to focus greater attention on the problems encountered by the private sector in obtaining financing during periods of rapid growth. These and similar areas of research are necessary to establish the basis for more responsive financing programs.

Analyses of the effects of project closure clearly require additional attention, but the data on such effects are very limited. Available information must be supplemented by analyses of historical cases from around the world. Only when a sound base of information has been established will it be possible to discern the common elements in such cases and the more general effects of project closure. In this area, nearly all dimensions require additional analyses.

Finally, there is a critical need for additional creativity to be shown in the development of policies to overcome the factors that limit the effectiveness of impact management programs. It is essential, for example, to develop mechanisms to overcome the jurisdictional infighting and jealousies that often inhibit the management process. Because the boundaries of impact areas often do not coincide with jurisdictional boundaries, means to effect better cooperation among jurisdictions are necessary. In like manner, attention should be given to the development of means to expedite cooperation between the public and private sectors in rapid-growth areas. The limited resources of rural areas often necessitate combining the resources of the public and private sectors to solve problems. In sum, it is essential that traditional policy patterns be re-evaluated as to their appropriateness in rapidly growing rural areas. The willingness to consider new approaches and to allow for different organizational arrangements is an important step toward the resolution of the problems inherent in impact management in rural areas.

Both the general and the specific research needs of impact management are thus extensive. The field's growth as a pragmatic set of activities has proceeded using the available knowledge base. Unfortunately, that base is often incomplete and requires extensive supplementation. Although additional research is required on nearly every dimension of impact analysis, these needs are particularly critical for impact management because decisions are being made and programs initiated on an ongoing basis. Immediate and continuing research is necessary to establish sounder bases for these decisions and programs.

Impact management is, as the content of this volume makes evident, a fledgling field in need of extensive development. It requires systematization, conceptual development, formulation of more extensive generalizations, and extensive evaluative and basic research if it is to move from a loose configuration of pragmatic activities to become an empirically and conceptually based process. It is our hope that this volume represents at least one small step toward the development of a more rigorous approach to the critical process of impact management.

References

Abrams, Nancy E., and Primack, Joel R. 1980. "Helping the Public Decide--The Case of Radioactive Waste Management." *Environment* 22:14-40.

Accola, John. 1983. "In Time of Boom, Government Going Bust." *USA Today* September 12.

AFL-CIO. 1982. *A Union Response to Plant Closings and Worker Displacement: A Program Guide.* Washington, D.C.: AFL-CIO, November.

Alberta Treasury. 1983. *Alberta Heritage Savings Trust Fund Annual Report 1982-83.* Edmonton, Alberta: Alberta Treasury.

Amok/Cluff Mining Ltd. 1981. *New Dimensions in Northern Participation.* Saskatoon, Saskatchewan.

Anderson, Robert, and Barkley, David L. 1982. "Rural Manufacturers' Characteristics and Probability of Plant Closings." *Growth and Change* 13(1): 2-8.

Armington, Catherine. 1983. *Further Examination of Sources of Recent Employment Growth Analysis of USEEM Data for 1976 to 1980.* Washington, D.C.: Brookings Institute.

Armington, Catherine, and Odle, Marjorie. 1982. *Sources of Employment Growth 1978-1980.* Washington, D.C.: Brookings Institute.

Arnstein, Sherry R. 1969. "A Ladder of Citizen Participation." *Journal of the American Institute of Planners* 35:216-24.

Aronson, Robert L., and McKersie, Robert B. 1980. *Economic Consequences of Plant Shutdowns in New York State.* Ithaca: New York State School of Industrial and Labor Relations, Cornell Univ., May.

Auger, C. S.; Allen, E.; Blaha, S.; Fahys, V.; Low, L.; Maurice, R.; Vestal, C.; and Walker, C. 1978. *Energy Resource Development, Socioeconomic Impacts, and the Current Role of Impact Assistance.* Boulder, Colo.: TOSCO Foundation.

Auger, C. S., and Zeller, M. 1979. *Siting Major Energy Facilities.* Boulder, Colo.: TOSCO Foundation.

Ayer, Harry W., and Layton, M. Ross. 1972. "Meeting the Economic Impact of Mine-Smelter Phase-Down in Bisbee-Douglas." *Arizona Review* 21(12): 1-5.

Bagshaw, Michael L., and Schnorbus, Robert H. 1980. "The Local Labor-Market Response to a Plant Shutdown." Federal Reserve Bank of Cleveland *Economic Review.* (January): 16-24.

Baker, Joe G. 1977. *Labor Allocation in Western Energy Development.* Human Resources Institute Monograph No. 5. Salt Lake City: Univ. of Utah.

Barbe, Nancy, and Daniels, Belden. 1982. "Resource-Rich States Break New Ground in Investing in Small Business." *The Entrepreneurial Economy* 1(2): 7-8.

Baril, R. G. 1981. "Community Impact Agreements and Monitoring." Presented at the Second International Forum on the Human Side of Energy, 16-19 August, at Edmonton, Alberta.

Barrows, Richard, and Charlier, Marj. 1982. "Local Government Options for Managing Rapid Growth." In *Coping with Rapid Growth in Rural Communities,* ed. Bruce A. Weber and Robert E. Howell. Boulder, Colo.: Westview Press.

Barth, Michael C. 1982. "Canada's Manpower Consultation Service: A Model for Adjustment Assistance?" *The Entrepreneurial Economy* 1(5): 12.

Bartholomew, Wayne; Joray, Paul; and Kochanowski, Paul. 1977. "Corporate Relocation Impact: South Bend." *Indiana Business Review* 52(1): 2-10.

Batey, Peter W. J., and Maden, Moss. 1983. "The Modeling of Demographic-Economic Change Within the Context of Regional Decline. Typescript. Liverpool, U.K.: Univ. of Liverpool, Dept. of Civic Design.

Batt, William, and Spring, William. 1982. *Plant Closings: What Can Be Learned from Best Practice.* Labor-Management Services Administration, U.S. Dept. of Labor. Washington, D.C.: GPO.

Bearse, Peter J., ed. 1982. *Mobilizing Capital: Program Innovation and the Changing Public/Private Interface in Development Finance.* New York: Elsevier Science Publishing Co.

Berger, Marguerite. 1983. "New State Approaches to Natural Resource-Based Development." *The Entrepreneurial Economy* 1(11): 10-12.

Berkey, E.; Carpenter, N. G.; Metz, William C.; Meyers, D. W.; Porter, D. R.; Singley, J. E.; and Travis, R. K. 1977. *Social Impact Assessment, Monitoring, and Management by the Electric Energy Industry: State of the Practice.* Washington, D.C.: Atomic Industrial Forum and Edison Electric Institute.

Berth, Michael C., and Reisner, Fritzie. 1983. *Worker Adjustment to Plant Shutdowns and Mass Layoffs.* Washington, D.C.: National Alliance of Business, March.

Betz, Marga R. 1980. "Community Stability in Resource Towns." Typescript. Calgary: Alberta Environment.

Birch, David. 1979. *The Job Generation Process.* Cambridge: MIT Program on Neighborhood and Regional Change.

Bisset, R. 1980. "Assessment of Social Impacts." Paper presented to WHO Seminar on Environmental Impact Assessment, 22 June-2 July, at Univ. of Aberdeen, Scotland.

Black, Robert E. 1983. "Public Participation in National Resource Management." In *Proceedings of the Alaska Symposium on the Social, Economic, and Cultural Effects of Natural Resource Development,* ed. Sally Yarie, pp. 124-30. Fairbanks: Univ. of Alaska.

Blalock, Hubert. 1969. *Theory Construction.* Englewood Cliffs, N.J.: Prentice-Hall.

Blasi, Joseph R., and Whyte, William Foote. 1982. "Worker Ownership and Pubic Policy." In *Public Policies for Distressed Communities,* ed. F. Stevens Redburn and Terry F. Buss. Lexington, Mass.: Lexington Books.

Bleiker, Hans. 1983. "How to Get Controversial Projects, Programs, and Plans Implemented." Presentation at the eleventh annual North Dakota State Planning Conference, 8-9 December, at Bismarck.

Bluestone, Barry, and Harrison, Bennett. 1980. *Capital and Communities: The Causes and Consequences of Private Disinvestment.* Washington, D.C.: The Progressive Alliance.

Bluestone, Barry, and Harrison, Bennett. 1982. *The Deindustrialization of America.* New York: Basic Books.

Blunck, Nancy L. 1983. "Public Participation on Complex Projects with a High Level of Conflict." In *Proceedings of the Alaska Symposium on the Social, Economic, and Cultural Effects of Natural Resource Development,* ed. Sally Yarie, pp. 131-34. Fairbanks: Univ. of Alaska.

Bowen, Richard L. 1983. "Economic and Fiscal Impacts of Decline." Typescript. Honolulu: Univ. of Hawaii, Dept. of Agr. Econ.

Bowen, Richard L., and Foster, David L. 1983. *A Profile of Displaced Pineapple Workers on Molokai.* Res. Ext. Series 031. Honolulu: Univ. of Hawaii, College of Tropical Agriculture and Human Resources, August.

Bradbury, J. H. 1979. "Towards an Alternative Theory of Resource-Based Town Development in Canada." *Economic Geography* 55:147-66.

Bradbury, Katharine L. 1982. "Fiscal Distress in Large American Cities." *New England Economic Review* (November/December): 33-44.

Bradbury, Katharine L. 1983. "Structural Fiscal Distress in Cities--Causes and Consequences." *New England Economic Review* (January/February): 32-43.

Bradley, Keith, and Gelb, Alan. 1983. *Worker Capitalism.* Cambridge: MIT Press.

Braid, Robert B., Jr. 1980. *Chronic Underprojections of Work Forces at Nuclear Power Plants.* Oak Ridge, Tenn.: Oak Ridge National Laboratory.

Braid, Robert B., Jr., and Kyles, Stephen D. 1977. *The Clinch River Breeder Reactor Plant: Suggested Procedures for Monitoring and Mitigating Adverse Construction-Period Impacts on Local Public Services.* Knoxville: East Tennessee Energy Projects Coordinating Committee.

Branch, Kristi M.; Hooper, Douglas A.; and Moore, James R. 1982. "Decision-Making Under Uncertainty." Paper presented at the Four Nations Energy Resource Communities Conference, 23-30 June, at Calgary and Edmonton, Alberta.

Brealey, T. B., and Newton, P. W. 1978. "Migration and New Towns." In *Mobility and Community Change in Australia,* ed. Ian H. Burnley, Robin J. Pryor, and Don T. Rowland. Brisbane, Australia: Queensland Univ. Press.

Brealey, T. B., and Newton, P. W. 1981. "Commuter Mining--An Alternative Way." In *Proceedings, Australian Mining Industry Council Environmental Workshop*. Canberra, Australia.

Brenner, M. Harvey. 1976. *Estimating the Social Costs of National Economic Policy*. A study prepared for the Joint Economic Committee, U.S. Congress. Washington, D.C.: GPO.

Briscoe, Maphis, Murray, and Lamont, Inc. 1978. *Action Handbook: Managing Growth in the Small Community*. A report for the U.S. Environmental Protection Agency. Washington, D.C.: GPO.

Bronder, Leonard D.; Carlisle, Nancy; and Savage, Michael D., Jr. 1977. *Financial Strategies for Alleviation of Socioeconomic Impacts in Seven Western States*. Prepared by Western Governors' Regional Energy Policy Office with Federal Energy Administration. Denver.

Brown, B. 1977. *The Impact of New Boomtowns*. Washington, D.C.: New Dimensions in Mental Health.

Browne, Bortz, and Coddington. 1981. *A Retrospective Analysis of the Jim Bridger Complex Socioeconomic Effects*. Denver: Browne, Bortz, and Coddington.

Browne, Bortz, and Coddington. 1982. *The 1981 Campbell County Socioeconomic Monitoring Report*. Denver: Browne, Bortz, and Coddington.

Brownrigg, Mark. 1980. "Industrial Contraction and the Regional Multiplier Effect: An Application in Scotland." *Town Planning Review* 51(2): 195-210.

Buckley, Walter. 1967. *Sociology and Modern Systems Theory*. Englewood Cliffs, N.J.: Prentice Hall.

Burchell, Robert W., and Listokin, David. 1978. *The Fiscal Impact Handbook*. New Brunswick, N. J.: Center for Urban Policy Research.

Burtco, Inc. n.d. Data on Various Mancamps. Seattle.

Business Week. 1980. "The Reindustrialization of America." Issue No. 2643(30 June): 55-142.

Business Week. 1983. The Fallout from "Whoops." Issue No. 2798(11 July): 80-88.

Buss, Terry F., and Redburn, F. Stevens. 1981. "How To Shut Down A Plant." *Industrial Management* 23(May-June): 4-9.

Buss, Terry F., and Redburn, F. Stevens. 1983. *Shutdown at Youngstown*. Albany: State Univ. of New York Press.

California Employment Development Department. 1983a. *Closed Businesses in California: February 1980 To April 1983*. Sacramento.

California Employment Development Department. 1983b. *Planning Guidebook for Communities Facing A Plant Closure or Mass Layoff*. Sacramento.

Carnes, S. A.; Copenhaver, E.; Reed, J.; Soderstrom, E.; Sorenson, J.; Peelle, Elizabeth; and Bjornstad, D. 1982. *Incentives and the Siting of Radioactive Waste Facilities*. Oak Ridge, Tenn.: Energy Division, Oak Ridge National Laboratories.

Carpenter, Richard A. 1981. "Balancing Economic and Environmental Objectives: The Question is Still, How?" *Environmental Impact Assessment Review* 2(2): 175-188.

Cavanagh, Charles R. 1980. "Impact Management for Project/Construction Managers." Socioeconomic Workshop II, Denver: Stone and Webster Engineering Company.

Cavanagh, Charles R., and Geiger, John P. 1982. "The Role of Impact Reduction Strategies in Construction Efficiency." Paper presented at the American Society of Civil Engineers 1982 National Spring Convention, 26-30 April, at Las Vegas.

CCREM. 1982. *Environmental Assessment in Canada*. Toronto, Ontario: Canadian Council of Resource and Environment Ministers.

Chalmers, James A. 1977. *Construction Worker Survey*. Denver: U.S. Bureau of Reclamation.

Chalmers, James A., and Anderson, E. J. 1977. *Economic-Demographic Assessment Manual*. Denver: U.S. Bureau of Reclamation.

Chalmers, James A.; Pijawka, D.; Branch, Kristi; Bergmann, P.; Flynn, Jim; and Flynn, Cynthia. 1982. *Socioeconomic Impacts of Nuclear Generating Stations*. U.S. Nuclear Regulatory Commission. NUREG/CR-2750. Washington, D.C.: GPO, July.

Chase, Robert A., and Leistritz, F. Larry. 1983. *Profile of North Dakota's Petroleum Work Force, 1981-82*. Agr. Econ. Rpt. No. 174. Fargo: North Dakota Agr. Exp. Sta.

Chase, Robert A.; Leistritz, F. Larry; and Halstead, John M. 1983. "Assessing the Economic and Fiscal Effects of Repository Development." In *Nuclear Waste: Socioeconomic Dimensions of Long-Term Storage*, ed. Steve H. Murdock, F. Larry Leistritz, and Rita R. Hamm. Boulder, Colo.: Westview Press.

Christenson, James A., and Robinson, Jerry W. 1980. *Community Development in America*. Ames: Iowa State Univ. Press.

Christofferson, Juline. 1983. "Experience of the State of Utah with the NWTS Program." In *Proceedings of Waste Management '83 Conference*, ed. Roy Post. Tucson, Ariz.

Clark, Redmond. 1983. Telephone interview by John M. Halstead. Assistant Director, Massachusetts Dept. of Environmental Management. Boston.

Clawson, Marion. 1980. "The Dying Community: The Natural Resource Base." In *The Dying Community*, ed. Art Gallaher, Jr. and Harland Padfield. Albuquerque: Univ. of New Mexico Press.

Cole, Janice Rae; Fargoni, Allison; and Ramage, Betty. 1983. "The Human Impacts of Large-Scale Development Projects: The Process and Legal Basis for Mitigation." In *Proceedings of the Alaska Symposium on the Social, Economic, and Cultural Impacts of Natural Resource Development*. Fairbanks: Univ. of Alaska.

Congressional Budget Office. 1982. *Dislocated Workers: Issues and Federal Options*. A CBO Study Background Paper. Washington, D.C.: GPO.

Conrad, Robert F., and Hool, R. Bryce. 1980. *Taxation of Mineral Resources*. Lexington, Mass.: Lexington Books.

Coon, R. C.; Mittleider, J. F.; and Leistritz, F. Larry. 1983. *Economic Analysis of the North Dakota Lignite Industry*. Agr. Econ. Misc. Rpt. No. 67. Fargo: North Dakota State Univ.

Copp, James H. 1982. "Rural Health and Rural Development." Keynote address at Sixth Annual Institute of the American Rural Health Association, 11-14 June, at Jeffersonville, Vt.

Cortese, Charles F. 1982. "The Impacts of Rapid Growth on Local Organizations and Community Services." In *Coping with Rapid Growth in Rural Communities*, ed. Bruce A. Weber and Robert E. Howell. Boulder, Colo.: Westview Press.

Cortese, Charles F., and Jones, Bernie J. 1977. "The Sociological Analysis of Boom Towns." *Western Sociological Review* 8:76-90.

Cortese, Charles F., and Jones, Bernie J. 1979. "The Sociological Analysis of Boomtowns." In *Boomtowns and Human Services*, ed. J. A. Davenport and J. Davenport. Laramie: Univ. of Wyoming.

Coser, Lewis A. 1956. *The Function of Social Conflict.* London: Free Press of Glencoe.

Council on Environmental Quality. 1973. "Preparation of Environmental Impact Statements: Guidelines." *Federal Register* 38 (147, August 1): 20550-20562.

Council on Environmental Quality. 1978. "National Environmental Policy Act." *Federal Register* 43 (230, November 29): 55978-56007.

Cummings, Ronald G., and Mehr, Arthur F. 1977. "Investments for Urban Infrastructure in Boom Towns." *Natural Resources Journal* 17(2): 223-40.

Cummings, Ronald G., and Schulze, William D. 1978. "Optimal Investment Strategy for Boom Towns. *American Economic Review* 68(3): 374-85.

Dahrendorf, Ralf. 1959. *Class and Class Conflict in Industrial Society.* Stanford, Calif.: Stanford Univ. Press.

Daicoff, Darwin W. 1973. "The Community Impact of Military Installations." In *The Economic Consequences of Reduced Military Spending*, ed. Bernard Udis. Lexington, Mass.: Lexington Books.

Dakota Country. 1983. "Montana Power Line Settlement Annouced." Vol. V, Issue X. Bismarck.

Daniels, Belden Hull. 1982. "Capital is Only Part of the Problem." In *Mobilizing Capital: Program Innovation and the Changing Public/Private Interface in Development Finance*, ed. Peter J. Bearse. New York: Elsevier Science Publishing Co.

Daniels, Belden Hull; Barbe, Nancy; and Lirtzman, Harry. 1981. "Small Business and State Economic Development." In *Expanding the Opportunity to Produce: Revitalizing the American Economy Through New Enterprise Development*, ed. Robert Friedman and William Schweke. Washington, D.C.: Corporation for Enterprise Development.

Daniels, Belden Hull, and Kieschnick, Michael. 1979. *Development Finance: A Primer for Policymakers.* Washington, D.C.: National Rural Center.

Davenport, J. A., and Davenport, J. 1979. "A Town and Gown Approach to Boomtown Problems." In *Boomtowns and Human Services*, ed. J. A. Davenport and J. Davenport. Laramie: Univ. of Wyoming.

Davenport, J. A., and Davenport, J. 1980. "Boom Towns and the Aged." In *Energy and Aging: A Symposium*, pp. 28-38. Laramie, Wyo.: Western Gerontological Society.

Deaton, Brady J. 1975. "Community Development Corporations." *Growth and Change* 6(1): 31-37.

Delli Priscoli, Jerry. 1979. "Implementing Public Involvement Programs in Federal Agencies." In *Citizen Participation in America*, ed. Stuart Landon. Lexington, Mass.: Lexington Books.

Denver Research Institute. 1979. *Socioeconomic Impact of Western Energy Resource Development*. Washington, D.C.: Council on Environmental Quality.

DePape, Denis. 1981. Personal communication with F. Larry Leistritz. Winnipeg, Manitoba: Intergroup Consulting Economists, Ltd.

DePape, Denis. 1982. "Government/Industry Agreements for Resource Development." Paper presented at CIM Annual General Meeting, 27 April, at Quebec City, Quebec.

DePape, Denis. 1983. "Alternatives to Single Project Mining Communities." Paper presented at Centre For Resource Studies Discussion Seminar *Mining Communities: Hard Lessons For the Future*, 27-29 September, at Kingston, Ontario.

Department of Regional and Economic Expansion. 1979. *Single Sector Communities*. Ottawa, Ontario: Dept. of Regional and Economic Expansion.

Detomasi, Don D. 1982a. "The Delivery and Financing of Housing." Paper presented at the Conference on Energy Resource Communities: Socioeconomic Impacts and Community Development Problems in Four Nations, June, at Calgary, Alberta.

Detomasi, Don D. 1982b. "Public Sector Fiscal Impacts." In *Energy Resource Communities*, ed. Gene F. Summers and Arne Selvik. Madison, Wisc.: MJM Publishing Co. for the Inst. of Industrial Economics, Bergen, Norway.

DeVeney, G. R. 1977. *Construction Employee Monitoring*. Knoxville: TVA.

Didur, Jan. 1983. Telephone interview by John M. Halstead. Alberta Environment. Edmonton, Alberta.

DiNoto, Michael, and Merk, Larry. 1982. "The Economic Status of Shoshone County, Idaho. Typescript. Moscow: Univ. of Idaho, Center for Business Development and Research, Dept. of Econ.

Dixon, Mim. 1978. *What Happened to Fairbanks? The Effects of the Trans-Alaska Oil Pipeline on the Community of Fairbanks, Alaska.* Boulder, Colo.: Westview Press.

Doricht, Terrell. 1982. Telephone interview by John M. Halstead. Challis, Idaho superintendent of schools.

Ducsik, Dennis. 1981. "Citizen Participation: Alladin's Lamp or Pandora's Box?" *Journal of the American Planning Association* April:154-66.

Ducsik, Dennis. 1982. Referenced in O'Hare et al., 1983.

Ducsik, Dennis. 1984. "Power Plants and People: A Profile of Electric Utility Initiatives in Cooperative Planning." *Journal of the American Planning Association.* Spring:161-74.

Duncan, Otis D. 1964. "Social Organization and the Ecosystem." In *Handbook of Modern Society,* ed. Robert Faris, pp. 36-82. Chicago: Rand McNally and Co.

Dunning, C. Mark. 1981. *Report of Survey of Corps of Engineers Construction Work Force.* Research Rpt. 81-R05. Fort Belvoir, Va.: U.S. Army Corps of Engineers, Inst. for Water Resources.

ECOS Management Criteria, Inc. 1982. *The Validation and Improvement of Socioeconomic Forecasting Methodologies.* Washington, D.C.: U.S. Geological Survey.

Ellis, Carl. 1982. "Managing Boom Growth in Wyoming--Yesterday and Today." Paper presented at the American Society of Civil Engineers 1982 National Spring Convention, 26-30 April, at Las Vegas.

Ellis, Carl. 1983. Telephone interview by John M. Halstead. Wyoming Industrial Siting Administration. Cheyenne.

Energy Information Administration, U.S. Department of Energy. 1983. *Nuclear Plant Cancellations.* DOE/EIA-0392. Washington, D.C.: GPO.

Faas, Ronald C. 1980. *Mitigation of Local Community Fiscal Impacts Related to Nuclear Waste Repository Siting.* Corvallis, Oreg.: Western Rural Development Center.

Faas, Ronald C. 1982. *Evaluation of Impact Mitigation Strategies.* Corvallis, Oreg.: Western Rural Development Center.

Federal Energy Administration. 1974. *Project Independence Blueprint, Final Task Force Report: Synthetic Fuels from Coal.* Washington, D.C.: GPO.

Federal Energy Administration. 1976. *Federal Assistance Programs and Energy Development Impacted Communities.* Washington, D.C.: Wendell Associates.

Fedrau, Ruth. 1982. "A Comprehensive State Response to Plant Closings and Mass Layoffs." *The Entrepreneurial Economy* 1(5): 7-9.

Finsterbusch, Kurt. 1982. "Boomtown Disruption Thesis." *Pacific Sociological Review* 25(3): 307-22.

Finsterbusch, Kurt; Llewellyn, Lynn G.; and Wolf, C. P., eds. 1983. *Social Impact Assessment Methods.* Beverly Hills: Sage Publications.

Finsterbusch, Kurt, and Wolf, C. P., eds. 1981. *Methodology of Social Impact Assessment.* 2d ed. Stroudsburg, Pa.: Dowden, Hutchinson, and Ross.

Fisher, Peter S. 1983. "The Role of the Public Sector in Local Development Finance." *Journal of Economic Issues* 17(1): 133-53.

Fitzsimmons, S. J.; Stuart, L. I.; and Wolf, C. P., eds. 1977. *Social Assessment Manual: A Guide to the Preparation of the Social Well-Being Account for Planning Water Resource Projects.* Boulder, Colo.: Westview Press.

Foltman, Felician F. 1982. "Managing and Adjusting To A Plant Closing." In *Public Policies for Distressed Communities,* ed. F. Stevens Redburn and Terry F. Buss. Lexington, Mass.: Lexington Books.

Fookes, T. W. 1981a. *Answers to People's Questions.* Final Rpt. No. 1. Huntly Monitoring Project. Hamilton, New Zealand: Univ. of Waikato.

Fookes, T. W. 1981b. *Expectations and Related Findings, 1973-81.* Hamilton, New Zealand: Univ. of Waikato.

Fookes, T. W. 1981c. *Huntly Power Project: A Description.* Final Rpt. No. 2. Huntly Monitoring Project. Hamilton, New Zealand: Univ. of Waikato.

Fookes, T. W. 1981d. *Public Participation Initiatives.* Hamilton, New Zealand: Univ. of Waikato.

Fosler, R. Scott, and Berger, Renee A., eds. 1982. *Public-Private Partnerships in American Cities.* Lexington, Mass.: Lexington Books.

Francaviglia, Richard V. 1983. "Bisbee, Arizona: A Mining Town Survives A Decade of Closure." *Small Town* 13(1): 4-8.

Freudenburg, W. R. 1982. "The Impacts of Rapid Growth on the Social and Personal Well-Being of Local Community Residents." In *Coping with Growth in Rural Communities,* ed. Bruce A. Weber and Robert E. Howell. Boulder, Colo.: Westview Press.

Freudenburg, W. R., and Olsen, D. 1983. "Public Interest and Political Abuse: Public Participation in Social Impact Assessment." *Journal of the Community Development Society* 14(2): 67-82.

Frovarp, S. 1984. Telephone interview with John M. Halstead. Hazen, N. Dak City Planner.

Fuchs, Richard P. 1982. "Rural Residents in the Exploration Phase of Newfoundland's Offshore Oil Industry, 1981." Paper presented at Second International Conference on Oil and the Environment, 16-19 August, at Halifax, Nova Scotia.

Garfield County, Colorado. 1983. County ordinances. Glenwood Springs, Colo.

Gartrell, John W.; Krahn, H.; and Sunahara, F. D. 1980. *A Study of Human Adjustment in Fort McMurray.* Report prepared for Alberta Oil Sands Environmental Research Program. Edmonton, Alberta: Thames Research Group, Inc.

General Electric Company. 1975. *Assessment of Energy Parks Versus Dispersed Electric Power Generating Facilities, Final Report.* Washington, D.C.: General Electric Co., Center for Energy Systems.

George, Critz. 1983. "Federal/State Relations in the NWTS Program." In *Proceedings of Waste Management '83 Conference,* ed. Roy Post. Tucson, Ariz.

Gibbs, Jack, and Martin, Walter. 1959. "Toward A Theoretical System of Human Ecology." *Pacific Sociological Review* 2:29-36.

Gilmore, John S. 1976. "Boom Towns May Hinder Energy Resource Development." *Science* 191:535-540.

Gilmore, John S. 1980. "Socioeconomic Impact Management: Are Impact Assessments Good Enough to Help?" Paper presented at Conf. on Computer Models and Forecasting Impacts of Growth and Development, 20-23 April, at Univ. of Alberta, Jasper Park Lodge.

Gilmore, John S. 1983. "Observations and Comments on the Roles of Federal, State, and Local Governments in Socioeconomic Impact Mitigation." In *Proceedings of the Alaska Symposium on the Social, Economic, and Cultural Impacts of Natural Resource Development*. Fairbanks: Univ. of Alaska.

Gilmore, John S., and Duff, M. K. 1975a. *Boom Town Growth Management: A Case Study of Rock Springs--Green River, Wyoming*. Boulder, Colo.: Westview Press.

Gilmore, John S., and Duff, M. K. 1975b. *The Sweetwater County Boom: A Challenge to Growth Management*. Denver: Denver Research Inst.

Gilmore, John S.; Flory, D. K.; Hammond, D. M.; Moore, Keith D.; and Coddington, D. C. 1977. *Socioeconomic Impact Mitigation Mechanisms in Six States*. Denver: Denver Research Institute.

Gilmore, John S.; Giltner, R. E.; Coddington, D. C.; and Duff, M. K. 1975. *Factors Affecting an Area's Ability to Absorb a Large-Scale Commercial Coal-Processing Complex*. Washington, D. C.: Energy Research and Development Administration.

Gilmore, John S.; Hammond, D. M.; Moore, Keith D.; Johnson, J.; and Coddington, D. C. 1982. *Socioeconomic Impacts of Power Plants*. Report prepared for Electric Power Research Institute. Denver: Denver Research Institute.

Gilmore, John S.; Moore, Keith D.; Hammond, D. M.; and Coddington, D. C. 1976. *Analysis of Financing Problems of Coal and Oil Shale Boom Towns*. Washington, D.C.: Federal Energy Administration.

Gold, R. 1981. *Industrial and Community Responses To A Plant Closing in Anaconda, Montana*. Missoula, Mont.: Social Research and Applications.

Gordon, John, and Mulkey, David. 1978. "Income Multipliers for Community Impact Analysis--What Size is Reasonable?" *Journal of Community Development Society* 9(2): 85-93.

Gordus, Jeanne Prial; Jarley, Paul; and Ferman, Louis A. 1981. *Plant Closings and Economic Dislocation*. Kalamazoo, Mich.: W. E. Upjohn Inst. for Employment Research.

Grayson, J. Paul. 1983. "The Effects of A Plant Closure on the Stress Levels and Health of Workers' Wives." *Journal of Business Ethics* 2(3): 221-25.

Greene, Marjorie, and Curry, Martha G. 1977. *The Management of Social and Economic Impacts Associated With the Construction of Large-Scale Projects*. Richland: Battelle Human Affairs Research Centers, Pacific Northwest Laboratories.

Gulley, David A. 1982. "Severance Taxes and Market Failure." *Natural Resources Journal* 22(3): 597-617.

Gulliford, Andrew. 1983. "From Boom to Bust: Small Towns and Energy Development on Colorado's Western Slope." *Small Town* 13(5): 15-22.

Habitat North, Inc. 1979. *Socioeconomic Impacts of Selected Foreign OCS Developments*. Tech. Rpt. No. 28, Alaska OCS Socioeconomic Studies Program. Anchorage: Bureau of Land Management, Alaska Outer Continental Shelf Office.

Hadden, Susan; Chiles, James; Anaejionu, Paul; and Cerny, Karl. 1981. *High Level Nuclear Waste Disposal*. Austin: Texas Energy and Natural Resources Advisory Council.

Halstead, John M.; Chase, Robert A.; and Leistritz, F. Larry. 1983. "Mitigating Impacts of Plant Closures." Paper presented at American Agricultural Economics Assoc. Annual Meeting, 1-3 August, at Purdue Univ., West Lafayette, Ind.

Halstead, John M., and Leistritz, F. Larry. 1983a. *Impacts of Energy Development on Mercer County, North Dakota*. Agr. Econ. Rpt. No. 170. Fargo: North Dakota Agr. Exp. Sta.

Halstead, John M., and Leistritz, F. Larry. 1983b. *Impacts of Energy Development on Secondary Labor Markets*. Agr. Econ. Rpt. No. 178. Fargo: North Dakota Agr. Exp. Sta.

Halstead, John M.; Leistritz, F. Larry; and Chase, Robert A. 1983. *Socioeconomic Impact Management For High-Level Nuclear Waste Repositories*. Fargo: North Dakota Agr. Exp. Sta.

Halstead, John M.; Leistritz, F. Larry; Rice, D. G.; Saxowsky, D. M.; and Chase, Robert A. 1982. *Mitigating Socioeconomic Impacts of Nuclear Waste Repository Siting*. Fargo: North Dakota Agr. Exp. Sta.

Halstead, Robert. 1982. Personal interview by John M. Halstead. Madison: Wisconsin State Energy Office.

Hannah, Richard, and Mosier, R. Kim. 1977. *An Examination of Occupational Bottlenecks in the Construction, Fueling, and Operation of Coal-Fired Power Plants*. Salt Lake City: Univ. of Utah, Human Resources Institute.

Hansen, Gary B., and Bentley, Marion T. 1981. *Problems and Solutions in A Plant Shutdown*. Logan: Utah Center for Productivity and Quality of Working Life, Utah State Univ., November.

Hansen, Gary B.; Bentley, Marion T.; and Davidson, Richard A. 1980. *Hardrock Miners in A Shutdown*. Monograph No. 1. Logan: Center for Productivity and Quality of Working Life, Utah State Univ., May.

Hansen, Gary B.; Bentley, Marion T.; Gould, Jeanni H.; and Skidmore, Mark H. 1981. *Life After Layoff*. Logan: Utah Center for Productivity and Quality of Working Life, Utah State Univ.

Hargreaves, A. W. 1982. "Future of Coal Industry." Paper presented at the Singleton Coal Day, 29 October, at Singleton, New South Wales, Australia.

Harnisch, A. A. 1978. *Chief Joseph Dam: Community Impact Report, Update III*. Fort Belvoir, Va.: U.S. Army Corps of Engineers, Inst. for Water Resources.

Harrison, Bennett, and Bluestone, Barry. 1982. "The Incidence and Regulation of Plant Closings." In *Public Policies for Distressed Communities*, ed. F. Stevens Redburn and Terry F. Buss. Lexington, Mass.: Lexington Books.

Harvey, Edward F. 1982. Personal communication with F. Larry Leistritz. Denver: Browne, Bortz, and Coddington.

Hassinger, Edward J. 1982. *Rural Health Organization*. Ames: Iowa State Univ. Press.

Hawley, Amos H. 1950. *Human Ecology: A Theory of Community Structure*. New York: Ronald Press.

Hayden, F. Gregory, and Swanson, Larry D. 1980. "Planning Through the Socialization of Property Rights: The Community Reinvestment Act." *Journal of Economic Issues* 14(2): 351-69.

Haynes, T. L. 1983. "The Socioeconomic Impacts of Resource Development on the Elderly." In *Proceedings of the Alaska Symposium on the Social, Economic, and Cultural Impacts of Energy Development*. Fairbanks: Univ. of Alaska.

Hekman, John S., and Strong, John S. 1980. "Is There A Case for Plant-Closing Laws?" *New England Economic Review* (July/August): 34-51.

Henry, Mark S. 1980. "On the Value of Economic-Demographic Forecasts to Local Government. *Annals of Regional Science* 14(1): 12-20.

Hertsgaard, T. A., and Leistritz, F. Larry. 1983. "Adjusting to the Socioeconomic Impacts of Energy Development in North Dakota." In *Proceedings of the Alaska Symposium on the Social, Economic, and Cultural Impacts of Natural Resource Development*. Fairbanks: Univ. of Alaska.

Hodge, Ian. 1984. *Employment Adjustments and the Economic Costs of Decline in a Small Rural Community*. Bul. No. 629. Moscow: Idaho Agr. Exp. Sta.

Holmes and Narver, Inc. 1981. *Life Support Facility Planning and Evaluation Concept Study for Construction and Deployment Personnel, M-X Weapons System*. San Francisco: U.S. Army Corps of Engineers.

Homans, George C. 1950. *The Human Group*. New York: Harcourt, Brace, and World.

Hooper, J. E., and Branch, Kristi M. 1983. *Big Horn and Decker Mine Worker Survey Report*. Billings, Mont.: Mountain West Research-North, Inc.

Housing Services, Inc. 1981. *Wright, Wyoming: A Planned Community Development*. Final Environmental Impact Statement. Denver.

Houstoun, Lawrence O., Jr. 1977. "Here's What Should be Done About the Energy Boom Towns." *Planning* 43(3): 18-20.

Howell, Robert E.; Olsen, M. E.; Olsen, D.; and Yuan, G. 1983. "Citizen Participation in Nuclear Waste Repository Siting." In *Nuclear Waste: Socioeconomic Dimensions of Long-Term Storage*, ed. Steve H. Murdock, F. Larry Leistritz, and Rita R. Hamm. Boulder, Colo.: Westview Press.

Huesflon, Lee. 1981. Personal communication with F. Larry Leistritz. Underwood, N. Dak.: Cooperative Power Assoc.

Hushak, LeRoy J., and Morse, George, eds. 1979. *Proceedings of the Ex Ante Growth Impact Models Conference*. Ames, Iowa: North Central Regional Center for Rural Development.

Hyman, Eric. 1982. "Wyoming's Industrial Siting Permit Process and Environmental Impact Assessment." *Environmental Management* 6(1): 1-7.

Ide, Peter, and Siegel, Beth. 1983. "Financing Agricultural Development." *The Entrepreneurial Economy* 1(12): 6-7.

IPMP. 1983. *The Consent-Builders' Bulletin.* Vol. 1, No. 2. Laramie, Wyo.: Inst. for Participatory Management and Planning.

Isard, Walter. 1960. *Methods of Regional Analysis.* Cambridge: MIT Press.

James Bay-Northern Quebec Agreements. 1976. Agreement between Government of Quebec, James Bay Energy Society, James Bay Development Corporation, Hydro-Quebec, Grand Council of the Crees, and the Northern Quebec Inuit Association.

Jamison, David. 1982. "The Emerging Public-Private Partnership." In *Mobilizing Capital: Program Innovation and the Changing Public/Private Interface in Development Finance,* ed. Peter J. Bearse. New York: Elsevier Science Publishing Co.

Johannesson, Cary L., and Plesuk, Brian W. 1982. "Operationalizing Socio-Economic Planning: 'Talk's Cheap--Whiskey Costs Money'." Paper presented at the Second International Conference on Oil and The Environment, 15-19 August, at Halifax, Nova Scotia.

Jones, Derek C., and Svejnar, Jan (eds.). 1982. *Participatory and Self-Managed Firms.* Lexington, Mass.: Lexington Books.

Jones, L. L., and Murdock, Steve H. 1978. "The Incremental Nature of Public Service Delivery." *American Journal of Agricultural Economics* 60(5): 955-60.

Kaldor, Nicholas. 1981. "The Energy Issues." In *Oil or Industry? Energy, Industrialization and Economic Policy in Canada, Mexico, the Netherlands, Norway and the United Kingdom,* ed. Terry Barker and Vladimir Brailovsky. London: Academic Press.

Kennedy, D. A. 1979. "Health Care in Boomtowns." In *Boomtowns and Human Services,* ed. J. A. Davenport and J. Davenport. Laramie: Univ. of Wyoming.

Kennedy, William V. 1980. "Environmental Impact Assessment in the Federal Republic of Germany." *Environmental Impact Assessment Review* 1(1): 92-94.

Keyes, Robert J.; Tunis, Edward; Reeves, J. E.; Hutchinson, R. D.; Lemieux, Andre; Porter, Nancy; and Kennedy, Mark. 1982. *Report of the Task Force on Mining Communities.* Ottawa, Ontario: Canada Energy, Mines, and Resources, September.

Knight, R. 1975. *Work Camps and Company Towns in Canada and the U.S.* Vancouver, British Columbia: Newstar Books.

Krawetz, N. M. 1981. *Overseas Energy Projects and Huntly.* Hamilton, New Zealand: Univ. of Waikato.

Krutilla, John V., and Fisher, Anthony C. 1978. *Economic and Fiscal Impacts of Coal Development: Northern Great Plains.* Baltimore, Md.: Johns Hopkins Univ. Press for Resources for the Future.

Labor Union Study Tour Participants. 1979. *Economic Dislocation: Plant Closings, Plant Relocations, and Plant Conversion.* Washington, D.C.: United Automobile Workers, United Steel Workers of America, and the International Association of Machinists.

Lamont, William; Beardsley, George; Briscoe, Andy; Carver, John; Harrington, Dan; Lansdowne, John; and Murray, James. 1974. *Tax Lead Time Study for the Oil Shale Region.* Denver: Colorado Geological Survey.

Lamphear, Charles F., and Emerson, M. Jarvin. 1975. *Urban and Regional Economics: Structure and Change.* Rockleigh, N.J.: Allyn and Bacon, Inc.

Langerman, Philip D.; Byerly, Richard L.; and Root, Kenneth A. 1982. *Plant Closings and Layoffs.* Des Moines, Iowa: Drake Univ., College for Continuing Education, November.

Lee, N., and Wood, C. 1978. "Environmental Impact Assessment of Projects in EEC Countries." *Journal of Environmental Management* 6(1): 57-71.

Leholm, A. G.; Leistritz, F. Larry; and Wieland, James S. 1976. *Profile of North Dakota's Electric Power Plant Construction Work Force.* Agr. Econ. Stat. Series No. 22. Fargo: North Dakota Agr. Exp. Sta.

Leifer, Nancy. 1982. "Investing the Energy Windfall in Resource-Rich States: The Montana Coal Tax Trust-Fund." In *Mobilizing Capital: Program Innovation and the Changing Public/Private Interface in Development Finance,* ed. Peter J. Bearse. New York: Elsevier Science Publishing Co.

Leistritz, F. Larry, and Chase, Robert A. 1982. "Socioeconomic Impact Monitoring Systems." *Journal of Environmental Management* 15:333-49.

Leistritz, F. Larry; Halstead, John M.; Chase, Robert A.; and Murdock, Steve H. 1982. "Socioeconomic Impact Management." *Minerals and the Environment* 4:141-50.

Leistritz, F. Larry, and Maki, Karen C. 1981. *Socioeconomic Effects of Large-Scale Resource Development Projects in Rural Areas: The Case of McLean County, North Dakota.* Agr. Econ. Rpt. No. 151. Fargo: North Dakota Agr. Exp. Sta.

Leistritz, F. Larry, and Murdock, Steve H. 1981. *Socioeconomic Impact of Resource Development: Methods for Assessment.* Boulder, Colo.: Westview Press.

Leistritz, F. Larry; Murdock, Steve H.; and Leholm, A. G. 1982. "Local Economic Changes Associated with Rapid Growth." In *Coping With Rapid Growth in Rural Communities,* ed. Bruce A. Weber and Robert Howell, pp. 25-62. Boulder, Colo.: Westview Press.

Leistritz, F. Larry; Toman, Norman E.; Murdock, Steve H.; and deMontel, John. 1981. "Cash-Flow Analysis for Energy Impacted Local Governments: A Case Study of Mercer County, North Dakota." *Socio-Economic Planning Sciences* 15(2): 165-74.

Lonsdale, R. E., and Seyler, H. L. 1979. *Nonmetropolitan Industrialization.* New York: John Wiley and Sons.

Lovejoy, Stephen B. 1983. "Employment Predictions in Social Impact Assessment." *Socio-Economic Planning Sciences* 17(2): 87-93.

Lovejoy, Stephen B.; Brown, D. J.; and Weitz, J. S. 1983. "Inmigrants in Nonmetropolitan Communities." *North Central Journal of Agricultural Economics* 5(2): 39-46.

Lovejoy, Stephen B.; Marotz-Baden, Ramona; and Baden, John. 1982. *Contracting for Public Service Delivery: An Alternative for Boom Towns.* WRDC Pub. No. 14. Corvallis, Oreg.: Western Rural Development Center.

Ludwig, Roger. 1983. Personal interview by John M. Halstead. Director, Garfield County Human Services Planning Dept. Glenwood Springs, Colo.

Luke, Ronald T. 1980. "Managing Community Acceptance of Major Industrial Projects." *Coastal Zone Management Journal* 7:271-96.

Lynch, John E. 1970. *Local Economic Development After Military Base Closures.* New York: Praeger Publishers.

MacDonnell, Lawrence; Moore, Keith D.; Lawson, Mark; Daniels, Belden; Klein, Steven; Posner, Bruce; and Browne, Ted. 1982. *Facilitating Private Sector Capital Availability in Rapid Growth Communities.* Denver: Denver Research Inst.

McGinnis, Karen, and Schua, Dean. 1983. "The Downside of Nuclear Plant Construction." Paper presented at Northwest Regional Economics Conference, 5-7 May, at Bellingham, Wash.

McHugh, H. H. 1982. "Reaching Out to Make A Town A Home." *Shale Country* April/May:6-8.

McKenzie, Richard B., ed. 1982. *Plant Closings: Public or Private Choices?* Washington, D.C.: Cato Institute.

McKersie, Robert B., and Sengenberger, Werner. 1983. *Job Losses in Major Industries: Manpower Strategy Responses.* Paris, France: Organization for Economic Cooperation and Development.

Malhotra, Suresh, and Manninen, Diane. 1980. *Migration and Residential Location of Workers at Nuclear Power Plant Construction Sites.* Vol. 1, *Forecasting Methodology* and Vol. 2, *Profile Analysis of Worker Surveys.* Seattle: Battelle Human Affairs Research Centers.

Markusen, Ann Roell. 1977. "Federal Budget Simplification: Preventative Programs Vs. Palliatives for Local Governments with Booming, Stable, and Declining Populations." *National Tax Journal* 30(3): 249-58.

Marshall, David W. I., and Scott, Paul F. 1982. "Environmental and Social Impact Assessment of the Beaufort Sea Hydrocarbon Production Proposal." Paper presented at the First International Conference on Social Impact Assessment, 25 October, at Vancouver, British Columbia.

Martin, Julie E. 1983. *New Resource-Based Developments in the North of Scotland.* Aberdeen, Scotland: Univ. of Aberdeen, Dept. of Geography.

Massachusetts. 1980. Massachusetts Hazardous Waste Facility Siting Act. Chapter 21D, Acts of 1980.

Mather, Tom. 1983. Telephone interview by John M. Halstead. Manager, Cypress Creek Camp. Holleran Services, Inc., Challis, Idaho.

Mazza, Jacqueline; Mayer, Virginia; Chione, Mary; Cutler, Leslie; Hauser, Timothy; and Spear, Amy. 1982. *Shutdown: A Guide for Communities Facing Plant Closings.* Washington, D.C.: Northeast-Midwest Institute.

Merton, Robert K. 1968. *Social Theory and Social Structure.* New York: Free Press.

Metz, William C. 1979a. *Socioeconomic Impact Management in the Western Energy Industry.* BNL-25545. Upton, N.Y.: Brookhaven National Laboratory.

Metz, William C. 1979b. *Worker-Vehicle Ratios at Major Eastern Power Plant Construction Sites.* BNL-27338. Upton, N.Y.: Brookhaven National Laboratory.

Metz, William C. 1980. "The Mitigation of Socioeconomic Impacts by Electric Utilities." *Public Utilities Fortnightly* 106(1): 34-42.

Metz, William C. 1981. *Construction Work Force Management: Worker Transportation and Temporary Housing Techniques.* Report prepared for Western Rural Development Center. Corvallis, Oreg.

Metz, William C. 1982a. "American Energy and Mineral Industry Involvement in Housing." *Minerals and the Environment* 4:131-40.

Metz, William C. 1982b. "Energy Industry Involvement in Worker Transportation." *Transportation Quarterly* 36(4): 563-84.

Metz, William C. 1983. "Industry Initiatives in Impact Mitigation." In *Proceedings of the Alaska Symposium on the Social, Economic, and Cultural Impacts of Natural Resources Development.* Fairbanks: Univ. of Alaska.

Michels, R. E. 1980. *The Atikokan Story.* Thunder Bay, Ontario: Municipal Advisory Committee.

Miller, Jack R. 1984. "Steel Minimills." *Scientific American* 250(5): 32-39.

Miller, James. 1983. Telephone interview by John M. Halstead. Director, Minnesota Public Interest Research Group (MPIRG). Minneapolis.

Miller, Michael K. 1982. "Health and Medical Care." In *Rural Society in the United States,* ed. Don A. Dillman and Daryl J. Hobbs. Boulder, Colo.: Westview Press.

Mills, C. Wright. 1948. *The Marxists.* New York: Harcourt, Brace, and World.

Moen, E.; Boulding, E.; Lilydahl, J.; and Palm, R. 1981. *Women and the Social Costs of Economic Development.* Boulder, Colo.: Westview Press.

Moore, James R.; Tomasik, Jack; Amacher, Ryan; and Whitworth, Regan. 1979. *Mineral Fuels Taxation in the Old West Region.* Prepared for the Univ. of Montana. Billings, Mont.: Mountain West Research, Inc.

Moore, Keith D. 1979. *Stimulating Energy-Related Growth.* Denver: Denver Research Institute.

Moore, R. 1982. *The Social Impact of Oil: The Case of Peterhead.* London: Routledge and Kegan Paul.

Morell, David, and Magorian, Christopher. 1982. *Siting Hazardous Waste Facilities.* Cambridge, Mass.: Ballinger Press.

Morse, George W. 1983. "Local Fiscal Impacts of Plant Closings." Paper presented at the annual meeting of the American Agricultural Economics Association, 1-3 August, at West Lafayette, Ind.

Morse, George W., and McDowell, George. 1982. "Estimating the Impacts of Growth on Local Governments." In *How Extension Can Help Communities Conduct Impact Analyses,* ed. Ron E. Shaffer. Bul. No. 1-04-82-IM-E. Madison: Univ. of Wisconsin Extension.

Mountain West Research, Inc. 1975. *Construction Worker Profile.* Washington, D.C.: Old West Regional Commission.

Mountain West Research, Inc. 1979. *Pipeline Construction Worker and Community Impact Surveys.* Billings, Mont.: Mountain West Research, Inc.

Muller, Thomas, and Soble, Carol E. 1982. *Financing Rapid Growth.* Community Guidance Manual VIII. Office of Economic Adjustment. Washington, D.C.: U.S. Dept. of Defense.

Murdock, Steve H. 1979. "The Potential Role of the Ecological Framework in Impact Analysis." *Rural Sociology* 44:543-65.

Murdock, Steve H.; Hopkins, P.; de Montel, J.; Hamm, Rita R.; Brown, T.; Bauer, M.; and Bullock, R. 1981. *Employment, Population, and Community Service Impacts of Uranium Development in South Texas.* College Station: Texas Agr. Exp. Sta.

Murdock, Steve H., and Leistritz, F. Larry. 1979. *Energy Development in the Western United States.* New York: Praeger Publishers.

Murdock, Steve H., and Leistritz, F. Larry. 1982. "Commentary." *Pacific Sociological Review* 25(3): 357-66.

Murdock, Steve H.; Leistritz, F. Larry; and Hamm, Rita R., eds. 1983. *Nuclear Waste: Socioeconomic Dimensions of Long-Term Storage*. Boulder, Colo.: Westview Press.

Murdock, Steve H.; Leistritz, F. Larry; and Schriner, Eldon C. 1982. "Local Demographic Changes Associated with Rapid Growth." In *Coping With Rapid Growth*, ed. Bruce A. Weber and Robert E. Howell, pp. 63-96. Boulder, Colo.: Westview Press.

Murdock, Steve H.; Wieland, James S.; and Leistritz, F. Larry. 1978. "An Assessment of the Validity of the Gravity Model for Predicting Community Settlement Patterns in Rural Energy Impact Areas in the West." *Land Economics* 54(4): 461-71.

Murphy and Williams, Consultants. 1978. *Socioeconomic Impact Assessment: A Methodology Applied to Synthetic Fuels*. Washington, D.C.: U.S. Dept. of Energy.

Murray, James A., and Weber, Bruce A. 1982. "The Impacts of Rapid Growth on the Provision and Financing of Local Public Services." In *Coping with Rapid Growth in Rural Communities*, ed. Bruce A. Weber and Robert E. Howell, pp. 97-113. Boulder, Colo.: Westview Press.

Myhra, David. 1975a. "Boomtown Planning: Examples of Successful Applications at Nuclear Power Plant and Western Coal Mining Sites." Paper presented at the 57th Annual Conference, *Planning 75: Innovation and Action*. San Antonio: American Institute of Planners.

Myhra, David. 1975b. "Colstrip, Montana . . . The Modern Company Town." Coal Age May.

Myhra, David. 1980. *Energy Plant Sites: Community Planning for Large Projects*. Atlanta: Conway Publications.

Nathanson, Josef. 1980. *Early Warning Information Systems for Business Retention*. Urban Consortium Information Bulletin. Washington, D.C.: U.S. Dept. of Commerce, Economic Development Administration.

Neil, C. C. 1982. "Development of Single Enterprise Resource Towns in Northern Australia." Paper presented at Conference of Association Universitaire Canadienne d'Etudes Nordique, at Montreal, Quebec.

Newhouse, Joseph P.; Williams, Albert P.; Bennett, Bruce W.; and Schwartz, William B. 1982. "Where Have All the Doctors Gone?" *Journal of the American Medical Association* 247:2392-96.

Newton, P. W. 1982. "Rapid Growth from Energy Projects: Assessing Population and Housing Impacts in the Gippsland Energy Resources Region, Victoria." *The Building Economist* 21(3): 99-107.

Nickens, J. C. 1983. "Impact Fee Legislation: Origins and Effect in Florida." *Economic Development Review* 1(1): 16-20.

North Dakota. 1981. North Dakota Facility Siting Act. Bismarck.

Northern Flood Agreement. 1977. Agreement among the Province of Manitoba, Manitoba-Hydro, the Northern Flood Committee, and the Canadian Government, Manitoba.

Northern States Power. 1982. Stipulation Agreement for Proposed Sherco 3 Generating Unit. Minneapolis.

Nothdurft, William E. 1983. *Renewing America: Natural Resource Investment and State Economic Development.* Washington, D.C.: Council of State Planning Agencies.

O'Connor, Patrick. 1983. Telephone interview by John M. Halstead. Community Development Coordinator. Knoxville: Tennessee Valley Authority.

OECD. 1979. *Analysis of the Environmental Consequences of Significant Public and Private Projects.* Paris, France: Organization for Economic Cooperation and Development.

O'Hare, Michael. 1977. "Not On My Block, You Don't--Facility Siting and the Strategic Importance of Compensation." *Public Policy* 25(7): 407-58.

O'Hare, Michael; Bacow, Lawrence; and Sanderson, Debra. 1983. *Facility Siting and Public Opposition.* New York: Von Nostrand Reinhold.

OIA. 1982. "OIA Participates in Impact Funding." *Overthrust News.* Iss. No. 3:4-5. Denver: Overthrust Industrial Association.

Olien, Roger M., and Olien, Diana Davids. 1982. *Oil Booms: Social Change in Five Texas Towns.* Lincoln: Univ. of Nebraska Press.

Olson, Dean F. 1981. "The Alaska Renewable Resources Corporation." In *Expanding the Opportunity to Produce: Revitalizing the American Economy Through New Enterprise Development,* ed. Robert Friedman and William Schweke. Washington, D.C.: Corporation for Enterprise Development.

ONWI-87. 1980. *Consultation and Concurrence Workshop Proceedings*. Office of Nuclear Waste Isolation. Columbus, Ohio: Battelle Memorial Inst.

Owens, Nancy J. 1983. "Is a Legal Basis for Impact Mitigation Necessary?" In *Proceedings of the Alaska Symposium on the Social, Economic, and Cultural Impacts of Natural Resource Development*. Fairbanks: Univ. of Alaska.

Paget, G., and Rabnett, R. A. 1981. "Planning for Large-Scale Energy Resource Developments." Paper presented at The Human Side of Energy Second International Forum, 16-19 August, at Edmonton, Alberta.

Parkinson, A.; Montgomery, S. W.; and Humphreys, R. D. 1980. *A Study of the Impact of Construction Camps on the People of Northeast Alberta*. Edmonton: Alberta Environment.

Parsons, Talcott. 1968. *The Structure of Social Action*. New York: Free Press.

Payne, Barbara A. 1982. "Patterns of Change in the Business Community in Energy Boomtowns." In *Proceedings of the Fifth Conference on the Small City and Regional Community*. Stevens Point: Univ. of Wisconsin-Stevens Point.

Pearson, Curtis. 1983. Telephone interview by John M. Halstead. Basin Electric Power Cooperative, Bismarck, N. Dak.

Pearson, Curtis. 1984. *ITAT Construction Work Force Report*. Bismarck, N. Dak.: Inter-Industry Technical Assistance Team (Basin Electric Power Coop.).

Peelle, Elizabeth. 1979. "Mitigating Community Impacts of Energy Development." Paper presented at the Annual Meeting of the American Association for the Advancement of Science, 3 January, at Houston, Tex.

Petak, William J. 1980. "Environmental Planning and Management." *Environmental Management* 4(4): 287-95.

Peters, Ted F. 1983. "Ethical Considerations Surrounding Nuclear Waste Repository Siting and Mitigation." In *Nuclear Waste: Socioeconomic Dimensions of Long-Term Storage*, ed. Steve H. Murdock, F. Larry Leistritz, and Rita R. Hamm. Boulder, Colo.: Westview Press.

Petro-Canada, Inc. 1982. *Registered Trapper's Compensation Program, Monkman Coal Project*. Calgary, Alberta.

Pietens, Brad. 1979. "Some Facts of Life About Boomtown Educations." In *Boomtowns and Human Services*, ed. J. A. Davenport and J. Davenport. Laramie: Univ. of Wyoming School of Social Work.

Pijawka, D., and Chalmers, James A. 1983. "Impacts of Nuclear Generating Plants on Local Areas." *Economic Geography* 59(1): 66-80.

Pinfield, Lawrence T., and Etherington, Lois D. 1982. *Housing Strategies of Resource Firms in Western Canada*. Burnaby, British Columbia: Simon Fraser Univ., Dept. of Business Administration.

Planning Center. 1982. *Louisiana Impacts of Declining OCS Petroleum Production: A Scoping Study*. Report prepared for the Louisiana Geological Survey, Dept. of Natural Resources. New Orleans.

Popper, Karl R. 1959. *The Logic of Scientific Discovery*. New York: Harper and Row.

President's Economic Adjustment Committee. 1981. *Community Impact Assistance Study*. Washington, D.C.: Intergovernmental/Interagency Task Force on Community Assistance.

Proctor and Redfern Group and Ontario Hydro. 1979. *A Social and Community Impact Monitoring and Review System*. Rpt. No. 79017. Toronto: Ontario Hydro Route Selection Division.

Pulver, Glen C. 1983. "Elements of a Comprehensive Community Economic Development Strategy." Paper presented at the Community Economic Development Strategies Conference, 1-3 March, at Omaha, Nebr.

Purdy, B. J.; Peelle, Elizabeth; Bronfman, B. H.; and Bjornstad, D. J. 1977. *A Post Licensing Study of Community Effects of Two Operating Nuclear Power Plants*. Oak Ridge, Tenn.: Oak Ridge National Laboratory.

Quality Development Associates, Inc. 1978. *Oil Shale Development: A Description of the Socioeconomic Mitigation Strategies at the Community and County Level*. Denver: Quality Development Associates, Inc.

Quinn, Sean. 1979. "The Impact of Lumber Mill Closure." *Northern California Review of Business and Economics*, pages 4-10.

Rabnett, R. A. and Associates. 1978. *Problems and Responses: Resource Community Development*. Victoria, British Columbia: Dept. of Municipal Affairs.

Rafferty, Timothy. 1981. Personal communication with F. Larry Leistritz. Spokane: Washington Water Power Co.

Rapp, Donald A. 1980. *Uranium Mining and Milling Work Force Characteristics in the Western United States.* LA-8656-MS. Los Alamos, N. Mex.: Los Alamos Scientific Laboratory.

Rathge, Richard W.; Leistritz, F. Larry; and Smutco, L. Steven. 1982. "Demographic Changes Associated With Energy Development Projects." Paper presented at Population Association of America Annual Meetings, 29-30 April, at San Diego.

Redburn, F. Stevens, and Buss, Terry F. 1979. "Public Policies for Communities in Economic Crisis: An Overview of the Issues." *Policy Studies Journal* 8(Fall): 143-50.

Reeder, Richard J. 1984. *Nonmetropolitan Fiscal Indicators: A Review of the Literature.* ERS Staff Rpt. No. AGEC 830908, Economic Development Division, ERS. Washington, D.C.: USDA.

Reese, M. H., and Cummings, J. C. 1979. "Energy Impacted Housing." In *Boomtowns and Human Services,* ed. J. A. Davenport and J. Davenport. Laramie: Univ. of Wyoming, School of Social Work.

Riley, R. W., and Hess, P. R. 1981. Letter to President Ronald Reagan. August 1. Washington, D.C.: State Planning Council on Radioactive Waste Management.

Rio Blanco County, Colo. 1979. County ordinances. Meeker, Colo.

Roberts, Richard; Kupfer, George; Walkey-Zaitzeff, Anna; and Morellato, Maria. 1980. *Development of Socio-Economic Principles and Practices.* Vancouver, British Columbia: Cornerstone Planning Group Ltd.

Robinson, Ira M. 1962. *New Industrial Towns on Canada's Resource Frontier.* Dept. of Geography Res. Paper No. 73. Chicago: Univ. of Chicago.

Robinson, Ira M. 1982. "New Resource Towns on Canada's Frontier." Paper presented at the Four Nations Energy Resource Communities Conference, 23-30 June, at Calgary and Edmonton, Alberta.

ROMCOE. 1982. *Rapid Growth Communities Project: Financing, Experiences, and Advise.* Boulder, Colo.: Rocky Mountain Center on Environment, Center for Environmental Problem Solving, July.

Root, Kenneth A. 1979. *Perspectives for Communities and Organizations on Plant Closings and Job Dislocations.* Ames, Iowa: North Central Regional Center for Rural Development.

Root, Kenneth A. 1982. "Phasing and Timing of Projects: Decommissioning and Shutdown Issues." Paper presented at the Energy Resource Communities Conference, 23-30 June, at Calgary/Edmonton, Alberta.

RSBC. 1979. Environment and Land Use Act. Victoria, British Columbia.

Sanderson, D. R. 1979. *Compensation in Facility Siting Conflicts.* Doc. No. 11. Cambridge: MIT Energy Impacts Project.

Santini, Danilo J.; South, David W.; and Stenehjem, Erik J. 1979. *Evidence of Future Increases in the Impact of Conventional Electric Facilities on Rural Communities.* ANL/EES-TM-152. Argonne, Ill.: Argonne National Laboratory.

Santini, Danilo J.; Stenehjem, Erik J.; and Meguire, Philip. 1978. *Methods of Eliminating Potential Socioeconomic Constraints on Near-Term Coal-Energy Development.* ANL/EES-TM-47. Argonne, Ill.: Argonne National Laboratory.

Sattalthite, William. 1983. Telephone interview by John M. Halstead. Public relations spokesperson. Cyprus Creek/Amoco, Challis, Idaho.

Schaeffer, John. 1983. "Social and Cultural Impact Issues." In *Proceedings of the Alaska Symposium on the Social, Economic, and Cultural Impacts of Natural Resource Development.* Fairbanks: Univ. of Alaska.

Schmickle, Sharon. 1983. "Riding the Boom: For 87 Iron Rangers, Working Means A 1,000-Mile Bus Ride." *Minneapolis Tribune,* October 2.

Schmidt, J. F.; Oehrtman, R. L.; and Doekson, G. A. 1978. "Planning Ambulance Service for a Rural Emergency Medical District." *Southern Journal of Agricultural Economics* July:127-133.

Schumpeter, Joseph. 1942. *Capitalism, Socialism, and Democracy.* New York: Harper and Row.

Schwarzweller, H. K. 1979. "Migration and the Changing Rural Scene." *Rural Sociology* 44(1): 7-23.

Schweke, William, and Friedman, Robert. 1983. "The Debate Over 'Who Generates Jobs'?" *The Entrepreneurial Economy* 1(8): 2-4.

Schweke, William, and Jones, Meriwether. 1982. *Economic Adjustment Resources*. Washington, D.C.: The Corporation for Enterprise Development.

Selvik, Arne; Summers, Gene F.; and Mackay, A. G. 1982. "External Linkages: Economic and Political Dependency of Energy Resource Communities." Paper presented at the Four Nations Energy Resource Communities Conference, 23-30 June, at Calgary and Edmonton, Alberta.

Serie, P. J.; Dressen, A. L.; and Aly, K. C. 1983. "Low-Level Waste Siting." In *Proceedings of Waste Management '83 Conference*, ed. Roy Post. Tucson, Ariz.

Sewel, J. 1983. *Social Consequences of Oil Developments*. Edinburgh: Scottish Development Dept.

Shaffer, Ron E. 1983. "Capital Markets and Community Economic Development." Typescript. Madison: Univ. of Wisconsin, Dept. of Agr. Econ.

Shapira, Philip. 1983. "Shutdowns and Job Loss in California." Typescript. Berkeley and Oakland: Univ. of California and Plant Closures Project, Dept. of City and Regional Planning.

Shen, Randolph F. C. 1980. "Estimating the Economic Impact of the 1973 Navy Base Closing." *Naval Research Logistics Quarterly* (No. 2): 335-44.

Shields, M. A.; Cowan, J. T.; and Bjornstad, D. J. 1979. *Socioeconomic Impacts of Nuclear Power Plants: A Paired Comparison of Operating Facilities*. Oak Ridge, Tenn.: Oak Ridge National Laboratory.

Shurcliff, Alice W. 1977. "The Local Impact of Nuclear Power." *Technology Review* (January): 40-47.

Siefried, Inga. 1983. Telephone interview by John M. Halstead. Alberta Environment. Edmonton, Alberta.

Sigurdson, Glenn. 1983. Telephone interview by John M. Halstead. Counsel for Northern Flood Agreement. Taylor, Brazzell, McCaffrey. Winnipeg, Manitoba.

Simmel, Georg. 1956. *Conflict and the Web of Group Affiliation*. Trans. Kurt H. Wolff. Glencoe, Ill.: Free Press.

Squire, Catherine A. 1982. "Options for Plant Retention in the Wake of an Anticipated Closure." *The Entrepreneurial Economy* 1(5): 9-10.

Staniforth, Sydney D., and Haggard, Joel P. 1982. "The Availability of Money in Rural Communities." *Economic Issues*. Iss. No. 70. Madison: Univ. of Wisconsin, Dept. of Agr. Econ.

Stinchcombe, Arthur L. 1968. *Constructing Social Theories*. New York: Harcourt, Brace, and World.

Stinson, Thomas F. 1978. *State Taxation of Mineral Deposits and Production*. Rural Development Res. Rpt. No. 2, Economic Development Div. Washington, D.C.: USDA.

Stinson, Thomas F. 1981. "Overcoming Impacts of Growth on Local Government Finance." *Rural Development Perspectives*. RDP-4. Washington, D.C.: USDA, ERS, September.

Stinson, Thomas F., and Temple, George S. 1983. *State Mineral Taxes, 1982*. Rural Development Res. Rpt. No. 36. USDA, ERS. Washington, D.C.: GPO.

Stinson, Thomas F., and Voelker, Stanley W. 1978. *Coal Development in the Northern Great Plains: The Impact on Revenues of State and Local Governments*. Economics, Statistics, and Cooperatives Service of USDA. Agr. Econ. Rpt. No. 394. Washington, D.C.: GPO.

Stinson, Thomas F., and Voelker, Stanley W. 1982. *Energy Development: Initial Effects on Government Revenues*. WRDC Pub. No. 15. Corvallis, Oreg.: Western Rural Development Center.

Storey, Keith. 1982. "Impacts and Implications of Regional Labour Preference Policies." Paper presented at the Second International Conference on Oil and the Environment, 16-19 August, at Halifax, Nova Scotia.

Stuart/Nichols Associates. 1979. *The Fiscal Impacts of Energy Development on Wyoming's Local Governments*. Denver.

Summers, Gene F.; Evans, S. D.; Clemente, F.; Beck, E. M.; and Minkoff, J. 1976. *Industrial Invasion of Rural America*. New York: Praeger Publishers.

Summers, Gene F., and Selvik, Arne, eds. 1979. *Nonmetropolitan Industrial Growth and Community Change*. Cambridge, Mass.: Lexington Books.

Susskind, Lawrence. 1980. *Citizen Participation in the Siting of Hazardous Waste Facilities*. Draft. Prepared for the National Governors' Assoc.

Susskind, Lawrence, and O'Hare, M. 1977. *Managing the Social and Economic Impacts of Energy Development.* Cambridge: MIT, Laboratory of Arch. and Planning.

Sweet, Morris L. 1981. *Industrial Location Policy for Economic Revitalization.* New York: Praeger Publishers.

Swerdloff, Sol. 1980. *A Guide for Communities Facing Major Layoffs or Plant Shutdowns.* Employment and Training Administration, U.S. Dept. of Labor. Washington, D.C.: GPO.

Symon, Mary Louise. 1980. Former member, State Planning Council. Letter to Governor Richard Riley, May 5.

Symon, Mary Louise. 1982. Personal interview by John M. Halstead. Former member, State Planning Council. Madison, Wis.

Teague, Carroll. 1982. "Private Sector Responsibility in a Plant Shutdown." *The Entrepreneurial Economy* 1(5): 6.

Tester, F. J., and Mykes, W., eds. 1981. *Social Impact Assessment: Theory, Method, and Practice.* Calgary, Alberta: Detselig Enterprises.

Thompson, Charles. 1983. Telephone interview by John M. Halstead. North Dakota Public Service Commission. Bismarck, N. Dak.

Thurow, Lester. 1980. *The Zero-Sum Society: Distribution and the Possibilities for Economic Change.* New York: Basic Books.

Time. 1984. "Pulling the Nuclear Plug." 123:34-38.

TOSCO Foundation. 1980. *Socioeconomic Impact Mitigation Program, NOSR-1.* Boulder, Colo.

Turner, Jonathan H. 1974. *The Structure of Sociological Theory.* Homewood, Ill.: Dorsey Press.

TVA. 1982. *Economic Revitalization Program, Phipps Bend, Yellow Creek and Hartsville.* Draft. Knoxville.

Tweeten, L., and Brinkman, G. L. 1976. *Micropolitan Development.* Ames: Iowa State Univ. Press.

Uhlman, J. M., and Olson, J. K. 1984. *Planning for Rural Human Services.* Denver: Office of Human Development Services, Dept. of Health and Human Services.

U.S. Bureau of the Census. 1982. *State Government Tax Collections in 1981*. Washington, D.C.: GPO.

U.S. Bureau of the Census. 1983. *Statistical Abstract of the United States, 1982-1983*. Washington, D.C.: GPO.

U.S. Department of Energy. 1980. *Management of Commercially Generated Radioactive Waste*. DOE/EIS-0046F. Washington, D.C.

U.S. Department of Energy. 1981. *Solvent Refined Coal-I Demonstration Project, Final Environmental Impact Statement*. DOE/EIS-0073. Washington, D.C.

U.S. Department of Housing and Urban Development. 1976. *Rapid Growth from Energy Projects: Ideas for State and Local Action*. Washington, D.C.: GPO.

U.S. Department of the Interior. 1982. *Proposed Outer Continental Shelf Oil and Gas Lease Sale, St. George Basin, Final Environmental Impact Statement*. Washington, D.C.: Minerals Management Service.

U.S. Department of the Interior, National Park Service. 1983. *Energy Impacted Communities: Challenges in Recreation, Open Space, and Historic Preservation*. Denver, Colo: National Park Service Regional Office.

U.S. Energy Research and Development Administration. 1976. *Managing the Social and Economic Impacts of Energy Developments*. Washington, D.C.: Centaur Management Consultants, Inc.

U.S. Environmental Protection Agency. 1980. *Using Compensation and Incentives When Siting Hazardous Waste Management Facilities*. Washington, D.C.

U.S. General Accounting Office. 1982. *Government-Industry Cooperation Can Enhance the Venture Capital Process*. Report to Senator Lloyd Bentsen, Joint Economic Committee. Washington, D.C.

U.S. Senate. 1980. *The Role of the Federal Government in Employee Ownership of Business*. Select Committee on Small Business. Washington, D.C.: GPO.

U.S. Small Business Administration. 1983. *The State of Small Business: A Report of the President*. Washington, D.C.: GPO.

Urban Systems Research and Engineering, Inc. 1980. *A Handbook for the States on the Use of Compensation and Incentives in the Siting of Hazardous Waste Management Facilities.* Prepared for U.S. Environmental Protection Agency. Cambridge, Mass.: Urban Systems Research and Engineering Inc.

Vatne, Eirik. 1980. "Structural Change, Industrial Linkages and Production Systems: The Case of a One-Company Town." Paper presented at the IGU Commission on Industrial Systems meeting, 25-31 August, at Tokyo, Japan.

Vatne, Eirik. 1981. "Single Sector Economies: The Resource Base Trap." Paper presented at the Sixth International Seminar on Marginal Regions, August, at Bergen and Sogndal, Norway.

Vaughan, Roger. 1980. *Local Business and Employment Retention Strategies.* Urban Consortium Bul. Washington, D.C.: U.S. Dept. of Commerce, Economic Development Administration.

Vincent, Nicholas. 1981. "Field Actualities of an Impact Monitoring Program." In *Social Impact Assessment: Theory, Method, and Practice,* ed. F. J. Tester and W. Mykes, pp. 254-268. Calgary, Alberta: Detselig Enterprises.

Voelker, Stanley W. 1981. *State and Local Taxes Affected by Energy Developments in Selected Western States.* Washington, D.C: U.S. EPA, Office of Research and Development.

Walsh, Pat. 1982. Personal interview by John M. Halstead. Former assistant attorney general, Wisconsin. Madison.

Wandesforde-Smith, Geoffrey. 1979. *Varieties of Environmental Impact Assessment: An International Analysis.* Netherlands: Mileiu en Recht.

Warrack, Allan A., and Dale, Lynne. 1981. "Megaprojects and Small Communities--Is It Progress?" Paper presented at The Human Side of Energy, Second International Forum, 16-19 August, at Edmonton, Alberta.

Watson, K. S. 1977. "Measuring and Mitigating Socioeconomic Environmental Impacts of Constructing Energy Projects." *Natural Resources Lawyer* 10:393-403.

Weber, Bruce A., and Howell, Robert E., eds. 1982. *Coping with Rapid Growth in Rural Communities.* Boulder, Colo.: Westview Press.

Weisz, R. 1979. "Stress and Mental Health in a Boom Town." In *Boomtowns and Human Services,* ed. J. A. Davenport and J. Davenport. Laramie: Univ. of Wyoming, School of Social Work.

Wernette, Dee R. 1980. "Estimation and Mitigation of Socioeconomic Impacts of Western Oil Shale Development." Paper presented at Seventh Annual Conference on Energy and the Environment, DOE and EPA, 30 November-3 December, at Phoenix, Ariz.

West, Stanley W. 1977. *Opportunities for Company-Community Cooperation in Mitigating Energy Facility Impacts.* Cambridge: MIT, Laboratory of Arch. and Planning.

Western Fuels, Inc. 1981. *Socioeconomic Impact Mitigation Agreement for the Deserado Mine, Bonanza Station and Associated Facilities.* Washington, D.C.

Western Research Corporation and Basin Electric Power Cooperative. 1983. *Socioeconomic Impact Monitoring Report: Final Summary.* Wheatland, Wyo.: Missouri Basin Power Project.

Wieland, James S., and Leistritz, F. Larry. 1978. *Profile of the Coal Creek Project Construction Work Force.* Agr. Econ. Misc. Rpt. No. 33. Fargo: N. Dak. Agr. Exp. Sta.

Wieland, James S.; Leistritz, F. Larry; and Murdock, Steve H. 1977. *Characteristics and Settlement Patterns of Energy-Related Operational Workers in the Northern Great Plains.* Agr. Econ. Rpt. No. 123. Fargo: North Dakota Agr. Exp. Sta.

Wieland, James S.; Leistritz, F. Larry; and Murdock, Steve H. 1979. "Characteristics and Residential Patterns of Energy-Related Work Forces in the Northern Great Plains." *Western Journal of Agricultural Economics* 4:57-68.

Wilkinson, K. P.; Thompson, J. G.; Reynolds, R. R.; and Ostresh, L. M. 1982. "Local Social Disruption and Western Energy Development." *Pacific Sociological Review* 25(3): 275-96.

Williams, Gary. 1982. *BLM Social Effects Project Community Report: Wheatland, Wyoming.* Billings, Mont.: Mountain West Research-North, Inc. in association with Western Research Corporation.

Wisconsin. 1981. Assembly Bill 555, Chapter 62, Laws of 1981.

Wolf, C. P. 1981. "Social Impact Assessment." *IAIA Bulletin* 1(1): 9-19.

Wolf, C. P. 1983. "Social Impact Assessment: A Methodological Overview." In *Social Impact Assessment Methods*, ed. Kurt Finsterbusch, Lynn G. Llewellyn, and C. P. Wolf, pp. 15-33. Beverly Hills: Sage Publications.

Wyoming. 1981. *Wyoming Industrial Development Information and Siting Act.* Cheyenne.

Young, Gordon M. 1981. "The Computer Model as a Municipal Management Tool." In *Computer Models and Forecasting Socio-Economic Impacts of Growth and Development.* Edmonton: Univ. of Alberta.

Zetterburg, Hans. 1965. *On Theory and Verification in Sociology.* 3d ed. Totowa, N.J.: Bedminster Press.

Index

For Product Safety Concerns and Information please contact our EU
representative GPSR@taylorandfrancis.com
Taylor & Francis Verlag GmbH, Kaufingerstraße 24, 80331 München, Germany

www.ingramcontent.com/pod-product-compliance
Lightning Source LLC
LaVergne TN
LVHW011121300926
849160LV00008B/466

* 9 7 8 0 3 6 7 3 0 3 3 0 3 *